Introduction to Machine Learning

Yves Kodratoff

Research Director
French National Scientific Research Council

MORGAN KAUFMANN PUBLISHERS

MORGAN KAUFMANN PUBLISHERS, INC.
2929 Campus Drive, Suite 260, San Mateo, CA 94403
Order Fulfillment: PO Box 50490, Palo Alto, CA 94303

© Yves Kodratoff

First published in Great Britain in 1988
by Pitman Publishing
128 Long Acre, London WC2E 9AN

First published in French as *Lecons
d'Apprentissage Symbolique Automatique*
by Cepadues-Editions, Toulouse, France (1986)

Library of Congress Catalog Card #: 88-046077

ISBN 1-55860-037-X

Printed in Great Britain at The Bath Press, Avon

Cover design by Eitetsu Nozawa

Contents

1 **Why Machine Learning and AI: The Contributions of AI to Learning Techniques** 1
   1   Historical sketch   1
   2   Various sorts of learning   2

2 **Theoretical Foundations for Machine Learning** 11
   0   Theoretical foundations for theory-haters   11
   1   Clauses   19
   2   Unification   26
   3   Resolution and inference on a set of clauses   32
   4   The Knuth–Bendix algorithm   39

3 **Representation of Complex Knowledge by Clauses** 42
   1   Some examples of logical knowledge representation   42
   2   The transformation of a given sentence into a theorem   47
   3   Representation of a hierarchy during resolution   49
   4   Representation by 'ternary quantified trees'   54

4 **Representation of Knowledge about Actions and the Addition of New Rules to a Knowledge Base** 59
   1   Truth maintenance   59
   2   Predicates in action mode/checking mode   60
   3   Main rules and auxiliary rules   62
   4   Organization of the program for the representation of actions   64
   5   The case of a new rule having the same premise as an old one   65
   6   New rule more specific than an old one   67
   7   Combination of rules   71
   8   Generalization of rules   72
   9   Rules for inference control   73

5 **Learning by Doing** 75
   1   The problem   75
   2   Version spaces (Mitchell 1982) seen as focussing   77
   3   Application to rule acquisition   83
   4   Learning by trial and error   86

6 **A Formal Presentation of Version Spaces** 93
   1   Different definitions of generalization   93
   2   Version spaces   110

7 **Explanation-Based Learning** 121
   1   Inductive versus deductive learning   122
   2   Intuitive presentation of EBL   123
   3   Goal regression   124
   4   Explantaion-based generalization   128
   5   Explanation-based learning   135

8   Learning by Similarity Detection: The Empirical Approach   138
1   General definitions   138
2   Description of the whole example   140
3   Recognition   142
4   Sparseness and the selection criteria for a 'good' function   144
5   The procedure of 'emptying the intersections'   145
6   Creation of recognition functions   148
7   Rules of generalization   151
8   Generalization of recognition functions   154
9   Application to soybean pathology   155
10   Application to an algorithm for conceptual clustering   157

9   Learning by Similarity Detection: The 'Rational' Approach   159
1   Knowledge representation   160
2   Description of a rational generalization algorithm   164
3   Using axioms and idempotence   171
4   A definition of generalization   172
5   Use of negative examples   178

10   Automatic Construction of Taxonomies: Techniques for Clustering   184
1   A measure of the amount of information associated with each descriptor   184
2   Application of data analysis   188
3   Conceptual clustering   193

11   Debugging and Understanding in Depth: The Learning of Micro-Worlds   202
1   Recognition of micro-worlds   205
2   Detection of lies   210

12   Learning by Analogy   216
1   A definition of analogy   216
2   Winston's use of analogy   220

Appendix 1   Equivalence Between Theorems and Clauses   228
1   Interpretation   228
2   The Herbrand universe of a set of clauses   233
3   Semantic trees   234
4   Herbrand's theorem   242

Appendix 2   Synthesis of Predicates   243
1   Motivation: an example of useful synthesis in ML   245
2   Synthesis of predicates from input/outputs   248
3   Approaches to automatic programming   256

Appendix 3   Machine Learning in Context   263
1   Epistemological reflections on the place of AI in science   263
2   Reflections on the social role of ML   273

Bibliography   287

Index   295

Foreword and Acknowledgements

This book has developed from a set of postgraduate lectures delivered at the University of Paris-Sud during the years 1983–1988.

All the members of my research group at the 'Laboratoire de Recherche en Informatique' helped me during the preparation of this text. Without several European grants, and particularly the ESPRIT programme, I would never have had the possibility of creating such a group.

In my group, I particularly thank Norbert Benamou, Jean-Jacques Cannat, Marta Franova, Jean-Gabriel Ganascia, Nicholas Graner, Michel Manago, Jean-Francois Puget, Jose Siquiera and Christel Vrain.

Outside my group, Toni Bollinger, Christian de Sainte Marie and Gheorghe Tecuci were also very helpful. Special thanks are due to Ryszard Michalski who re-read Chapter 8 which concerns his own contribution to inductive machine learning.

Special thanks are also due to my wife Marta. Besides the comfort she provides me as a wife, she is also a first-rate researcher and helps me a lot in my scientific work in addition to doing her own. She entirely re-read this English version and found many mistakes that had been left in the original French version.

This English edition has been produced by Stephen Thorp who read and understood most of it while translating it. He pointed out many of my ambiguous French ways of speaking so this edition may be easier to understand than the French one.

Yves Kodratoff
LRI, Paris, 1988

1 Why Machine Learning and Artificial Intelligence?
The Contribution of Artificial Intelligence to Learning Techniques

The approach to learning developed by Artificial Intelligence, as it will be described here, is a very young scientific discipline whose birth can be placed in the mid-seventies and whose first manifesto is constituted by the documents of the "First Machine Learning Workshop", which took place in 1980 at Carnegie-Mellon University. From these documents a work was drawn which is the "Bible" of learning in Artificial Intelligence, entitled "Machine Learning: An Artificial Intelligence Approach". "Machine Learning" is written ML throughout this book.

1 HISTORICAL SKETCH

The first attempts at learning for computers go back about 25 years. They consist principally of an attempt to model self-organization, self-stabilization and abilities to recognize shapes. Their common characteristic is that they attempt to describe an "incremental" system where knowledge is quasi-null at the start but grows progressively during the experiments "experienced" by the system.

The most famous of these models is that of the perceptron due to F. Rosenblatt [Rosenblatt 1958], whose limitations were shown by Minsky and Pappert [Minsky & Pappert 1969]. Let us note that these limitations have been rejected recently by the new connectionist approach [Touretzky & Hinton 1985].

The most spectacular result obtained in this period was Samuel's (1959, 1963). It consists of a system which learns to play checkers, and it achieved mastery through learning. A detailed study of this program enables us to understand why it disappointed the fantastic hopes which emerged after this success (of which the myth of the super-intelligent computer is only a version for the general public). In fact, Samuel had provided his program with a series of parameters each of which was able to take numerical values. It was these numerical values which were adjusted by experience and Samuel's genius had consisted in a particularly judicious choice of these parameters. Indeed, all the knowledge was contained in the definition of the parameters, rather than in the associated numerical values. For example, he had defined the concept of "move centrality" and the real learning was done by inventing and recognizing the importance of this parameter rather than its numerical value, so that in reality it was done by Samuel himself.

During the Sixties another approach emerged: that of symbolic learning, oriented toward the acquisition of concepts and structured knowledge. The most famous of the supporters of this approach is Winston (1975) and the most spectacular result was obtained by Buchanan's META-DENDRAL program [Buchanan 1978] which generates rules that explain mass spectroscopy data used by the expert system DENDRAL [Buchanan 1971].

As written above, a new approach began about ten years ago, it does not reject the two previous ones but includes them. It consists in recognizing that the main successes of the past, those of Samuel or Buchanan for example, were due to the fact that an important mass of knowledge was used in their systems implicitly. How could it now be included explicitly? And above all how could it be controlled, augmented, modified? These problems appear important to an increasingly high proportion of AI researchers. At this moment ML is in a period of rapid growth. This is principally due to the successes encountered by the initiators of the AI approach to Learning.

2 VARIOUS SORTS OF LEARNING

Keep it clearly in mind that many other approaches to automatic knowledge acquisition exist apart from AI: the Adaptive Systems of Automata Theory, Grammatical Inference stemming from Shape Recognition, Inductive Inference closely connected with Theoretical Computer Science and the many numerical methods of which Connectionism is the latest incarnation.

But it turns out that even within the AI approach there are numerous approaches to the automatic acquisition of knowledge: these are the ones that we shall devote ourselves to describing.

In Appendix 2, we shall describe some problems of inductive inference and program synthesis which, although marginal, seem nevertheless to belong to our subject.

Before describing the main forms of learning, it must be emphasized that three kinds of problem can be set in each of them.

The first is that of clustering, (which is called "classification" in Data Analysis): given a mass of known items, how can the features common to them be discovered in such a way that we can cluster them in sub-groups which are simpler and have a meaning? The immense majority of procedures for clustering are numerical in nature. This is why we shall recall them in chapter 10.

The problem of conceptual classification is well set by a classic example due to Michalski.

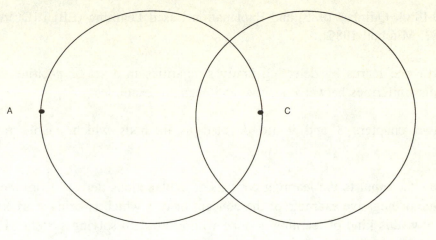

The points A and C are very far apart. Must they belong to the same sub-group?

The second problem (of discrimination) is that of learning classification procedures.

Given a set of examples of concepts, how is a method to be found which enables each concept to be recognized in the most efficient way? The great majority of existing methods rest on numerical evaluations bound up with the diminution of an entropy measure after the application of descriptors. This is described in chapter 10.

We shall also present a symbolic approach to this problem.

The third problem is that of generalization. Starting from concrete examples of a situation or a rule, how can a formula be deduced which will be general enough to describe this situation or this rule, and how can it be explained that the formula has this descriptive capacity? For example, it can be asked how starting from a statement like:

"France buys video-recorders from Japan", the more general rule can be derived:

"Countries which have not sufficiently developed their research in solid- state physics buy electronic equipment from countries which have."

It is not yet reasonable to expect from a learning system that it should be really capable of making such inferences without being led step by step. The rest of the book is going to show how we are at least beginning to glimpse the solution to this problem.

2.1 SBL versus EBL

It was during the 1985 "International Workshop in Machine Learning" that was defined the distinction between Similarity Based Learning (SBL) [Lebowitz 1986,

Michalski 1984, Quinlan 1983] and Explanation Based Learning (EBL) [DeJong 1981, Silver 1983, Mitchell 1985].

In SBL, one learns by detecting firstly similarities in a set of positive examples, secondly dissimilarities between positive and negative examples.

The two chapters 8 and 9 are devoted to methods which enable this to be achieved.

In EBL, the input to the learning consists of explanations derived from the analysis of a positive or negative example of the concept or rule which is being learned.

Generally, this kind of learning is done with a problem-solving system. Each time the system arrives at a solution it is, of course, either a success or a failure (in that case one talks of negative examples). A module then analyzes the reasons for this success or failure.

These reasons are called "explanations" and they are used to improve the system.

A detailed study of several approaches of this type will be found in chapter 5, 6, and 7.

2.1.1 A simple example of SBL

Let us consider the positive examples: {B, D, E, F, H, K, L}. The reader can detect that these are all capital letters which have in common the fact that their biggest left-hand vertical line touches two small horizontal lines to its left.

Let us suppose we are given: {C} as a negative example to the above series; then we detect that the similarity found above does indeed separate the positive examples from the negative ones.

If we now add: {M, N} as negative examples then we have to look for a new similarity between the positive examples which must be a dissimilarity from the negative examples. A suggestion: they are capital letters whose biggest left-hand vertical line touches two small horizontal lines to its left, and if there is a big line toward the right beginning from the top of the vertical line, then this line is horizontal.

2.1.2 A simple example of EBL

An explanation is always, in practice, a proof. This proof points (in the sense of pointing with the finger) to the important piece of knowledge which is going to have to be preserved.

Suppose we had a complete description of a hydrogen balloon with its dimensions, its color, the fact that it is being rained on, the political context in which it was inflated, etc...

An SBL system would ascertain that a red balloon rises in air, that a blue balloon does too, that a green balloon does too etc... to conclude that the color has nothing to do with whether the balloon rises in air.

An EBL system, on the other hand, given a single example of a red balloon that flies off, will seek to prove that it must indeed rise. To cut a long argument short, it will ascertain in the end that if the weight of the volume of air displaced is bigger than the weight of the balloon, then it must rise. The arguments will be about the weight of the balloon's envelope, the density of hydrogen, the temperature and the degree of humidity of the air. It will conclude with certainty that color and politics have nothing to do with the matter, and that, on the other hand, the data contained in the arguments are the significant descriptors for this problem.

2.2 Numerical versus conceptual learning

These two forms of learning are opposite in their means and their goals. The numerical approach aims to optimize a global parameter such as entropy in the case of Quinlan's ID3 program [Quinlan 1983] or such as distance between examples in Data Analysis [Diday & al. 1982].

Its aim is to show up a set of descriptors which are the "best" relative to this optimization. It also has as a consequence the generation of "clusters" of examples.

It is well-known that the numerical approach is efficient and resistant to noise but that it yields rules or concepts which are in general incomprehensible to humans.

Conversely, the symbolic approach is well-suited to interaction with human experts, but it is very sensitive to noise.

It aims at optimizing a recognition function which is synthesized on the basis of examples. This function is usually required to be complete, which means that it must recognize all the positive examples, and to to be discriminant, which means that it rejects all the negative examples.

Its aim is to attempt to express a conceptual relationship between the examples.

The examples of EBL and SBL given above are also examples of symbolic learning. Examples of numerical learning will be found in chapter 10.

2.3 Learning by reward/punishment

Weightings are associated with each concept or rule to indicate the importance of using it. In this kind of learning, the system behaves a bit like a blind man who gropes in all directions.

Each time it obtains a positive outcome (where the notions of positive and negative are often very dependent on the problem set), the system will assign more weight to the rules which brought it to this positive outcome. Each time it obtains a negative result, it reduces the weighting for the use of the rules it has just used.

This kind of learning is very spectacular, since it makes it possible to obtain systems which are independent of their creator once they begin to work.

On the other hand, you can well imagine that the definition of the concepts or rules, the definition of positive and negative depend closely on the problem set. These systems are very hard to apply outside their field of specialization and are very difficult to modify.

2.4 Empirical versus rational learning

In empirical learning, the system acquires knowledge in a local manner. For example, if a new rule helps it with a problem it is solving, the rule is added to the knowledge base, provided it does not contradict the others already there.

Learning is said to be rational, on the other hand, when the addition of the new rule is examined by a module which seeks to connect it with the other global knowledge about the Universe in which the system is situated.

So it is clear that rational learning will be able to introduce environment-dependent data naturally, whereas empirical learning is going to be frustrated by this type of question.

In the case of learning by testing examples, a similar difference exists. Since the difference between the empirical and rational approaches is always illustrated by EBL, we, in contrast, are now going to give an example of the difference between these two approaches using SBL.

- An example of rational versus empirical similarity detection

2.4.1 Studying the positive examples

Let us suppose that we wish to learn a concept given the two following positive examples.

E_1 : *DOG(PLUTO)*
E_2 : *CAT(CRAZY) & WOLF(BIGBAD)*

where PLUTO, CRAZY and BIGBAD are the names of specific animals.

In both cases one still uses general pieces of knowledge of the universe in which the learning takes place.

Suppose that we know that dogs and cats are domestic animals, that dogs and wolves are canids, and that they are all mythical animals (referring to Walt Disney's 'Pluto', R. Crumb's 'Crazy Cat' and the 'Big Bad Wolf' of the fairy-tales).

This knowledge is known by theorems like

$Eg1_{empirical}$ $[WOLF(x) \Rightarrow CANID(x)]$.

Empirical learning will use one such piece of knowledge to find one of the possible generalizations.

For example, it will detect the generalizations:

$Eg1_{empirical}$ $CANID(x)$ & $NUMBEROFOCCURRENCES(x) = 1$
$Eg2_{empirical}$ $DOMESTIC(x)$ & $NUMBEROFOCCURRENCES(x) = 1$
$Eg3_{empirical}$ $MYTHICAL\text{-}ANIMAL(x)$ & $NUMBEROFOCCURRENCES(x) = 1$ OR 2

which says that there is a canid in each example etc... The negative examples will serve to choose the "right" generalization (or generalizations), as we shall see a little farther on.

Rational learning is going to try to find the generalization which preserves all the information which can possibly be drawn from the examples.

The technique used for this has been called **structural matching**.

Before even attempting to generalize, one tries to structurally match the examples to use the known features.

The examples are going to be re-written as follows.

E_1' : $DOG(PLUTO)$ & $DOG(PLUTO)$ & $DOMESTIC(PLUTO)$ & $CANID(PLUTO)$ & $MYTHICAL\text{-}ANIMAL(PLUTO)$ & $MYTHICAL\text{-}ANIMAL(PLUTO)$

E_2' : $CAT(CRAZY)$ & $WOLF(BIGBAD)$ & $DOMESTIC(CRAZY)$ & $CANID(BIGBAD)$ & $MYTHICAL\text{-}ANIMAL(CRAZY)$ & $MYTHICAL\text{-}ANIMAL(BIGBAD)$

In these expressions all the features of the domain have been used at once, duplicating them if necessary, to improve the matching of the two examples.

Here we use the standard properties of the logical connectives

$A \Leftrightarrow A$ & A, and $A \Rightarrow B$ is equivalent to A & $B \Leftrightarrow A$

to be able to declare that

$$E_1 \Leftrightarrow E_1'$$
$$E_2 \Leftrightarrow E_2'.$$

In the final generalization we only keep what is common to both examples, so it will be

$Eg_{rational}$: $DOMESTIC(x)$ & $CANID(y)$ & $MYTHICAL\text{-}ANIMAL(x)$ & $MYTHICAL\text{-}ANIMAL(y)$.

2.4.2 Studying the negative examples

In the empirical case, the total number of possible generalizations will be enormous, and in the rational case, the length of the generalization is what will be enormous.

In both cases, negative examples are used to limit the combinatorial explosion.

Let us suppose that the concept to be invented on the basis of the two examples above allows of the negative example

$$CE_1 : FOX(WILD)$$

where 'WILD' is the name of a specific wild fox.

Since foxes are also canids, these pieces of knowledge are given by the two theorems

$$\forall x \; [FOX(x) \Rightarrow CANID(x)]$$
$$FOX(WILD) \Rightarrow \neg DOMESTIC(WILD)$$

Let us note that there are mythical foxes which are wild, so there is no theorem eliminating the possibility of WILD also being mythical.

Empirical learning always looks for a complete and discriminant concept. Only

$$Eg2_{empirical} : DOMESTIC(x) \; \& \; NUMBEROFOCCURRENCES(x) = 1$$

makes it possible to reject CE_1. It becomes the empirical generalization, taking account of E_1, E_2 and CE_1.

In rational learning, one studies the formula

$$E_g \; \& \; \neg CE_1$$

to detect what is contradictory in it.

It emerges from this that the negative example contradicts only the fact that the positive examples are about a canid.

So the generalization which is deduced is

$$Eg_{rational} : DOMESTIC(x) \; \& \; MYTHICAL\text{-}ANIMAL(x) \; \& \; MYTHICAL\text{-}ANIMAL(y)$$

where the possibility of x and/or y being mythical has been preserved.

2.4.3 Discussion

These examples enable us to see better what the two approaches are good for. It is clear that the rational approach enables the information to be better controlled. On the other hand, if knowledge concerning the negative examples is forgotten (for example, if it had been forgotten that WILD is not in fact a mythical animal), then there would be a risk of the generalization recognizing certain negative examples.

In fact, the empirical method allows us to ensure that the concepts learned are indeed discriminant, which often has great practical importance.

Conversely, the rational method makes possible a much richer description, preserving links which seem redundant relative to the negative examples, but giving better explanations of the reasons why these examples belong to the same concept.

Quite often, the examples need only serve to suggest the general form of the concepts we wish to acquire, they need not serve to draw definitive conclusions, hence it can be unfortunate to eliminate any information they may share.

2.5 (Deductive versus inductive) versus inventive learning

This distinction is relative to the inventiveness required from the system.

Learning will be called deductive when all the necessary knowledge is given explicitly at the beginning. Learning "by heart" is a particularly trivial case of it, but numerical learning can also be described as deductive, and, as we shall see in chapter 10, it is far from being trivial.

Inductive learning is that in which although all the knowledge is given to the system, some of it has an implicit form. For example, when the system begins with an inadequate description and modifies it itself, with known descriptors.

Inventive learning is that in which it is necessary for the system to create a certain piece of knowledge from nothing, for example a descriptor which is going to make possible the definition of a more useful concept. It is known as the invention of genius, and we should not expect to meet systems capable of such abilities soon.

Appendix 2 shows how it has already been possible to automate certain types of creativity, and chapter 7 gives more details about the difference between inductive and deductive learning.

2.6 Explanatory learning

The reader will not fail to wonder what the difference can be between learning on the basis of explanations and explanatory learning.

It is a question of purpose.

The purpose of EBL is to use explanations to improve its performance.

The purpose of explanatory learning is to improve the quality of the explanations that the system can provide its user with, in some cases even at the cost of a slight loss of efficiency.

When a system has to acquire common-sense knowledge, such as learning to ride a bicycle, the notion of explanation is not very meaningful. In this case, one might say that the learner has to keep his center of gravity between his points of contact with the ground, but this is just as true of standing still upright as it is of walking a tight-rope over the Niagara Falls. The explanations that we are able to provide ourselves are pretty poor: "Make sure you pay attention", "You have to be brave" - nothing in all that helps the learner. So learning is only done in an indirect way, by exercises which experience has shown to be instructive and by exercising in a repetitive way: "Practice makes perfect".

So it will be noticed that the notion of banality is purely anthropomorphic: a piece of common-sense knowledge is one about which the human cannot provide explanations capable of helping learners.

Conversely, expert knowledge can be defined as that where a reasoning operation enables somebody who is capable of performing certain actions to explain his capability and these explanations make the beginners' task easier.

One of the aims of ML is to show the characteristics of what is banal and what is expert. The teaching of expert knowledge is fundamentally different from that of banal knowledge.

It is clear that EBL is an ideal candidate to become explanatory, since if everything goes off well, the system must progressively discover reasons which are refined more and more as the learning progresses. It can then be considered to be capable of providing better explanations to its user.

The example above also shows that rational SBL has the claim to be more explanatory than empirical SBL.

Chapter 11 is also going to show how to build systems which refine the relations between possible micro-worlds. Explanations of the kind "I do this because I am in this or that micro-world, whereas in these others I would do something else" are extremely important because they describe the context in which such-and-such an action can take place.

In practice they also have value as a strategy for using a system.

This is why we believe that the learning of strategies takes place through an improvement in the techniques of explanatory learning.

2 Theoretical Foundations for Machine Learning

This chapter contains the following sections.

0 - Theoretical foundations for theory-haters. Simplification of the LISP/PROLOG debate.

1 - Definition of clauses, conversion into normal form, Skolemization, some examples of the translation of natural languages sentences into theorems and clauses.

2 - Unification, terms, substitutions.

3 - Resolution, inference on a set of clauses.

4 - The Knuth-Bendix completion.

0   THEORETICAL FOUNDATIONS FOR THEORY-HATERS

This section is "reserved" for those who do not like theory. They will then be able to pass on directly to chapter 3.

Those who like theory risk being shocked by some short-cuts in the descriptions of Resolution and Logic Programming.

This book uses PROLOG clause notation as a convention, since a convention has to be chosen.

The aim of this section is to show the link between this convention and the others.

We are going to use the example of the Socratic syllogism. In natural language, this syllogism is expressed by

> $Form_1$
>> *All men are mortal.*
>> *Socrates is a man.*
>> *Therefore, Socrates is mortal.*

Numerous ways exist of transcribing these sentences into logical form (see section 1.2); this is not the problem we wish to study now. So let us assume that they are first transcribed thus:

Form$_2$

> *If x is a man then x is mortal*
> *(or again: ∀ x [MAN(x) ⟹ MORTAL(x)])*
> *Socrates is an x such that MAN(x) is true.*
> *Socrates is an x such that MORTAL(x) is true.*

where x is a variable.

The first problem which interests us here is the transition from the form *Form$_2$* to forms contained in programming languages. Note that the ' Therefore ' has disappeared from *Form$_2$*; we shall see later how this ' therefore ' does get represented after all, in accordance with the representation chosen.

0.1   Knowledge representation (without inferences)

0.1.1   Using IF ... THEN ...

We then have

Form$_3$

> IF MAN(x) THEN MORTAL(x)
> MAN(SOCRATES) = TRUE
> MORTAL(SOCRATES) = TRUE

It must be remembered that the expression ' IF MAN(x) THEN MORTAL(x) ' means precisely: If MAN(x) is true, then I know that MORTAL(x) is true also. On the other hand, if MAN(x) is false, then I do not know anything about MORTAL(x). This is one interpretation already of ' All men are mortal ' !

0.1.2   Use of LISP functions

Let us first recall that LISP provides the means of defining functions by using the symbolic form

(LAMBDA Function-name (variable-list)(function-body)).

It thus enables us to define conditionals which constitute the body of the functions and have the form

(COND((A_1)(B_1)) ... ((A_i)(B_i)) ...)

where the value of the expression is the first B_i whose A_i takes the value TRUE. So they are equivalent to

IF A_1 THEN B_1 ELSE ... IF A_i THEN B_i ELSE ...

The correspondences between this knowledge and its LISP representations are not absolutely immediate.

We can either define predicates as LISP functions, or we can use LISP lists whose contents implicitly represent what we wish.

In this section we are going to use the functional representation. An example of representation by lists will be given in section 0.2.2.

To represent

$$MAN(SOCRATES) = TRUE$$

we shall have to define a predicate (i.e. a function with values in {TRUE, FALSE}) which yields the value TRUE when ' SOCRATES ' is the value of its variable. It will be written

> (LAMBDA MAN (x)(COND
> ((EQ x SOCRATES) TRUE)
> ((EQ x ...) TRUE)
> . . .
> (TRUE NIL)))

where the dots represent other values of ' x ' for which (MAN x) is TRUE.
Notice also that we use LISP notation in LISP expression. For instance, MAN(x) is written (MAN x) when met in a LISP expression.

To represent

$$MORTAL(SOCRATES) = TRUE$$

a predicate ' MORTAL ' has to be defined in a similar manner. We shall not do so explicitly. However, we shall now give a different definition of ' MORTAL ' from this one.

There are several ways of representing

$$IF\ MAN(x)\ THEN\ MORTAL(x)$$

depending on the type of inference desired, as we shall see farther on. In any case, we can of course represent an implication by agreeing to represent the indeterminate value by NIL. This is the value which MORTAL(x) must take when MAN(x) is FALSE.

One can then define:

> (LAMBDA MORTAL(x) (COND
> (MAN(x) TRUE)
> (TRUE NIL)))

Be careful; the two definitions of MORTAL we have just given are incompatible in the same LISP program!

It must be carefully noted that

> (COND(MAN x) (MORTAL x))

does not represent what we want, since it expresses the fact that

$$IF\ MAN(x)\ THEN\ \mathbf{EVALUATE}\ MORTAL(x)$$

where MORTAL(x) can then take the value FALSE just as well as the value TRUE.

0.1.3   Condition/action pair + data

You can see immediately that *Form₃* and the LISP representation are equivalent to a condition/action pair with data. We have

Condition: MAN(x), Action: MORTAL(x),

Data: MAN(SOCRATES) & MORTAL(SOCRATES)

In this specific example, the "action" MORTAL(x) does not say very much because 'MORTAL' is obviously the precondition for subsequent actions.

We shall not see condition/action pairs with a "real" action before chapter 4. In chapter 4 section 2, we shall discuss the contribution of the notion of a real action (essentially: an implicit temporality) to representation.

0.1.4   Use of representation by clauses

Form₄

MORTAL(x) :- MAN(x)

MAN(SOCRATES) :-

MORTAL(SOCRATES) :-

0.1.5   **Comparison of** *Form₃* with *Form₄*

Obviously to write   A :- B   amounts to write   IF B THEN A   so that the ' :- ' sign is an   IF. The order of reading is reverse; instead of   ' IF B THEN A ' we say   ' A IF B '.

The formula   ' A :- '   says that A is always true.

The formula   ' :- A '   says that A is always false.

More generally, there are the equivalences (denoted by the symbol ' ~ ')

Let us also denote the logical AND by & , the logical OR by $\vee$, the implication by $\Rightarrow$, the negation by $\neg$.

A; B; C   :-   D, E, F   ~   IF (D & E & F) THEN (A $\vee$ B $\vee$ C)

A   :-   ~   A = TRUE

:-   A   ~   A = FALSE

By using these equivalences, the reader can himself re-write all the assertions shown by this book as clauses in ' IF ... THEN ... ' form.

0.2 Representation of inference

0.2.1 Inference from data with *Form₃*

In this form we first consider the rule
$$IF \ MAN(x) \ THEN \ MORTAL(x)$$
and notice that the fact
$$MAN(SOCRATES) = TRUE$$
satisfies the condition of the rule for the value ' SOCRATES ' of the variable x.
We thus have
$$IF \ TRUE \ THEN \ MORTAL(SOCRATES)$$
which simplifies to
$$MORTAL(SOCRATES) = TRUE.$$

The inference is thus represented by the search for constants which give the value TRUE to the predicates of the conditions.

The programmer is free to choose any method he wants to find these constants.

When we compare LISP and PROLOG, this freedom is a characteristic of LISP (the functional versus logical programming style is the other difference, but it is not our subject here.)

0.2.2 Inference in a LISP representation

There are several cases depending on what is to be represented

First case.

We want to stop after the inference and print the fact that MORTAL(SOCRATES) = TRUE. The solution can then be:

```
(LAMBDA MORTAL(x) (COND
    ((MAN x) (PRINT 'MORTAL( x ') '= 'TRUE))
    . . .
    (TRUE NIL) ))
```

Second case.

We want to transfer the fact that MORTAL(SOCRATES) = TRUE into our data-base. Then we shall have to define a LISP data-base (i.e. a list, of course), in which we shall write that Socrates is mortal, and an inference function which, when evaluated, will add the fact that Socrates is mortal to the list of known facts.

To avoid having too trivial a representation, let us deal at the same time with the inference
$$IF \ WOMAN(x) \ THEN \ MORTAL(x)$$

Letting ' x ' be the variable containing the list of facts, ' x ' is given the beginning value:

$$((MORTAL())(MAN(SOCRATES\ ARISTOTLE...))(WOMAN(MARTA\ BEATA...)))$$

where ' ARISTOTLE ' is also a man, where ' MARTA ' and ' BEATA ' are women, and where the dots represent other known men and women.

Executing the inference simply amounts to transferring the content of the lists that follow ' MAN ', ' WOMAN ', and other mortals into the list that follows 'MORTAL'.

To achieve this, we can use the function ' INFER-MORTAL ' defined as follows

```
(LAMBDA INFER-MORTAL (x) (PRINT (INFER-MORTAL2 (CAR x) (CDR x))))
```

```
(LAMBDA INFER-MORTAL2 (x y)
   (COND
      ((EQ y NIL) x)
      ((EQ (CAAR y)  'MAN) (INFER-MORTAL2 (INSERT-VAL x (CADAR y))(CDR y)))
      ((EQ (CAAR y) 'WOMAN) (INFER-MORTAL2 (INSERT-VAL x (CADAR y))(CDR y)))
      . . .
      (TRUE NIL)))
```

where the row of dots is there to indicate that other inferences on ' MORTAL ' are easy to insert, and where ' INSERT-VAL ' is defined by ;

```
(LAMBDA INSERT-VAL (x v)
   (CONS (CAR x) (LIST (APPEND (CADR x) v))))
```

We shall see in section 0.2.5 that this case is that of forward-chaining (or fact propagation) in a data-base.

Third case.

We do not want to write all the possible consequences of an inference, but only to use it when we need it. Hence we need to represent the inference by a LISP function, as we did in section 0.1.2.

```
LAMBDA MORTAL(x) (COND
      ((MAN x) TRUE)
      (TRUE NIL) ))
```

defines the function ' MORTAL ' which will take the value TRUE when the function MAN(x), defined elsewhere, takes the value TRUE.

0.2.3 General resolution in inference from data

General resolution starts with $Form_4$ and compares the two clauses

MORTAL(x) :- MAN(x)

MAN(SOCRATES) :-

and, as in the preceding case, it has to notice that ' MAN ' occurs on either side of the ' :- ' sign. This leads to the resolution of these two clauses. The mechanism of resolution can be summarized as: the predicates on either side of the ' :- ' are reduced and transmit their instantiations. A rigorous description is given in section 3.

Here, we obtain

MORTAL(SOCRATES) :-

So in our example, the LISP resolution and the general resolution are equivalent. We shall see farther on how they differ.

0.2.4 **PROLOG resolution**

In PROLOG inference is not on the basis of data. In fact, PROLOG does not possess a general resolution mechanism, so that the clauses

MORTAL(x) :- MAN(x)

MAN(SOCRATES) :-

are not reduced, and nothing is concluded at all. PROLOG resolution only starts when a problem is set. Suppose here that we invoke the query

Is Socrates mortal?

The clause which says that Socrates is mortal is

MORTAL(SOCRATES) :-

PROLOG works by refutation. The user has to set the problem by denying its conclusion. So here, the user would have to write

:- MORTAL(SOCRATES)

to invoke the query of whether Socrates is mortal. Then the complete system is

MORTAL(x) :- MAN(x)

MAN(SOCRATES) :-

:- MORTAL(SOCRATES)

Hence only the clauses whose concluding parts can be resolved with the query are used. Here, the conclusion of the clause

MORTAL(x) :- MAN(x)

can be resolved with

:- MORTAL(SOCRATES)

This generates the new query

:- MAN(SOCRATES)

This new problem could in turn generate other problems. Here this is not the case because

:- MORTAL(SOCRATES) and MORTAL(SOCRATES) :-

contradict each other, since it is obviously contradictory to declare at the same time that Socrates is mortal and that he is not mortal.

This contradiction is called the empty clause. As is standard in refutation arguments, we deduce from the empty clause that it was absurd to have denied ' MAN(SOCRATES) ', and hence that it should have been asserted.

Hence we do have

MORTAL(SOCRATES) :-

Clearly this way of reasoning is extremely rigid, but this is what makes it efficient in execution.

0.2.5 Forward versus backward chaining

Thus, PROLOG's only way of working is to set itself problems and to generate the associated sub-problems until it arrives at the empty clause.

This way of proceeding, by studying the conclusions of clauses instead of their conditions, is called **backward chaining**. The fact that a clause is added denying the query is called **refutation**.

So PROLOG works by backward chaining and by refutation.

Inference from data, as presented in 0.2.1 and 0.2.2, is called **forward chaining**.

It is well-known that EMYCIN, for instance, essentially works by backward chaining, even though it is a product of the LISP school [Waterman & Hayes-Roth 1978].

This clearly shows that in practice the creators of Expert Systems and the creators of PROLOG, all faced with the same problem of accelerating the speed of inference, chose similar solutions.

Today's usage shows that PROLOG is a language particularly well suited to writing Expert Systems. This tends to bridge the gap which separates the supporters of LISP from those of PROLOG.

The choice between backward versus forward chaining is not tied to the representation chosen.

In the representation of *Form₃*, backward chaining behaves as follows.
The initial rule is always considered
$$IF \ MAN(x) \ THEN \ MORTAL(x)$$
but now, instead of seeking the values which make the condition TRUE, a query is invoked, here:
$$Is \ Socrates \ mortal? \quad \tilde{} \quad MORTAL(SOCRATES) = TRUE \ ?$$

Only then is it noticed that one of the conditions for Socrates being mortal is that
$$MAN(SOCRATES) = TRUE.$$

With such a small number of clauses, the difference between forward chaining and backward chaining is not striking.

So let us imagine that we face a data-base containing thousands of clauses. Then there is a big difference between the two. In one case, we try to use all the available knowledge by propagating truth through forward chaining. In the other case, on the contrary, we ask a precise question and only seek the information relevant to this problem.

In LISP representation, if we choose to put the facts into lists, then we are rather led to use forward chaining, since the known facts will be propagated within the lists of facts. Conversely, if we choose a functional representation of inference, we shall be more likely to chain backward, since the inference will only be carried out when the function it represents is evaluated.

Exercise 1
****

Using the predicates
MAN(x), WOMAN(x), GOD(x), MORTAL(x), SICK(x), TO-BE-TREATED(x)
which take the value TRUE if ' x ' is a man, woman, God, mortal or somebody being treated, put the following sentences into IF ... THEN form, condition-action pairs, clauses, LISP lists and LISP programs.

All men are mortal. All women are mortal. No God is mortal. All sick mortals must be treated. Beatrice is a woman. Christel is a woman. Marta is a woman. Nadia is a woman. Sophie is a woman. Sylvie is a woman. Socrates is a man. Zeus is a God. Socrates is sick.
Propagate the system's knowledge by forward chaining.
Answer the queries: Must Socrates be treated? Must Zeus be treated?

****

Note to readers in a hurry.
You certainly will not do this exercise. Nevertheless, be aware that if you are not capable of "seeing" how it can be solved, then you will not be able to understand the rest.

1 CLAUSES

1.1 Definitions

A procedure exists which we shall now take a rather quick look at which is called: **conversion into conjunctive normal form**.

The importance of conversion into conjunctive normal form is that there is a theorem which (almost) all automatic theorem-proving is based on. Let A be a formula of first-order logic and let A' be this same formula put into conjunctive normal form. This theorem says:

A and A' are not equivalent but A is unsatisfiable if and only if A' is.

Appendix 1 is entirely devoted to this theorem. It includes the background knowledge, so that a person who has not studied standard logic can perfectly well understand it.

In Logic, we use the label **connective** to denote logical symbols finite in number and known in advance, whose definition is a part of Logic.

For example, the logical AND: & , the logical OR: $\vee$, implication: $\Rightarrow$, negation: $\neg$, are connectives of this kind.

We use the label **elementary atom** (or, equivalently: **atomic formula**) to refer to symbols for the facts. The **predicates** are the symbols from which these formula are built.

For example, RED(x) is a particular fact, called an atomic formula, (' RED ' is a predicate) which takes the value TRUE when x is red and the value FALSE when it is not.

Anything which is either an elementary atom or the negation of an elementary atom is called a **literal**.

For example, RED(x) and $\neg$ RED(x) are literals.

Conversion into normal form consists in transforming a quantified formula A into a formula without quantifiers whose form is:

$$A_1 \ \& \ A_2 \ \& \ ... \ \& \ A_n$$

where each A_i is a disjunction of literals, and where all variables are implicitly universally quantified.

So each A_i has the form:

$$A_{i1} \vee A_{i2} \vee ... \vee A_{ip} \vee \neg A_{ip+1} \vee ... \vee \neg A_{iq}$$

where we suppose that there are p positive literals and q - p negative literals.

Clearly, logical implication can be expressed as a function of other logical connectives, for if P and Q are two propositions then

$$P \Rightarrow Q \text{ is equivalent to } \neg P \vee Q.$$

All this is elementary but it is at the heart of applications of Logic to AI.

Since each A_i is in the above form, we can write it

$$A_{ip+1} \ \& \ ... \ \& \ A_{iq} \Rightarrow A_{i1} \vee ... \vee A_{ip}.$$

Introducing an "IF" notation (written :-), we have:

$$A_{i1} \vee ... \vee A_{ip} :- A_{ip+1} \ \& \ ... \ \& \ A_{iq}.$$

Such an expression is called a clause. It is most often seen in the form

$$A_{i1}; ...; A_{ip} :- A_{ip+1}, ..., A_{iq}$$

where it is implicit that the ' ; ' to the left of the ' :- ' stand for $\vee$ and the ' , ' to the right of the ' :- ' stand for &.

A Horn clause is a clause where p = 1, i.e. it has the form

$$A_{i1} :- A_{i1+1}, ..., A_{iq}.$$

where q > 0. In particular, if q = 1, a Horn clause of the form

$$A_{i1} :-$$

is often called a fact.

Let us return to the starting formula A. It will be represented by a set of clauses which will be required, taken together, to take the value TRUE.

Thus, when two clauses are put together, they are always required to be simultaneously satisfied, since they are assumed to have come from the same formula which has been converted into normal form.

In the same way, when working with Horn clauses like

$$A_{i1} :- A_{i1+1}, ..., A_{iq}$$

we require all the atoms $A_{i1+1}, ..., A_{iq}$ to be simultaneously satisfied.

So finally the equivalence theorem we spoke of becomes a theorem of equivalence between logical formulae and a set of clauses.

The Skolemization of a formula consists in suppressing the quantifiers in accordance with the convention that the variables within the scope of a ∃ sign are replaced by functions (called Skolem functions) depending on universally quantified variables whose ∀ occurs in front of the ∃ concerned. Of course, it follows that when a ∃ comes first, the variable under its scope is turned into a constant.

The choice of an appropriate Skolem function is a problem which nobody has envisaged an automatic solution to as far as we know. However, as the following examples clearly show, it is quite all right to convert a sentence expressing a feature into a theorem when its conversion into a clause (or rule) requires a Skolemization which can only be done well by a domain expert. Techniques for acquiring knowledge to construct Expert Systems must not fail to get the expert to point out the right Skolem functions.

Example 3 below illustrates this problem. In due course it will become clear that Skolemization and the classification of variables are two facets of one and the same problem.

1.2 Problems involved in the conversion of sentences into clause form

In this section we shall only see the most elementary problems; chapter 3 and the beginning of chapter 4 will treat them in greater depth.

Attempts to convert even the simplest sentences into theorems immediately run up against difficulties which are usually passed over in discrete silence. These difficulties are due to the fact that the sentence can mean several different things.

The "semantic networks" solution to this problem is to postpone it until the time when the semantic network will actually be used. If a logical representation is required for a piece of knowledge then choices have to be made immediately, since the only way of using it is through theorem derivation.

Example 1: 'Iron is a metal'.

This sentence means that everything made of iron is metal but that not all metals are iron.

To express that in logic there are 3 solutions.

1- One is to say that METAL is a unary predicate METAL(x) which takes the value TRUE when x = IRON.

This is represented by the clause
       METAL(IRON):-

2- Another solution is to say that METAL and IRON are two unary predicates, one of which implies the other.

So we have the theorem
$$\forall x \ [IRON(x) \Rightarrow METAL(x)]$$
which can be represented by the clause
       METAL(x) :- IRON(x)

3- Another is to rely directly on a hierarchy and to say that the class IRON is a subclass or "descendant" of the class METAL.
       Type IRON: IRON1
       Type METAL: METAL1
       Class IRON < METAL
where IRON1 and METAL1 are constants, in this case some particular object made of iron and hence of metal.

This last representation is of a different order from the other two since the standard resolution procedure cannot be directly applied to it. It is used as a piece of meta-knowledge for controlling resolution; we shall see how in chapter 3.

Example 2: 'Man is fallible '.

This simple sentence is capable of a multitude of interpretations.
We shall give just some of them below, but it must be said that some are rather unlikely and serve rather to illustrate the difficulty of choosing the right representation.

1- Taken on its own, it generally means that fallibility is one of the characteristics of humanity, which is written:
       $\forall x \ [MAN(x) \Rightarrow FALLIBLE(x)]$
       FALLIBLE(x) :- MAN(x)
which gives FALLIBLE the same type of dependence on Man that METAL had on IRON in interpretation 2 above.

A *refusal to accept that iron is to metal what man is to fallible forces us to choose between two different representations.*

2- In certain contexts the 'the' in 'the man' will point to a particular individual being referred to. This usage is more common when the aim is to warn somebody, for instance, referring to a quite specific person, to say 'Look out, the man is irritable'.

In this case, letting 'Robert' be the man in question, the logical representation must refer to him directly:

MAN(Robert) & FALLIBLE(Robert) *represented by the two clauses*
MAN(Robert) :-
FALLIBLE(Robert) :-

3- This sentence could also mean that 'fallible' is a necessary and sufficient characteristic of humanity, saying implicitly that other beings cannot be fallible. Of course, it would have been better then to say:

'Only man is fallible and all men are.'

$$\forall x \ [FALLIBLE(x) \Leftrightarrow MAN(x)]$$

Equivalence is represented by two clauses (which introduce a computation loop in resolution. Many methods have been proposed to deal with such loops; we shall see only the Knuth-Bendix completion here, in section 2.4.)

MAN(x) :- FALLIBLE(x)
FALLIBLE(x) :- MAN(x)

4- If the meaning were 'only Man is fallible', then we should have to write

$$\forall x \ [FALLIBLE(x) \Rightarrow MAN(x)]$$

MAN(x) :- FALLIBLE(x)

5- If we interpret it by: 'There are men who are fallible' then we have to write

$$\exists x \ [MAN(x) \Rightarrow FALLIBLE(x)]$$ *which can be put into clause form provided an instance of x <<no quotes?> is available, say, 'Robert'*

FALLIBLE(Robert) :- MAN(Robert)

6- If it is interpreted by: 'Fallible can characterize certain men' then we must write it:

$$\exists x \ [FALLIBLE(x) \Rightarrow MAN(x)]$$ *Still for the sake of Skolemization, this is also written*

MAN(Robert) :- FALLIBLE(Robert)

Finally, if the meaning required had been: ' There is no human who is not fallible', then we would have had to write:

$$\forall x \ [\neg \, FALLIBLE(x) \Rightarrow \neg \, MAN(x)]$$ *which amounts to form 1- above.*

Exercise 2
****

Discuss the interpretations 1 to 7 above.

Look for an interpretation for the formula ∃x [FALLIBLE(x) ⟺ MAN(x)]

****

Example 3: 'Everybody makes mistakes.'

a - form in first-order logic
        ∀x ∃ y [HUMAN(x) ⟹ DOES(x, y) & MISTAKE(y)]

b - transformations
The variable ' y ' under the scope of the ∀ quantifier ' x ' has to be Skolemized.
We could bring in an arbitrary Skolem function and transform
        ∀x ∃y [DOES(x, y) & MISTAKE(y)] *into*
        'DOES(x, g(x))'. *where g has to express the dependence between an agent*
'x' and what he does.

In practice, it would be awkward to neglect the information we have about the
predicate 'does', which tells us that what is done is called an 'action'. For this rea-
son we transform
        ∀x ∃y [DOES(x, y) & MISTAKE(y)] *into*
        'DOES(x, action(x)) & MISTAKE(action (x))' where the function
'action(x)' can if necessary stand for known features (e.g. that an action has a
cause and an effect, that there is a situation of failure if the action is not followed
by effects, etc ...).

Looking back now at the first solution to example 1, it emerges that this function
'action(x)' is only there to specify the type of y = action(x). Assuming that the type
'action' exists, then we could just as well Skolemize
        ∀x ∃y [DOES(x, y) & MISTAKE(y)] *into*
        [type y: action] DOES(x, y) & MISTAKE(y).*

Thus, we obtain
        b_1:   [HUMAN(x) ⟹ DOES(x, action(x)) & MISTAKE(action(x))]
        b_2:   [¬ HUMAN(x)] ⋁ [DOES(x, action(x)) & MISTAKE(action(x))]

        b_3:   [¬ HUMAN(x) ⋁ DOES(x, action(x))] & [¬ HUMAN(x) ⋁
MISTAKE(action(x))]

c - CLAUSES:

        DOES(x, action(x)) :- HUMAN(x)
        MISTAKE(action(x)) :- HUMAN(x)

Example 4: 'One person is the ancestor of another either if he or she is the parent of another or if he or she is the ancestor of an ancestor of another.'

a - form in first-order logic:

$\forall x \, \forall y \, [PARENT(x, y) \lor \exists z \, [ANC(x, z) \,\&\, ANC(z, y)] \Rightarrow ANC(x, y)]$

b - transformations

b_1: $ANC(x, y) \lor [\neg \, PARENT(x, y) \,\&\, \forall z \, \neg \, [ANC(x, z) \,\&\, ANC(z, y)]]$

c - CLAUSES:

$ANC(x, y)$:- $PARENT(x, y)$
$ANC(x, y)$:- $ANC(x, z) \,\&\, ANC(z, y)$

Example 5: 'A supplier is preferred when all the things he delivers arrive on time'

$\forall x \, [[SUPPLIER(x) \,\&\, \forall u \, [DELIVERS(x, u) \Rightarrow ARRIVEONTIME(u)]] \Rightarrow$
$\qquad PREFERRED(x)]$.
$\forall x \, [PREFERRED(x) \lor \neg \, SUPPLIER(x) \lor$
$\qquad \neg \, \forall u \, [\neg \, DELIVERS(x, u) \lor ARRIVEONTIME(u)]]$
$\forall x \, [PREFERRED(x) \lor \neg \, SUPPLIER(x) \lor$
$\qquad \exists u \, [DELIVERS(x, u) \,\&\, \neg \, ARRIVEONTIME(u)]]$

So the variable ' u ' has to be Skolemized. As you see, the last disjunct asserts the existence of something which gets delivered, which we are going to call goods.

It can be proved that the initial theorem has an interpretation if and only if the clause obtained by replacing ' u ' by $f(x)$ is unsatisfiable. On the other hand, it is worth choosing an f which makes the existential true. For this reason the problem of choosing the right Skolemization function, although it is totally uninteresting in automatic theorem-proving, becomes very important when the Skolem function ' f ' really has to be chosen from among the functions with known features. For example, the function ' $goods(x)$ ' can have instances in the data-base which are important to reckon with. As we have said already in section 1.1, it is the problem of choosing the right type of variable.

$\forall x \, [PREFERRED(x) \lor \neg \, SUPPLIER(x) \lor [DELIVERS(x, goods(x)) \,\&\,$
$\qquad \neg \, ARRIVEONTIME(goods(x))]]$
$[PREFERRED(x) \lor \neg \, SUPPLIER(x) \lor DELIVERS(x, goods(x))] \,\&\,$
$\qquad [PREFERRED(x) \lor \neg \, SUPPLIER(x) \lor \neg \, ARRIVEONTIME(goods(x))]$.

Which gives the following set of clauses:

$PREFERRED(x)$:- $SUPPLIER(x), ARRIVEONTIME(goods(x))$
$PREFERRED(x); DELIVERS(x, goods(x))$:- $SUPPLIER(x)$

2 UNIFICATION

2.1 Terms

There are plenty of formal presentations which start with the definitions you need in order to know how to use terms, so that you then understand the problems bound up with unification.

In view of the importance of the problem of unification in ML (as in AI generally) our definition now is going to be more intuitive, and illustrated by some examples.

Let V = {x, y, z, ...}, a denumerable set of variables and let Φ = {f, g, h, ...}, a finite or denumerable set of functional symbols, at least one of which has arity greater than one.

2.1.1 Terms

A **set of terms**, written T, will be the set recursively defined as follows:
- the members of V are terms,
- for any functional symbol f of arity n and any series of n terms M_1, ..., M_n; $f(M_1, ..., M_n)$ is a term.

> *Example 6*
> *The functional symbol for addition, +, has an arity of 2.*
> *With the use of this symbol (of arity greater than one), ' 27 ' and ' 38 ' (which are functions of arity zero) and the variables x and y, we can construct a set of terms*
> *{x, y, 27, 38, (x + y), (x + 27), ..., ((x + y) + x), ...}.*

Remarks
People habitually confuse functional symbols with the evaluation of the functional operation associated with them. This is convenient as long as the features of the functions are disregarded, which is what this account does at first.

In other words, terms are ordered trees and no feature is attached to their nodes.

The term 2 + 3 is different from the term 3 + 2, even though they both evaluate to 5. Here , the property of commutativity of + is disregarded.

A constant is a function of arity zero; they will be written A, B, C, ...
The current term of T will be written t.

2.1.2 Various definitions

Let us define a number of intuitively clear concepts applicable to terms, and let us illustrate our discussion as we go along by the terms

$T_1 = f(g(h(x, A)), h(g(z), g(z)))$ and $T_2 = f(z, w)$ where x, z and w are variables and where A is a constant.

The representation of T_1 as a tree is

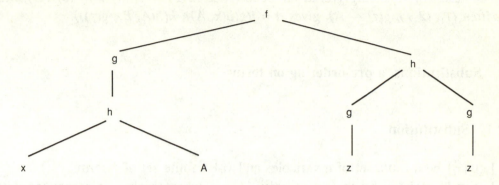

The set of **variables of a term** is defined as the set formed by the variables which occur in the term, taken without repetition.

The set of variables of T_1 is $\{x, z\}$.

The **size of a term** is defined as the number of links present when it is represented as a tree.

The size of T_1 is 9, that of T_2 is 2.

Every time that a node is a function of arity n, each child of this node can be denoted by a number between 1 and n.

We choose to number the child nodes from left to right in the tree representation of a term. In other words, the tree associated with a term is numbered in prefix order and the occurrences in these terms are lists of integers made from these numbers.

The root of the tree is numbered 0, its left-hand child by 1, its lefthand-lefthand grandchild by 11, etc...

In T_1, the child 1 of f is g, child 2 is h.

An occurrence of a term is defined as the place of one of the nodes of the term. This place is referred to by the series of integers showing the path from the root of the term to the node in question.

In T_1, the occurrence of x is (1 1 1), the occurrence of A is (1 1 2), the leftmost occurrence of z is (2 1 1).

A sub-term ' t' ' of ' t ' at the occurrence ' u ' is the term whose root is at the occurrence ' u ' of t.

Let us consider the occurrence (2 1) of T_1.

The sub-term ' t' ' occurring at the occurrence (2 1) of T_1 is g(z), which is the leftmost g(z) of T_1.

The **replacement** of the sub-term ' t' ' at the occurrence ' u ' of ' t ' by the term t" (the result of which will be called tt) is denoted by

$$(t, u, t' \leftarrow t").$$

It consists in replacing the sub-term ' t' ' at the occurrence ' u ' by the term t".

The result of replacing g(z) at the occurrence (2 1) of T_1, by t" = h(A, B), which is written (T_1, (2 1), g(z) ← t"), gives tt = f(g(h(x, A)), h(h(A, B), g(z))).

2.2   Substitutions, a pre-ordering on terms

2.2.1   Substitution

Let $\{x_i\}$ be a finite set of n variables and $\{t_i\}$ a finite set of n terms.

Let σ be defined by the set of pairs $\{x_i, t_j\}$, where each x_i is associated with a different t_j. We say that σ is a substitution when this definition is extended to the set of terms T by requiring:

For any f of arity n, f ∈ Φ, $\sigma(f(t_1, ..., t_n)) = f(\sigma(t_1), ..., \sigma(t_n))$.

From now on we shall write σ(t) as σ.t and the composition of the two substitutions σ and ρ by σ.ρ.

Clearly this composition, without which the notion of the most general unifier cannot be understood, is defined by:

$$\forall \, t \in T, \, [\sigma.\rho].t = \sigma.[\rho.t].$$

It follows that the composition of substitutions is not commutative.

Example 7

$\{x \leftarrow cons(x, A)\}.\{x \leftarrow cons(A, B)\} = \{x \leftarrow cons(A, B)\}$ *and*

$\{x \leftarrow cons(A, B)\}.\{x \leftarrow cons(x, A)\} = \{x \leftarrow cons(cons(A, B), A)\}$.

A **permutation** is a special substitution in which some variables are substituted for other variables.

The permutations of T will be written χ.

2.2.2   Generalization

We say that ' t ' is more general than ' t' ', written t ≤ t', if a substitution σ exists such that σ.t = t'. This definition induces a partial ordering of the terms. Some of them are not comparable because there is no such substitution. On the other hand, whenever such substitution exists, either it is a simple permutation and one says that t = t' (relative to this partial ordering), or it different from a permutation and t < t' or t > t'.

We also say that ' t' ' matches ' t ', or that ' t' ' is an instance of ' t ', that σ is the matching substitution of ' t' ' toward ' t ', that the operation of finding σ is a pattern-matching.

Example 8

Let t = cons(x, cons(B, cons(y, NIL))). That is, ' t ' is the LISP list: (x B y).

Also let t' = cons(cons(A, NIL), cons(B, cons(C, NIL))). That is, ' t' ' is the LISP list: ((A) B C).

The term ' t ' is more general than ' t' ', since σ.t = t', with σ = {x ← cons(A, NIL), y ← C}.

Negative examples.

1- The term t = cons(x, A) is neither more nor less general than t' = cons(B, y), since no σ exists such that either σ.t = t' nor such that σ.t' = t.

2- the term t = cons(x, x) is no more general than t' = cons(A, B), since the application of σ = {x ← A, x ← B} to a term is undefined, since there is no knowing whether x is to be replaced by A or by B.

3- the term t = cons(x, A) is no more general than the term t' = cons(x, B), since the replacement {A ← B} at occurrence 2 of ' t ' is not a substitution.

Negative negative example.

The term t = cons(x, A) is more general than the term t' = cons(cons(A, x), A), since the substitution σ = {x ← cons(A, x)} is indeed such that σ.t = cons(cons(A, x), A) = t'. In other words, there is no "occur check" when executing matchings.

This last negative negative example is historically interesting, since PROLOG underwent a dispute due to the fact that, in general, PROLOG's unification algorithm does not look for the occur check.

Exercise 4
****

Verify that in the absence of functions there can be no occur check in a unification.

Analyze the complication introduced into PROLOG when the use of functional expressions is authorized.

****

2.2.3 Properties of matching substitution

These properties will be given here without proof.

Uniqueness

$\forall$ t, t', σ, σ': [t' = σ.t] & [t' = σ'.t] $\Rightarrow$ σ = σ'.

Equivalence of two terms

The term ' t ' is equivalent to t' if and only if a permutation χ exists such that t = χ.t'.

Pre-ordering on substitutions

σ $\Leftarrow$ σ' if and only if there exists a ρ such that σ' = ρ.σ.

So the pre-ordering on substitutions derives from the concept of the composition of two substitutions.

Equivalence of two substitutions

σ is equivalent to σ' if and only if a permutation χ exists such that σ = χ.σ' .

2.2.4   The "nearest" generalization

Depending on the authors, this concept is called either the "least" or the "greatest" generalization. Intuitively, it is the generalization of two terms that keeps the most of their common properties. This is why we shall call it the "nearest", and also, by abbreviation, "the" generalization.

Let ' t ' and ' t' ' be two terms. There is a proof of the uniqueness of t_g, the nearest generalization of ' t ' and ' t' ', defined by the Sup of the generalizations of ' t ' and ' t' '. If $\{t_i\}$ is the set of terms of T which are more general (i.e. smaller) than ' t ' and ' t' ', then $t_g = \text{Sup}\{t_i\}$, where ' Sup ' refers to the partial ordering defined in section 2.2.2.

Trivially, the most general generalization of two terms is a variable ' x ', since for any couple of terms (t, t') there exists always the required two substitutions, namely {x ← t} and {x ← t'}. Clearly, those loose all the information common to t and t'. This shows why one tries to find a term that is a generalization of t and t', but also that stays as near as possible of both t and t'.

The algorithm for calculating the nearest generalization of t and t' is the following.

Let G(t, t') be the nearest generalization of ' t ' and ' t' ' and let ' v ' be a variable which receives ' t ' and ' t' ',

1- if ' t ' and ' t' ' are variables and if t = t' then G(t, t') = t.

2- If t and ' t' ' are different (i.e. different variables, different functions, or one is a variable and the other is a function), then G(t, t') = v.

3- if ' t ' and ' t' ' are functions and t = $f(t_1 ..., t_n)$ and t' = $f(t_1' ..., t_n')$, then G(t, t') = $f(G(t_1, t_1'), ..., G(t_n, t_n'))$.

It is presupposed that each triplet (v, t, t') is preserved during the execution of the algorithm and that if a triplet (v', t, t') appears, then v = v'.

2.2.5   Forced matching

(The phrase is derived from J. Darlington's PhD thesis).

   Example 9

   Let us assume that we want to match t_1 = cons(x, cons(cons(x, NIL), NIL)) and t_2 = cons(A, cons(cons(B, cons(C NIL))NIL)).

   This matching fails. Let us refer to the replacements which allow the transition

from t_1 to t_2 as σ_{12}.

$\sigma_{12} = \{(t_1, 1, x \leftarrow A), (t_1, 211, x \leftarrow B), (t_1, 212, nil \leftarrow cons(C, nil))\}.$

Note that the third replacement is considered as being done in t_1. This is because the size (defined in section 2.2.1) of NIL is less than the size of cons(C, NIL).

If the algorithm of the nearest generalization is applied to t_1 and t_2, it yields t' = cons(u, cons(cons(v, w), nil)).

Definition
The triplet consisting of the nearest generalization of t_1 and t_2, the replacements in t_1 allowing the transition from t_1 to t_2, and the matching substitution of t_2 toward t' is called the **forced matching** of t_2 against t_1.

In example 9, the triplet is (t', σ_{12}, σ' = {u $\leftarrow$ A, v $\leftarrow$ B, w $\leftarrow$ cons(C, NIL)}).

Failure of forced matching
If the replacements in the two terms contradict the ordering on the size of the terms, then there is said to be a **failure of forced matching**.

Example 10

If the NIL at 22 of t_2 is replaced by a variable y, then (t_1, 22, NIL $\leftarrow$ y) contradicts the ordering on the terms, since in all the orderings which are possible and suggested in the literature, a variable is always lower than a function.

2.3 Unification

Let there be two terms, t_1 and t_2. They are said to have been unified when a substitution σ has been found such that $\sigma.t_1 = \sigma.t_2$.

This substitution σ is called the **unifier** of t_1 and t_2, and the term $\sigma.t_1$ (= $\sigma.t_2$, of course) is called the **unification** of t_1 and t_2.

In a sense, this means solving the equation $t_1 = t_2$, since it finds the conditions under which these two terms will become equal.

Let $U(t_1, t_2)$ be the set of unifiers of t_1 and t_2.

What Robinson's Unification Theorem says is that any pair of terms t_1 and t_2 whose variables are separate (they have no variables in common) and which have a common upper bound must have a unique most general unifier σ where σ is the very smallest element of $U(t_1, t_2)$ in accordance with the inherent order on substitutions defined above.

This result is true of terms as defined here and in first-order logic. It is important to note that it becomes false when functional variables are introduced. This is a major theoretical result for AI. For years researchers have been aware that the solution to their problems lies in "changing to higher-order", without recognizing that the problem of the recognition of terms then becomes insoluble. This does not prohibit changing to higher- order, but it implies that certain precautions have to be taken.

This being so, the difficult problem consists in finding the smallest substitution, if it exists, which unifies two terms that can have variables in common. This is what Robinson did first; his algorithm has been followed by a series of others which improve on its complexity.

It must also be remembered that the majority of unifications are merely matchings and that the majority of this majority do not include an "occur check". So when applying a unification algorithm in practice, it is essential to study its speed in relation to the task it is given.

Examples 11 and negative examples

1- The unified representation of cons(x, cons(A, NIL)) and cons(A, cons(A, NIL)) is cons(A, cons(A, NIL)) with $\sigma = \{x \leftarrow A\}$. As you see, this is trivially lower than the substitution $\sigma' = \{x \leftarrow A, x \leftarrow A\}$ which is obtained first.

2- The terms $t_1 = cons(x, cons(A, NIL))$ and $t_2 = cons(B, cons(x, NIL))$ have no common unification , since $\sigma = \{x \leftarrow A, x \leftarrow B\}$ yields no common unified representation. It will be noticed that t_1 and $t_2' = t_2[(11) \leftarrow y]$ have a unified representation now that they no longer have any variables in common.

3- $t_1 = cons(x, A)$ and $t_2 = cons(cons(A, x), A)$ have no common unified representation. This can be seen by calculating $\sigma.t_1$ and $\sigma.t_2$. This is the "occur check" already mentioned which consists in noticing that there is a variable on either side of the substitution.

4- $t_1 = cons(x, cons(x, A))$ and $t_2 = cons(cons(y, A))$ have no variables in common, and yet $\sigma = \{x \leftarrow cons(y, A), y \leftarrow cons(y, A)\}$ is not a unifying substitution, as can be seen by calculating $\sigma.t_1$ and $\sigma.t_2$. Another way of looking at it is to calculate the minimum substitution required by carrying out the substitution $\sigma' = \{y \leftarrow Cons(x, A)\}$ on σ. We now have $\sigma'.\sigma = \{x \leftarrow cons(cons(x, A), A), y \leftarrow cons(A, x)\}$. This substitution now reveals an occur check.

3   RESOLUTION AND INFERENCE ON A SET OF CLAUSES

3.1   The Kowalski resolution algorithm

In a clause $A_1, ..., A_m :- B_1, ..., B_n$ the terms A_i are called the conclusions of the clause and the terms B_j are called the conditions of the clause.

We shall give a resolution algorithm for the case where the clauses have different variable names (otherwise they would have to be re-named). Here is a definition of the function ' resolves(x, u, y, v, σ) ', which resolves a condition ' u ' of the clause x with a conclusion ' v ' of the clause y.

clause x: ... :- ..., u, ...

clause y: ..., v, ... :- ...

which are such that ' u ' and v can be unified by the substitution σ.

Assume, then, that we have a (known) function ' member ', which tests whether or not an atom is a member of a set, and a (known) function ' unifies' which returns the value TRUE when ' u ' and ' v ' can be unified and which assigns their most general unifier to σ. This is written

resolves(x, u, y, v, σ) :- member(u, cond(x)), member(v, concl(y)), unifies(u, v, σ)

where cond(x) is the set of conditions of x and concl(y) is the set of conclusions of ' y '.

When ' u ' and ' v ' are atoms which unify, let us now refer to the resolvent of x and y as ' rst ', so that we have rst(x, u, y, v). Let us see what is required for an atom w to be part of the conditions of this resolvent.

1- It stems from one of the atoms in the conditions of x or y, to which the substitution σ has been applied. Let ' w' ' be this original atom. Let us call the function that applies a substitution ' applies '. Then

applies(w', σ, w)

must be true.

2- Of course, ' w' ' and ' u ' must be different, since ' u ' disappears during the resolution. Let ' different ' be the function which checks this. Then we must have

different(w', u).

3- The term ' w' ' was required to belong to the condition of x or y. Let ' union ' represent the union operation of set theory. Then we have

member(w', union(cond(x), cond(y))).

4- Lastly, ' u ' and ' v ' are required to resolve ' x ' and ' y ' with the substitution ' σ ', so we must have

resolves(x, u, y, v, σ).

We conclude by writing:
 member(w (cond(res(x, u, y, v))) :- resolves(x, u, y, v, σ), member(w', union(cond(x), cond(y))), different(w', v), applies(w', σ, w)

Of course, we need the symmetrical function for ' concl ':
 member(w (concl(res(x, u, y, v))) :- resolves(x, u, y, v, σ), member(w', union(concl(x), concl(y))), different(w', u), applies(w', σ, w).

Negative example
Let x, y, u, v be integers and S the successor function.
Consider the clauses

$$S(x) \vee S(y) :-$$
$$:- S(u), S(v).$$

Resolving them, for example, through S(x) and S(u), we obtain
$$S(y) :- S(v)$$

By renaming these two clauses for the unifications, we shall be able to resolve this last clause either with S(x') ∨ S(y') :- or with :- S(u'), S(v').

With S(x') ∨ S(y') :- we obtain S(y) ∨ S(y') :- , which, except for a renaming, is identical with S(x) ∨ S(y) :- .

With :- S(u'), S(v') we shall obtain :- S(v), S(v') , which is identical, except for a renaming, with :- S(u), S(v) .

So in both cases we have introduced an infinite loop of resolution, when we know the "empty clause" solution with {x ← u, y ← v}.

So Kowalski's method is not complete unless we add the **factorization rule**: When two atoms in the same condition or the same conclusion are identical except for a renaming of their variables, then they must be identified.

Resolution, seen as problem-solving, enables the "&-∨" trees of AI to be represented.

The origin of the "&" signs is the desirability of on the one hand simultaneously satisfying all the clauses while on the other hand simultaneously satisfying the atoms to the right of the :- .

When the clauses are not Horn clauses, the origin of the "∨" signs is also double.

On the one hand, the atoms to the left of the :- form a disjunction.

For instance, the clause A_1; A_2 :- A_3 means that if A_3 is true, then it can be concluded either that A_1 is true or that A_2 is true.

On the other hand, during the resolution it is possible for several clauses to be candidates; hence either the one clause or one of the others can be chosen.

For example, if we have the set of clauses:

> *HUMAN(x) :- MAMMAL(x), ... (the ... represent the other conditions*
for a mammal being human)
> *:- HUMAN(Fido)*
> *:- HUMAN(Blanchette)*

the resolution can follow two paths by choosing to propagate either the fact that Fido is not human or the fact that Blanchette is not human.

3.2 A complete example *(Example 12)*

This example is actually an exercise, the solution of which will be given at once.

Study the information contained in the following 7 assertions.

1- Animals are offended if I pay no attention to them.
2- Animals which are not in this meadow do not belong to me.
3- No animal can solve a riddle if it has not received an education.
4- None of the animals in this meadow is a racoon.
5- When an animal is insulted, it yelps.
6- I pay no attention to an animal which does not belong to me.
7- No animal that has received an education yelps.
8- Oscar is a racoon.

Translate assertions 1-7 into clauses, after having put them into disjunctive normal form. Use only the following predicates:
Attention(x), Insulted(x), InMeadow(x), BelongsToMe(x), Education(x), Yelps(x), CanSolveRiddle(x), Racoon(x).

Solution
The following set of clauses is obtained:

(C_1) *Insulted(x) $\vee$ Attention(x) :-*
(C_2) *InMeadow(x) :- BelongsToMe(x)*
(C_3) *Education(x) :- CanSolveRiddle(x)*
(C_4) *:- InMeadow(x), Racoon(x)*
(C_5) *Yelps(x) :- Insulted(x)*
(C_6) *BelongsToMe(x) :- Attention(x)*
(C_7) *:- Yelps(x), Education(x)*

We have a set of clauses here, which is hence equivalent to theorems. To ask what information is available about racoons, for example, is to ask which theorems concern racoons and which can be deduced concerning them.
The only theorem containing "Racoon" is C_4, from which it follows that the information can only be deduced by "backward chaining".

We have C_4, then from C_4 and C_2 we deduce:

(C_8) *:- BelongsToMe(x), Racoon(x)*

from C_8 and C_6 we deduce:

(C_9) *:- Attention(x), Racoon(x)*

from C_9 and C_1 we deduce:

(C_{10}) *Insulted(x) :- Racoon(x)*

from C_{10} and C_5 we deduce:

(C_{11}) *Yelps(x) :- Racoon(x)*

from C_{11} and C_7 we deduce:

(C_{12}) *:- Education(x), Racoon(x)*

from C_{12} and C_3 we deduce:

(C_{13}) *:- CanSolveRiddle(x), Racoon(x)*

3.3 Using Resolution

We insisted in section 1.1 of this chapter on the importance of the equivalence between the incoherence of a theorem and the incoherence of the set of clauses derived from it by the procedure of conversion into conjunctive normal form. This assertion will now be illustrated.

Logic uses well-known **inference rules** that are to be found in all the introductory texts. We are now giving Modus Ponens and its mirror-image Modus Tollens.

Modus Ponens: A, A $\Rightarrow$ B / B

Modus Tollens: $\neg$ A, B $\Rightarrow$ A / $\neg$ B

This is read

Modus Ponens: from A and from A implies B, infer B.

Modus Tollens: from A = FALSE and from B implies A, infer B = FALSE.

Modus Ponens is merely the mirror-image of Modus Tollens, since the implication

A $\Rightarrow$ B is also written

$\neg$ A $\vee$ B.

Thus, replacing A by $\neg$ A and B by $\neg$ B, Modus Ponens is written

$\neg$A, $\neg\neg$A $\vee$ $\neg$B / $\neg$B

and, using the equivalence $\neg\neg$A $\Leftrightarrow$ A, it is clear that

$(\neg\neg$A $\vee$ $\neg$B $) \Leftrightarrow ($ A $\vee$ $\neg$B $) \Leftrightarrow ($ B $\Rightarrow$ A $)$.

Let T be a theory (i.e. a set of already known axioms and theorems containing no contradictions) and let ' t ' be a new theorem. Suppose our problem is to prove that ' t ' is a consequence of T.

One kind of solution is **natural deduction**. This sets up rules of inference and constructs a finite and ordered series of inferences whose last member is ' t ' and whose other members are all formulae which are valid in T.

Another kind of solution is **proof by refutation**. In this we add $\neg$ t to the theory T and, using only Modus Tollens as a rule of inference, attempt to deduce a contradiction (i.e. that a proposition A is both true and false, i.e. that we have A and $\neg$ A).

So a proof by refutation is carried out by propagating negation through Modus Tollens. Assume, then, that we can deduce a contradiction from T & ¬ t. Then, since T contains no contradiction, T & ¬ t can only be contradictory if ' t ' is just what is contained, more or less implicitly, by T, thus enabling the contradiction t & ¬ t to be found.

Now let us consider the set of clauses T' deduced from T by converting T to normal form and the set of clauses ¬t' obtained by converting ¬t to normal form. What Herbrand's theorem, given in appendix 1, says is that even though T & ¬t and T' & ¬t' may not be equivalent, the one leads to a contradiction if and only if the other also leads to a contradiction. Here is the reason for the importance of this theorem, since many methods of proof used in AI (in particular the language PROLOG) are based on refutation.

In AI, it is customary to call a coherent theory by a special name: it is a **coherent knowledge base**, or, more simply, a **knowledge base**.

> **So in a proof by refutation, the problem of "proving t'" will be dealt with by adding "¬ t'" to the knowledge base.**

In most cases ¬ t' is a purely negative clause of the form
$$:- A, B, C, ...$$
We call it a **problem** or **question**.

The constituents A, B, ... are called **sub-problems**.

In the same way, each new negative clause generated by the refutation proof is called a **sub-problem generated** by the initial problem.

When we obtain a contradiction in a system of clauses, i.e. a pair of clauses of the form
$$A :-$$
$$:- A$$
we say we have obtained the **empty clause**.

The success of refutation is due to its ability to aim the proof toward the desired result. In fact there are plenty of theorems whose negation could be added to the system of clauses T' to derive a contradiction, and not all of them are relevant to the negation of t. By including ¬ t in T', the problem we set is precisely the problem set by ¬ t, and nothing else.

It must be clearly realized that proof by refutation does not specify the *strategy* required.

If we consider the purely negative clauses and seek to resolve them with the positive parts of other clauses, then we say we are using a strategy of *backward chaining.*

We shall give a complete example later on, but for the moment, let us consider the trivial system

$$A :-$$
$$:- A$$

We are doing backward chaining if we take :- A to unify it with A :- .

It we take the purely affirmative clauses and seek to resolve them with the the negative parts of other clauses, then the strategy we use is called forward chaining.

In the trivial system

$$A :-$$
$$:- A$$

We are chaining forward if we think of A :- as being unified with :- A .

In a slightly more convincing manner, let us consider the three clauses

$$A :- B$$
$$:- C$$
$$D :-$$

In forward chaining, we seek to unify D with C or B; in backward chaining we seek to unify C with D or A.

In this case there is clearly a difference between forward and backward chaining.

Example 13

Let us consider two rules saying that ' x ' is son (or daughter) of father ' y ' and mother ' z ' if ' y ' is the father of ' x ' and ' z ' is the mother of ' x '.

$$son(x, y, z) :- father(y, x), mother(z, x)$$
$$daughter(x, y, z) :- father(y, x), mother(z, x)$$

Let us assume also that we have a weighty fact base about who is father or mother of who. The "..." stand for thousands of facts.

$$father(GEORGE, ROBERT) :-$$
$$father(GEORGE, ANATOLE) :-$$

$$...$$

$$mother(ANNIE, ROBERT) :-$$
$$mother(ANNIE, JOSETTE) :-$$

$$...$$

Supposing that the question is asked whether ROBERT is the son of GEORGE and ANNIE, then we are going try to deduce the empty clause by adding to the fact base:

$$:- son(ROBERT, GEORGE, ANNIE).$$

Of course, since there are thousands of facts, it is pure luck that the

"interesting" facts in our example should be so conveniently located in the fact base.
    Here,

           son(x, y ,z) :- father(y, x), mother(z, x) and
           :- son(ROBERT, GEORGE, ANNIE)

resolve while generating two new sub-problems
           :- father(GEORGE, ROBERT)
           :- mother(ANNIE, ROBERT)

which will both yield the empty clause with the corresponding facts:
           father(GEORGE, ROBERT) :-
           mother(ANNIE, ROBERT) :-

If we had wanted to crack this nut with the sledgehammer of forward chaining, we would have started by deducing all the true facts in the fact base. For instance, from

           son(x, y ,z) :- father(y, x), mother(z, x)
           daughter(x, y ,z) :- father(y, x), mother(z, x)
           father(GEORGE, ROBERT) :-

we deduce

           son(ROBERT, GEORGE, z) :- mother(z, GEORGE)
           daughter(ROBERT, GEORGE, z) :- mother(z, GEORGE)

The second deduction concerning daughters will never be any use, nor will a huge number of these deductions.

This example was designed to illustrate the efficiency of backward chaining. Nobody should believe that it is always like this. On the contrary, the example given in section 3 of chapter 3 will illustrate a case where forward chaining would be more efficient. We shall show then how variables must be typed in order to preserve the efficiency of backward chaining.

Furthermore, as we said in the example, it is a case of using forward chaining like a sledgehammer. It is quite obvious that (meta-)strategies could be imagined that would control forward chaining more efficiently as a function of the problem set, for example by restricting inferences to those connected with the predicate of the problem.

4 THE KNUTH-BENDIX COMPLETION ALGORITHM

It happens very often that knowledge about a system is given in the form of equivalences (and not of implications) between expressions, and that it is natural to learn it in this form. For example, Physics sets out its results as identities.

It follows that we are often confronted with the problem of finding a property which is true modulo the equivalence, the problem being that we often have to use both senses of equivalence.

Let the axiom system be
1 - union(Empty, x) = x
2 - union(x, empty) = x
3 - union(union(x, y), z) = union(x, union(y, z))
4 - subset(x, union(x, y)) = TRUE
5 - subset(Empty, x) = TRUE
6 - subset(x, x) = TRUE

Prove that t_1 = union(x, union(y, z)) is a subset of t_2 = union(union(x, y), union(z, u))). Check that you use one axiom in both directions.

****

Rewrite systems or, to put it more exactly, their completion, which we are now going to describe, are used to solve this kind of problem. They are also starting to become efficient tools for automatic theorem-proving [Hsiang 1982].

Let $g_i \rightarrow d_i$ and $g_j \rightarrow d_j$ be two rules having no variables in common (if they have, they must first be renamed). We say that these rules **overlap** when an occurrence ' u ' of g_j exists such that
g_i and the sub-term of g_j at the occurrence ' u ' are unifiable.

This sub-term will be written g_j/u, and hence we have σ, which is the *MOST GENERAL* unifier of g_i and g_j/u.

We then define a **critical pair** as being the pair:
$\{\sigma.d_j, \sigma.g_j[u \leftarrow d_i]\}$.
So this pair is formed by the right-hand part of rule j and the left-hand part of rule j where the sub-term at the occurrence ' u ' of g_j has been replaced by the right-hand part of rule i, and by also applying the substitution σ.

Example 14
Let there be two rules:
*(i) x * I(x) → e*
*(j) (a * b) *c → a * (b * c).*
- *g_i unifies with the sub-term at the occurrence 1 of g_j using the substitution σ = [a ← x, b ← I(x)]. So we have σ d_j = x * (I(x) * c), σ d_i = e, which is to replace (a * b) at occurrence 1 of g_j. Hence the critical pair*
        *{x * (I(x) * c), e * c}.*
- *g_i also unifies with the sub-term at the occurrence 0 of g_j (i.e. with g_j) using the (secondary) substitution [x ← (a * b), c ← I(x)]. This is given to make it clear that we want the most general unifier, i.e., σ = [x ← (a * b), c ← I(a * b)].*

It follows that $\sigma.d_j = a * (b * I(a * b))$. Besides, since $\sigma.d_i = e$ is to replace the occurrence 0 of g_j, it is thus transformed into e, whence the critical pair:
$$\{a * (b * I(a * b)), e\}.$$

After obtaining the critical pairs, we use the rewrite system to convert each constituent into normal form, and if they are not syntactically identical we create a new rule, ordering the pair according to what we assume are known ordering criteria.

In practice we use easier ways of calculating critical pairs.

For example, we write $\{\sigma.g_j, \sigma.d_j\}$ and apply the rewrite system while taking care to apply rule i first at occurrence u.

In the first case above we have
$$\{(x * I(x)) * c, x * (I(x) * c)\}$$
and the second case
$$\{(a * b) * I(a * b), a * (b * I(a * b))\}$$

The iterated application of the process for creating new rules described above is called **completion**.

The application of axioms to an expression often leads to looping, because an axiom is applied first in one direction and then in the other. It would be interesting to be able to use a rewrite system which was equivalent to the initial set of axioms and which calculated a unique form in a finite number of steps for each term it was applied to. In this case, the rewrite system is said to be **complete**.

It can be shown that when the completion process stops, then the system is exactly complete: any expression it is applied to will after a finite number of steps take a unique form, known as **canonical form**.

In AI we very often use transformation rules (that could be formalized as rewrite rules), and we try to use these rules to get the "right" form of the expressions.

The "right" form means a canonical form, even if the rules are heuristics.

For example, the conversion of a natural language sentence into internal representation is nothing but a search for a canonical form for the sentence. Rules for disambiguation are nothing but rules which ensure the uniqueness of the normal form.

It is not the aim of this book to give an interpretation of the AI work which takes the form of rewrite rules; however, we do think that this profound link between rewrite rules and AI ought to be pointed out.

3 Representation of Complex Knowledge by Clauses

Kowalski [Kowalski 1979] was the first to uphold the thesis that

PROGRAMS = LOGIC + CONTROL

where it is assumed that "LOGIC" means "first-order logic", since the "control" represents the higher orders. We are going to adapt Kowalski's idea to try and show that

"KNOWLEDGE REPRESENTATION = LOGIC(FIRST-ORDER) + CONTROL".

The approach we wish to illustrate is very pragmatic. On the one hand, we shall not worry here about the way knowledge is represented in living creatures endowed with intelligence. On the other hand, we know that the only way of doing inferences without too many risks is to relentlessly confine ourselves to inference on first-order clauses.

In view of this, we are reduced to translating the other knowledge by control procedures. For the rule of the game is that if we are going to restrict our control too much, then our inference procedures will be too complex. Conversely, if we do not use first-order inference enough, then the procedures are going to become incomprehensible (to other people, but also to their authors).

The problem we are setting here of the balance between control and clauses has not been solved, and the aim of this chapter is to give some indications about the way it can be tackled.

1 SOME EXAMPLES OF LOGICAL KNOWLEDGE REPRESENTATION

1.1 Example 1 : The age of Jean's mother

The example in question can be summarized by the knowledge contained in the following sentences:

Marie is Jean's mother.

Marie is 50 years old.

Jean is 25 years old.

Jean is a human being.

Marie is a human being.

Any mother of a human being is a human being.

Any human being has an age.

Let us ask the question: What is Jean's mother's age?

Let us put these sentences into Horn clause form.

Marie is Jean's mother.	=	MOTHER(Marie, Jean)	:-	
Marie is 50 years old.	=	AGE(Marie, 50)	:-	
Jean is 25 years old.	=	AGE(Jean, 25)	:-	
Jean is a human.	=	HUMAN(Jean)	:-	
Marie is a human.	=	HUMAN(Marie)	:-	
Any mother of a human is a human.	=	HUMAN(x)	:-	MOTHER(x, y), HUMAN(y)
Any human has an age.	=	AGE(x, SKOL(x))	:-	HUMAN(x)
What is Jean's mother's age?	=		:-	AGE(m, t), MOTHER(m, Jean)

It is simpler to write the Skolem function "SKOL(x)", since most PROLOGs authorize the use of functions.

Here SKOL(x) is a function which takes the age of ' x ' as its value.

The last clause is understood as follows: It is a question so it will be interpreted as the negation of the assertion corresponding to the question. This assertion is that Jean's mother has an age, i.e.:

$$Th: \exists x \exists y [MOTHER(x, Jean) \& AGE(x, y)]$$

and the reason for linking this theorem with this assertion will become clear very soon. The negation of this theorem is:

$$\neg Th = \forall x \forall y \neg [MOTHER(x, Jean) \& AGE(x, y)]$$

which is indeed the last clause in the list above.

We can now leave the PROLOG interpreter to unwind;

The second and the last clauses combine with the substitution $\{m \leftarrow Marie, t \leftarrow 50\}$ generating:

$$:- MOTHER(Marie, Jean)$$

which will in turn combine with the first clause to give the empty clause.

Exercise 6
****

Deal with the case where the last clause is changed to

:- MOTHER(Marie, Jean), Age(m, t)
Deal with the case where the clause
AGE(x, SKOL(x))   :- HUMAN(x)
is placed as the first one.
Deduce everything that can be deduced from this data-base.
****

One of the problems of the logical representation of knowledge will immediately become clear: it is very sensitive to the order in which resolution chooses the clauses. This is obviously a problem of control, which we can only talk about a little bit here.

1.2   Example 2 : Purple mushrooms and contexts

The sentence: "Purple mushrooms are poisonous in North America" can obviously be represented by the Horn clause:
POISONOUS(x) :- PURPLE(x), MUSHROOM(x), GROWSINNORTHAMERICA(x).

While being very simple, this example touches on more problems than it seems to.
The notion of "Purple mushroom" can be represented by PURPLE(x) & MUSHROOM(x). Indeed the class of purple objects is not particularly interesting, at least in the universe whose knowledge we seem to be representing.
On the other hand, it is possible that the class of things that happen in North America could be an interesting class. In this case and only in this case (and we insist that it must be a piece of non-universal knowledge) it is possible for "In North America" to be considered as a context which is to be used as a "condition" (later on we shall say "modulation") for using the rule. We should then prefer to represent the above phrase by:
[MODULATION: In North America] POISONOUS(x) :- PURPLE(x), MUSHROOM(x).

The rules for using and combining modulations will not be tackled here.

1.3   The problem of exceptions

The problem of exceptions has generated an abundant literature. This is due to the need to find a clever solution to the two following problems:
1 - since there is an exception, the logical database is bound somewhere to contain a contradiction. How is it to be controlled?
2 - the mode of inference must reflect the fact that "in general" the exception does not arise (otherwise it would not be one).

1.3.1 Solution by inventing the predicate "EMPTY".

Example 3.

An elephant is an animal.	=	ANIMAL(x)	:-	ELEPHANT(x)
Any animal has a mother.	=	MOTHER(SKOL(x), x)	:-	ANIMAL(x)
Clyde is a pink elephant.	=	ELEPHANT(Clyde)	:-	
		PINK(Clyde)	:-	
Clyde has no mother.	=	MOTHER(EMPTY, Clyde)	:-	

The fact that Clyde is an exception to the rule is explicitly indicated by giving a particular value to the "name" of his mother. So to avoid making heaps of inferences about Clyde's mother, this information has to be considered right away. One solution in PROLOG is to begin with some clauses, the exception clauses - this is a control solution but a simple one.

1.3.2 Solution by inventing an "EXCEPTION" predicate

PROLOG's standard NOT predicate is used: NOT-A takes the value FALSE if A can be proved and the value TRUE if A cannot be proved (this is what "unless there is an exception" really means). So when the query invoked is :- NOT-A, TRUE will be read out if A can be proved and FALSE if A cannot be proved.

Example 4. Let the data-base be the following.

FLIES(x)	:-	BIRD(x), NOT-EXCEPTBIRDFLIES(x)
BIRD(x)	:-	OSTRICH(x)
BIRD(x)	:-	PENGUIN(x)
EXEPTBIRDFLIES(x)	:-	OSTRICH(x)
EXEPTBIRDFLIES(x)	:-	PENGUIN(x)
OSTRICH(Kiki)	:-	
	:-	FLIES(Kiki)

It represents some information about the ostrich Kiki, and the question of whether Kiki flies.

Clearly we cannot conclude that Kiki flies, which is quite interesting because we can conclude it for birds other than penguins and ostriches.

A grave defect of this representation is that all the exceptions are going to be checked each time. It could be avoided by defining another procedure for calculating "NOT".

1.3.3 Solution by controlling an inconsistent data-base

All the information is entered in the form of Horn clauses. In the above example, leaving out the penguins, we have:

Example 5.

```
FLIES(x)          :-    BIRD(x)
BIRD(x)           :-    OSTRICH(x)
                  :-    FLIES(x), OSTRICH(x)
OSTRICH(Kiki)     :-
```

Then given this incoherent data-base, we can either invoke queries such as:

```
:-   FLIES(Kiki)
```

which lead to the empty clause by pure backward chaining, or we can use the negations of queries (which are hence assertions) and start chaining forward:

```
FLIES(Kiki)     :-
```

which also leads to the empty clause.

Detecting an incoherence like this can be called special treatment if you wish. The strategy can, of course, be elaborated a bit more than it is here, while preserving this principle.

This is the debugging strategy where mistakes are only corrected after they have been noticed. For more details see [Duval & Kodratoff 1986].

1.3.4   Solution by environments

We can also tell ourselves that, basically, it is true that birds fly, that mammals have legs etc... in the universe we are familiar with. In some universes, the exceptions cannot be significant. If such universes are considered to be interesting, then why not put these universes inside a modulation?

[MODULATION: Our familiar universe] FLIES(x) :- BIRD(x)

Conversely, there are cases where exceptions really are significant, but in that case checking whether or not each inference is an exception cannot be said to be a waste of time.

For example, if you say that every mushroom of the genus Amanita with a grey-green top and little streaks at the edge of the top is edible except the phalloid one, which has no streaks, then you had better check the exceptional case each time you apply it. By the way, many people have neglected to do so and died of it. Of course, this is just the kind of case where common sense is caught out, and to the extent that we are trying to simulate common sense, we need not feel too concerned by this negative example. However, it seems to us that common sense should not be simulated when it makes bad sense to do so.

2.1 Logical description of concepts

When doing concept learning, a concept can be defined by its recognition function, which is a atomic formula P(x). The variable x is free, i.e. P(x) takes the value TRUE for instances of x which are instances of the concept and the value FALSE for instances of x which are not instances of the concept. From then on, the concept itself is nothing but a name, let us call it *Concept*$_1$ and define a predicate *Concept*$_1$ by the relation

$$\forall x[P(x) \Rightarrow Concept_1(x)]$$

We then take it that the name *Concept*$_1$ represents the concept *Concept*$_1$. To make this more convincing, it has to be specified that a concept must never be defined by a single recognition function, which is why we can say that *Concept*$_1$, for example, is defined by a set of n definitions:

$$\forall x[P_1(x) \Rightarrow Concept_1(x)]$$

$$. . .$$

$$\forall x[P_n(x) \Rightarrow Concept_1(x)]$$

So we define a concept by its recognition function $P_i(x)$.

In what follows, since we shall be working on a toy problem, we can accept having just one definition.

Example 6: Three representations of a "grain-eating animal"
In this example we shall give three definitions for the predicate 'EATSGRAIN'.

1 - A grain-eating animal is an animal which eats nothing but grain can be represented by : IF ANIMAL(x) & EATSGRAIN(x, y) THEN GRAIN(y).

This definition can be criticized by saying, very properly, that the concept is ANIMAL(x) & [IF EATSGRAIN(x, y) THEN GRAIN(y)]. The two representations are not exactly equivalent.

****
Exercise 7   Demonstrate their differences.
****

The logical formula associated with the first of the above descriptions is:

∀y [ANIMAL(x) & EATSGRAIN(x, y) ⇒ GRAIN(y)]

Here the free variable is x, which must be instantiated by an arbitrary animal which eats grains for the recognition function to take the value TRUE.

If certain parts of the sentence characterize a predicate, then this predicate is implied by these parts of the sentence as soon as a universal quantifier governs this implication. Intuitively, it isn't very clear why the same interpretation of the above English sentence could not be written:

∀y [ANIMAL(x) & EATSGRAIN(x, y) ⇔ GRAIN(y)].

This would be perfectly possible, but it is just what our interpretation opposes: we have given the sentence a direction. It is clear that the sentence corresponding to the above biconditional would be: "An animal is a grain-eating animal if it eats nothing but grain and eats all grains", which is "unnatural" language!

Another possibility would be

$$\forall y \ [ANIMAL(x) \ \& \ EATSGRAIN(x, y) \ \& \ GRAIN(y)].$$

The non-equivalence argument given above applies again, and besides, it defines a universe where animals can only like grains, which is not at all what the sentence implies.

2 - A grain-eating animal is an animal which eats all sorts of grains.
In this case, the taste for grain is characterized by:

$$\forall y \ [ANIMAL(x) \ \& \ GRAIN(y) \Rightarrow EATSGRAIN(x, y)]$$

3 - A grain-eating animal is an animal which eats certain grains.
In this case, the definition of the new concept is not an implication, but a simple juxtaposition of properties :

$$\exists y \ [ANIMAL(x) \ \& \ EATSGRAIN(x, y) \ \& \ GRAIN(y)]$$

The English sentence is now symmetrical relative to the two properties "liking a foodstuff" and "being a grain", because it is not a reciprocal implication; it simply observes that these two properties occur together. Again, we cannot write

$$\forall y \ [IF \ ANIMAL(x) \ \& \ EATSGRAIN(x, y) \Leftrightarrow GRAIN(y)]$$

now because in a universe where each limb of the biconditional took the value FALSE, the biconditional itself would remain TRUE, which does not correspond to the meaning of the English sentence.

2.2 Logical description of statements

Example 7: "All mechanics repair all cars"
This sentence has to quantify simultaneously over mechanics and cars, just like
"All cars are repaired by all mechanics"

In our opinion, if one of these were going to be quantified universally and the other existentially then transition from the active to the passive form is not going to do it; it must be done by transition from the use of "all" to the use of "some".

"All mechanics repair all cars" and
"All cars are repaired by all mechanics"

both mean

$$\forall x \ \forall y \ [MECHANIC(x) \ \& \ CAR(y) \Rightarrow REPAIRS(x, y)]^*$$

---

* Translator's note: This is not such a trivial paraphrase in the French, because where

However, there could be cases where the active/passive form is heavily loaded with meaning, and where it would be a mistake to give the same normal form to both sentences.

For example, in the same vein, we would tend to say that
$$\exists x \, \forall y \, [MECHANIC(x) \, \& \, CAR(y) \Rightarrow REPAIRS(x, y)] \text{ means that}$$
"Some mechanics repair all cars" whereas
$$\forall y \, \exists x \, [MECHANIC(x) \, \& \, CAR(y) \Rightarrow REPAIRS(x, y)] \text{ would tend to mean}$$
"All cars can be repaired by some of the mechanics".

3 REPRESENTATION OF A HIERARCHY DURING RESOLUTION

The following example is due to L. Schubert of the University of Alberta, and was published by C. Walther of Karlsruhe [Walther 1984], who submitted it to various automatic theorem-provers which could not deal with it in its original form. Walther introduced a methodology for reducing the search space of the resolution, which is particularly large in this case. This methodology is based on the notion of many-sorted resolution.

Notice, however, that this problem which generated a quite abundant literature is now recognized as relatively simple, and one is quite surprised that it could have been a failure case for a theorem prover.

Example 8.

In this example, capital letters will denote predicates or functions, small letters denote constants and x_i the variables.

Let the task be to transform the following text into a set of clauses.

Wolves, foxes, caterpillars, birds and snails are animals and each of these species is represented.
There is also grain, and grain is a plant.
Every animal likes to eat
　　　　either all plants
　　　　or all animals smaller than themselves which like to eat plants.
Caterpillars and snails are much smaller than birds, birds are much smaller than foxes, which are themselves much smaller than wolves.
Wolves do not like to eat foxes, nor grain, whereas birds like to eat caterpillars but not snails.
Snails and caterpillars like to eat plants.

English-speakers would say "all", the French would merely use the definite article.

Consequently, there exists an animal which likes to eat an animal which likes to eat grain.

The following 27 clauses are obtained.

1 - WOLF(wolf) :-

2 - BIRD(bird) :-

3 - SNAIL(snail) :-

4 - FOX(fox) :-

5 - CATERPILLAR(caterpillar) :-

6 - GRAIN(grain) :-

7 - ANIMAL(x_1) :- WOLF(x_1)

8 - ANIMAL(x_1) :- FOX(x_1)

9 - ANIMAL(x_1) :- BIRD(x_1)

10 - ANIMAL(x_1) :- CATERPILLAR(x_1)

11 - ANIMAL(x_1) :- SNAIL(x_1)

12 - PLANT(x_1) :- GRAIN(x_1)

13 - LIKEAT(x_1, x_2) $\vee$ LIKEAT(x_1, x_3) :-
   ANIMAL(x_1), PLANT(x_2), ANIMAL(x_3), PLANT(x_4), MSMALLER(x_3, x_1), LIKEAT(x_3, x_4)

14 - MSMALLER(x_1, x_2) :- CATERPILLAR(x_1), BIRD(x_2)

15 - MSMALLER(x_1, x_2) :- SNAIL(x_1), BIRD(x_2)

16 - MSMALLER(x_1, x_2) :- BIRD(x_1), FOX(x_2)

17 - MSMALLER(x_1, x_2) :- FOX(x_1), WOLF(x_2)

18 -   :- FOX(x_1), WOLF(x_2), LIKEAT(x_2, x_1)

19 -   :- GRAIN(x_1), WOLF(x_2), LIKEAT(x_2, x_1)

20 - LIKEAT(x_1, x_2) :- BIRD(x_1), CATERPILLAR(x_2)

21 -   :- BIRD(x_1), SNAIL(x_2), LIKEAT(x_1, x_2)

22 - PLANT(FOODCATER(x_1)) :- CATERPILLAR(x_1)

23 - LIKEAT(x_1, FOODCATER(x_1)) :- CATERPILLAR(x_1)

24 - PLANT(FOODSNAIL(x_1)) :- SNAIL(x_1)

25 - LIKEAT(x_1, FOODSNAIL(x_1)) :- SNAIL(x_1)

26 - GRAIN(EATS(x_1, x_2)) :- ANIMAL(x_1), ANIMAL(x_2), LIKEAT(x_1, x_2)

27 -   :- ANIMAL(x_1), ANIMAL(x_2), LIKEAT(x_1, x_2), LIKEAT(x_2, EATS(x_1, x_2))

There is no very easy way of proving the consistency of this set of clauses and the reason is that the search space is too large.

The underlying reason is that a large number of explanations are given about the knowledge level "wolves, snails, etc...", whereas the real conclusion is required at the level "animals"; this is what is very difficult.

This is even more difficult when you realize that automatic theorem-provers are generally used in a context where they are required to prove a theorem in which implicitly universally-quantified variables appear. In practice, this means that their strategies are oriented (explicitly or implicitly) toward backward chaining, because to find all the knowledge available from the system would be a combinatorially explosive task. If the system has slightly complex rules, then even if there are not many facts, the number of facts derivable can be immense.

Conversely, if there are a lot of facts and not many rules, then it would be preferable to use a "forward-chaining" strategy which propagates facts rather than sub-problems.

Actually, our problem is slightly different. It involves a large quantity of sub-problems but a relatively small quantity of facts, and so our choice should be to resolve it by forward chaining.

Nevertheless, in order to follow Walther's argumentation we shall continue to tackle the problem by backward chaining. The conclusion, namely that unification must be typed to represent knowledge of hierarchies, would be valid for any resolution strategy.

Walther tackles the problem by introducing sorts and types as well as a sorted unification, as the example shows.

Before following him, let us see how theorems can be associated with the natural language sentences given above.

Somebody who says "the wolf is an animal" may (and this choice has already been discussed in section 1.2 of chapter 2) be wishing to express the fact that any instance of x giving the value TRUE to the atomic formula WOLF(x) is also an instance of x which makes the atomic formula ANIMAL(x) TRUE. So this is written $\forall x \ [WOLF(x) \Rightarrow ANIMAL(x)]$, which is immediately translated as clause 7.

For clause 13, assume that the corresponding expression is written

$$\forall x_1 \ [[\forall x_2 \ [ANIMAL \ (x_1) \ \& \ PLANT(x_2) \Rightarrow LIKEAT(x_1, x_2)]] \ \vee$$
$$[\forall x_3 \ [[ANIMAL(x_1) \ \&$$
$$ANIMAL(x_3) \ \&$$
$$MSMALLER(x_3, x_1) \ \&$$
$$\exists x_4 \ [PLANT(x_4) \vee LIKEAT(x_3, x_4)]]$$
$$\Rightarrow LIKEAT(x_1, x_3)]]].$$

So in normal form, this yields

$$\forall x_1 \ [[\forall x_2 \ [\neg \ ANIMAL(x_1) \vee \neg \ PLANT(x_2) \vee LIKEAT(x_1, x_2)]] \ \vee$$
$$[\forall x_3 \ [[\neg \ ANIMAL(x_1) \ \vee$$
$$\neg \ ANIMAL(x_3) \ \vee$$
$$\neg \ MSMALLER(x_3, x_1) \ \vee$$
$$\forall x_4 \neg \ PLANT(x_4) \ \& \ \neg \ LIKEAT(x_3, x_4)]]$$
$$\vee LIKEAT(x_3, x_4)]]].$$

So it can be reduced to a single clause without Skolemization, since all the variables are universally quantified. It is clause 13.

For clauses 26 and 27, the last expression is translated by

$$\exists x_1 \ x_2 \ [ANIMAL(x_1) \ \& \ ANIMAL(x_2) \ \& \ \forall x_3[GRAIN(x_3) \Rightarrow LIKEAT(x_2, x_3)] \ \& \ LIKEAT(x_1, x_2)].$$

But this last expression is the query being invoked, so this theorem must be denied before we introduce it in clause form and try to show that the whole set is inconsistent. So this negation is written:

$\forall x_1 \, \forall x_2 [\neg \, ANIMAL(x_1) \lor \neg \, ANIMAL(x_2)$
$\qquad \exists x_3 [GRAIN(x_3) \, \& \, \neg LIKEAT(x_2, x_3)] \, \lor \, \neg LIKEAT(x_1, x_2)].$

In normal form:

$\forall x_1 \, x_2 \, \exists x_3 [\neg \, ANIMAL(x_1) \lor \neg \, ANIMAL(x_2) \, \lor \, GRAIN(x_3) \lor \neg \, LIKEAT(x_1, x_2)] \quad \&$
$\qquad [\neg \, ANIMAL(x_1) \lor \neg \, ANIMAL(x_2) \, \lor \, GRAIN(x_3) \, \lor \, \neg \, LIKEAT(x_1, x_2)]]$

Replacing x_3 by the skolem function EATS(x_1, x_2), 26 and 27 above are indeed obtained.

Let us now see how these clauses can be transformed to take account of the hierarchical relationships involved in the taxonomies of the animals and plants.

The variables of type ANIMAL will be called A_1, A_2, ..., those of type BIRD B_1, B_2, etc...

In unification, a variable x will only be able to receive a substitution it if t belongs to a type which is equal to or lower than the type x belongs to.

Clauses 1 - 6 become definitions of the types of the constants wolf, bird,...

1 - type wolf : WOLF
2 - type bird : BIRD
3 - type snail : SNAIL
4 - type fox : FOX
5 - type caterpillar : CATERPILLAR
6 - type grain : GRAIN

Clauses 7 - 12 become hierarchical relations between the sorts.

7 - sort WOLF < ANIMAL
8 - sort FOX < ANIMAL
9 - sort BIRD < ANIMAL
10 - sort CATERPILLAR < ANIMAL
11 - sort SNAIL < ANIMAL
12 - sort GRAIN < PLANT

Relation 13 becomes a relation between plants and animals, as it is explicitly in the text.

For this reason we go through 13 word by word, replacing ANIMAL(x_1) by the fact that ' x_1 ' belongs to the sort ANIMAL, and thus eliminating the parts of 13 which indicate membership of a sort. A_1 replaces x_1, P_1 replaces x_2, A_2 replaces x_3, P_2 replaces x_4, so that:

13 - LIKEAT(A_1, P_1) $\lor$ LIKEAT(A_1, A_2) :- MSMALLER(A_2, A_1), LIKEAT(A_2, P_2)

The same happens to the other clauses. For example, 14 is now going to say that instances of CATERPILLAR are much smaller than those of BIRD.

14 - MSMALLER(C_1, B_1) :-
15 - MSMALLER(S_1, B_1) :-
16 - MSMALLER(B_1, F_1) :-
17 - MSMALLER(F_1, W_1) :-
18 -   :- LIKEAT(W_1, F_1)
19 -   :- LIKEAT(W_1, G_1)
20 - LIKEAT(B_1, C_1) :-
21 -   :- LIKEAT(B_1, S_1)

Now the Skolem functions are typed too, and since, for example, *FOODCATER(x)* *replaces a variable of the sort PLANT, it must take its sort as well. On the other hand, since its variable is of the sort CATERPILLAR, this too has to be said.*

22 - type FOODCATER(CATERPILLAR): PLANT

From this comes 23, where the declaration of sort implicit in CATERPILLAR(x_1) *has been suppressed and C_1 has replaced x_1 in the remainder.*

23 - LIKEAT(C_1, FOODCATER(C_1)) :-
24 - type FOODSNAIL(SNAIL) : PLANT
25 - LIKEAT(S_1, FOODSNAIL(S_1)) :-

Clause 26 requires special treatment. First of all, we have to include an indication *that the function GRAIN is meaningless unless it is applied to variables of the sort GRAIN: this is what 26 below expresses.*

26 - type EATS(ANIMAL, ANIMAL) : GRAIN

Now the procedure already described can be used to obtain 26':

26' - GRAIN(EATS(A_1, A_2)) :- LIKEAT(A_1, A_2)
27 -   :- LIKEAT(A_1, A_2), LIKEAT(A_2, EATS(A_1, A_2))

So let us consider the two clauses 13 and 27.

13 - LIKEAT(A_1, P_1) $\vee$ LIKEAT(A_1, A_2) :- MSMALLER(A_2, A_1), LIKEAT(A_2, P_2)
27 -   :- LIKEAT(A_1, A_2), LIKEAT(A_2, EATS(A_1, A_2))

In these clauses, P_1 et A_2 do not belong to the same sort. It follows that LIKEAT(A_1, P_1) cannot be unified to LIKEAT(A_1, A_2). The sort of EATS(A_1, A_2) is GRAIN, it follows that only LIKEAT(A_1, P_1) can be unified with LIKEAT(A_2, EATS(A_1, A_2)), for instance by the substitution $\{A_1 \leftarrow A_2, P_1 \leftarrow EATS(A_1, A_2)\}$. So only two possible resolutions of these two clauses are possible, instead of the four in the previous representation.

Choosing now to resolve the LIKEAT(A_1, A_2) of 13 with the ¬LIKEAT(A_1, A_2) of 27, *we find the resolvent:*

28 - LIKEAT(A_1, P_1) :- MSMALLER(A_2, A_1), LIKEAT(A_2, P_2), LIKEAT(A_2, EATS(A_1, A_2)).

But we then use a rule called subsumption, which basically says that if a clause C_1 *is more general than a clause C_2 (or if an atom A_1 is more general than an atom A_2 in the same clause), then the sets containing C_1 and C_2 (or A_1 and A_2) are inconsistent if and only if they only contain C_2 (or A_2). In other words, during the resolution the more general clause or atom is eliminated. This is what is done here, resulting in:*

28' - LIKEAT(A_1, P_1) :- MSMALLER(A_2, A_1), LIKEAT(A_2, EATS(A_1, A_2)) *which is combined with*

17 - MSMALLER(F_1, W_1) :- which is possible since F_1 and W_1 both belong to the sort ANIMAL. We have

29 - LIKEAT(W_1, P_1) :- LIKEAT(F_1, EATS(W_1, F_1)) which is resolved with

19 - :- LIKEAT(W_1, G_1) for $\{P_1 \leftarrow G_1\}$ is possible, so that

30 - :- LIKEAT(F_1, EATS(W_1, F_1))

By 16 - MSMALLER(B_1, F_1) :- and 28' above we have

31 - LIKEAT(F_1, P_1) :- LIKEAT(B_1, EATS(F_1, B_1))

If we now resolve 30 and 31 with the substitution $\{P_1 \leftarrow EATS(W_1, F_1)\}$, we obtain

32 - :- LIKEAT(B_1, EATS(F_1, B_1)) We now resolve 13 and 21:

33 - LIKEAT(B_1, P_1) :- MSMALLER (S_1, B_1), LIKEAT(S_1, P_2)),

then 32 and 33 (where B_1 is implicitly renamed B_2) and with the substitution

$\{B_2 \leftarrow B_1, P_1 \leftarrow EATS(F_1, B_1)\}$:

34 - :- LIKEAT(S_1, P_2), MSMALLER(S_1, B_1)

The MSMALLER(S_1, B_1) is cancelled against 15 and the LIKEAT(S_1, P_2) against 25, which of course yields the empty clause. So the set is inconsistent, showing we had indeed been wrong to deny the existential theorem given above. And so there are indeed animals which eat animals which are grain-eaters; it turns out that the set of instantiations during the resolution shows that foxes eat birds which themselves eat all grains.

4 REPRESENTATION BY "TERNARY QUANTIFIED TREES"

To give an account of the deep meaning of natural language sentences, Colmerauer's group at Lumigny (1977, 1979, then P. Saint-Dizier 1985) introduced representation by ternary trees.

The ternary predicates introduced all have the form

$$HEAD(x, RESTR(x), REM),$$

that is

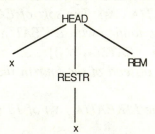

where HEAD is the "head" of the predicate. As farther examples show, this head may be either a logical connective or some kind of quantifier. RESTR is the type of x and REM is the remainder of the sentence. REM has the same form as HEAD, except when it is terminal. When it is terminal, REM is an n-ary predicate that describes relationships among variables of its HEADs.

For example, the statement

"Each worker possesses a car"
is to be represented, using the three "heads" ' ALL ', ' A ' and ' TO HAVE ', by

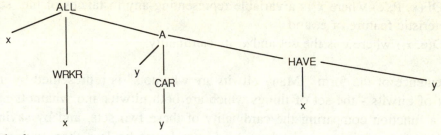

or alternatively

ALL(x, WRKR(x), A(y, CAR(y), HAVE(x, y)))) :-

where WRKR is a predicate which "restricts" (whence RESTR above) x to belonging to the type ' WORKER ', and where ' HAVE ' is a binary predicate expressing a relationship between the variables of ' A ' and ' ALL '.

Of course, this formalism has to be coherent for the PROLOG evaluation to be executed correctly.

This formalism enables nouns, verbs, and relative and interrogative clauses to be represented satisfactorily.

Here is an example of the representation of a verb.

Example 9.

The sentence

"The workers go by bus to the factory." *which contains two senses of the verb to go, viz.* "to go to a place" *and* "to go by a given means of locomotion", *can be rendered by an ' AND ' head, the logical AND, which allows the paraphrase*

"the workers go by bus AND the workers go to the factory"

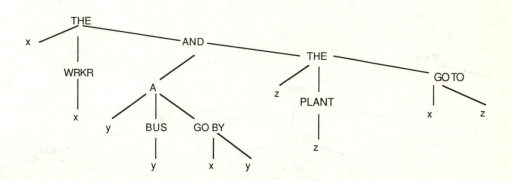

Now we are to normalize some of the commonest heads, such as

1 - one, some, ...
2 - all, each, the, ...
3 - none, no, ...
4 - one, two, at least four, ...
5 - some, many, most, ...

To illustrate this, here is how heads of type 5 are written.

Two basic functions are used:

SET-OF(x, P, e) where x is a variable representing any instances of the set e, and P a characteristic feature of e, and

CARD(e, x_1) where e is the set and x_1 its cardinality.

A sentence of the form "Many nitwits are whatnots" is represented by introducing - the set of nitwits - the set of things which are both nitwits and whatnots at the same time. - a function comparing the cardinality of these two sets, and by saying that the cardinality of the "nitwits and whatnots" is not lower by less than such-and-such an amount than the cardinality of the "nitwits".

Let f be the function fulfilling this office.

If n is the cardinality of the set of nitwits and n_1 is that of the set of nitwits and whatnots, we can express

' many ' by $f(n_1, n) = n_1 > 0.5 * n$,

' almost all ' by $f(n_1, n) = n_1 > 0.8 * n$, etc ...

Finally, let

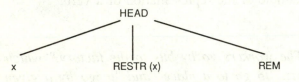

where HEAD is of type 5, it will be rewritten

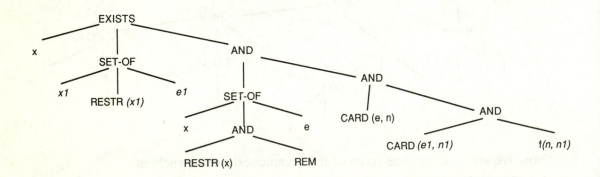

Example 10.

"Many workers have a car."

is represented by

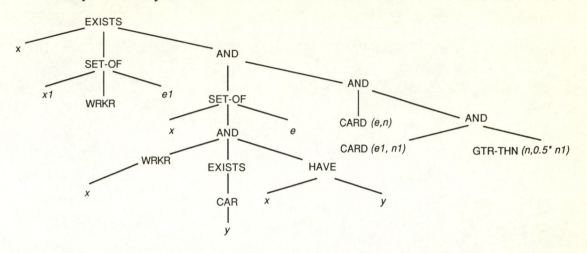

CONCLUSION

This chapter attempted to show how clauses can be used even when complex information has to be represented, and we have used PROLOG clauses.

At this point, let us reflect a little upon the importance of this representation.

Firstly, it must be understood that anything that is represented by Semantic Nets can also be represented by equivalent sets of clauses. Nevertheless, as the immediately preceding section shows, as soon as the complexity of the information represented rises somewhat, the complexity of clause representation quickly becomes tremendous. In practice, we felt that as long as the simple examples of a tutorial book are to be presented, clause representation is so much simpler that it would be sinful not to use it. On the contrary, when big applications, maybe already described as semantic nets, are in view, they may become less cumbersome to use. To end this with a joke, let us also stress that Semantic Nets representation has already been so much used in AI books that we felt "compelled" to use an other one.

Secondly, when you use PROLOG clauses to represent knowledge, it does not mean at all that you use PROLOG resolution strategy to propagate knowledge in these clauses. An instance of this fact will be given in Chapter 4 where we will even forbid its use. In Chapter 4, the resolution strategy underlying our clauses must be forward chaining (see the definition of forward and backward chaining in Chapter 2) instead of the backward-chaining which is used in PROLOG.

The reader must keep these two remarks in mind when reading the rest of this book, not forgetting that when standard PROLOG resolution is not valid for the application in hand we shall always say so.

4 Representation of Knowledge About Actions and the Addition of New Rules to a Knowledge Base

The normal practice in ML is to assume that we should concentrate on the problem of acquiring the "right" rules.

This is not enough, because a learning system presupposes the ability to consider what happens when a new rule is added to a group of old ones. Here again, there is a normal practice of assuming that the only problem is to ensure the global coherence of the system. This is called "truth maintenance" and has been very widely studied in the context of data-bases.

But still this is not enough, for a learning system must also be capable of structuring its knowledge "intelligently", must be capable of rejecting rules which are correct, redundant and dangerous, and, on the other hand, of accepting rules which are correct, redundant and useful (with the problem of what is dangerous and what is useful, of course).

The problem of rule acquisition is dealt with in other chapters. We are now going to quickly study the problem of truth maintenance, referring the reader to [Doyle 1979] for farther details. We are going to give more details and some partial solutions to the problems involved in wholesale intelligent re-structuring as soon as a new rule arrives.

1 TRUTH MAINTENANCE

So in principle, the problem is that of detecting contradictions in a database and correcting them.

We immediately come up against the logic of exceptions, non-monotonic logic and temporal logic.

Each of these problems has created a significant specialist literature. The problem to be tackled here, as in [Doyle 1979], is that of dealing with all these problems simultaneously. Furthermore, since we are still assuming that a PROLOG-like interpreter is available to us, we can ask how the involvement of sequential evaluation (given the present state of our interpreters, parallel interpreters are still being built) can enable temporal problems to be dealt with.

In chapter 3 we have already given many examples of the logical way of dealing with exceptions; we shall not repeat that here.

Our approach to non-monotonicity uses two well-known characteristics of PROLOG: micro-worlds and the commands ASSERT and RETRACT.

There are many PROLOGs which offer a relative modularity which is in fact nothing other than the right to declare micro-worlds independent or linked by a microworld taxonomy.

The command ASSERT enables a clause to be added in a file, if need be in one of the micro-worlds. Symmetrically, the command RETRACT enables a clause to be eliminated.

By reviewing some recent work by [Steels and Van de Welde˙1985, 1986], we are now going to show how temporality can be dealt with by using non-temporal transformations of clauses generated in sequence.

We shall also show how the notions of main predicate and auxiliary predicate can be rendered by using the PROLOG "NOT".

2   PREDICATES IN ACTION MODE / CHECKING MODE

The reader is asked to bear in mind that the description offered here of predicates in action/checking mode is not a standard one. PROLOG enables predicates in checking mode to be expressed marvelously well, but on the other hand it is rather ill suited to action mode. The interested reader can consult e.g. [Porto 1983] on this subject. A solution is given here whose only merit is that it is easy to understand. A realistic implementation would require far more work (which is included in the research work of the group I lead).

An expert system must in general contain two sorts of predicates: predicates in the action mode and predicates in the checking mode.
For example, a predicate in the checking mode (call this a "check" predicate) in an Expert System for car repair could be: Check that the starter button has been pushed.
The "action of checking" consists, for the robot, in going and checking whether or not the starter button has been pushed.

The same predicate can become a predicate in the action mode (call this an "act" predicate) in the form: *Push the starter button.*

From the point of view of classical logic, these two forms seem to be equivalent because they imply each other.

In fact, there are two main differences between the two modes.

- Firstly, a "check" predicate does not call the same procedures as the corresponding "act" predicate. This has to be borne in mind.

For example, when you burst a tire in muddy terrain , you can soon check that "tires inflated?" evaluates to FALSE, but it takes a very long time, with a jack that slides or sinks in, to change the wheel. Hence the "execution of tires inflated" only takes the value TRUE after a long effort.

- Secondly, they are not identical from the temporal point of view. To understand this, assume that the system executes a predicate in the checking mode (call this P') at time t, then the same predicate in the action mode (call this P) at time t + n.

It is implicitly assumed that between times t and t + n, P' evaluates to FALSE, whence the need to execute P. So this is part of the normal running of the program.

Suppose now that P is executed at time t and P' at time t + n. Then it is implicitly assumed that there has been a failure between t and t + n, and that we are checking whether the execution of P was successful. So to check P' after the execution of P amounts to casting doubt on whether P was performed, which amounts to casting doubt on the validity of the procedures attached to P. So this is not part of the normal running of the program but a process of debugging.

In the same line of thought it has to be realized that there exists a complexity order on predicates, and that this order is very important for the writing of the rules.

By the way, the complexity orders on checkings and on their executions differ widely.

Checks that the starter button has been pushed or that a tire has burst are of the same order of complexity, whereas their executions have different complexities.

Once again, this is connected with the fact that the procedures called in order to give the value TRUE to the concerned predicate.

Rather than using a temporal logic, the representation of the difference between action and checking offered here will be a transformation of clauses which takes account of their temporal succession. These transformations, in the form given here, were inspired by [Steels & Van de Welde 1985] and do not rely on temporal operators. The evaluator is what introduces the notion of time through a sequential evaluation.

In the rest of the chapter, each predicate will depend on a variable which, when instantiated by "check", makes it a predicate in the checking mode, and then instantiated by "act", makes it a predicate in the acting mode. For notation, we shall say that the predicates designated by letters, like A, B, AA etc ... are predicates in the acting mode and that those designated by primed letters, like A', B', AA' etc ... are predicates in the checking mode.

Note carefully the practical importance of these remarks. This point is usually neglected in Expert Systems as they are designed today, which is quite wrong. Typically, indeed, knowledge of this kind is what we normally depend on the expert for; some of it is good for changing the wheels and some of it is good for changing the contact points, and anyone who wants to design an Expert System to be independent of facts of this kind is going to be forced to introduce very complicated meta-rules which will, of course, always remain bad.

3 MAIN RULES AND AUXILIARY RULES

Some of the data of the system are called the main data because they are very important and need to be checked immediately to enable the running process to continue. Others are called auxiliary because their importance is lesser and because they serve to confirm things that are already known rather than to control the reasoning.

Intuitively, it might be thought that the main rules have to be executed first. This will be shown to be false by the very simple examples used here.

In practice, a main rule is a rule whose truth must be checked in order to apply it. An auxiliary rule, on the other hand, can be considered as being true as long as it has not been shown to be false.

We are touching on default logic, which was discussed above. In this particular case I propose the following solution, linked to the closed world hypothesis which is always given in PROLOG, and to the manner in which the PROLOG "NOT" is always implemented.

The closed world hypothesis consists in assuming the availability of all possible information about the world the theorem is being proved in. Consequently, failure to prove the theorem shows that it is false, since proving its truth would require additional information, which is impossible since the world is closed.

The implementation of the PROLOG "NOT" follows from the closed world hypothesis.

In PROLOG, NOT - A takes the value FALSE when A can be proved true, and takes the value TRUE when nothing can be proved about A.

Note carefully that it is not the logical NOT (everywhere written "¬" in this book) since ¬ A takes the value TRUE only when A can be proved FALSE.

Hence, in order to distinguish what is auxiliary in the rules from what is main, the difference will be marked as follows.

Let us assign each predicate a variable which takes the value ' yes ' when we want to test that the predicate is TRUE and the value ' no ' when we want to test that the predicate is FALSE. So this assumes the case where the predicate is considered as being main.

If we want to turn it into the auxiliary case, then to test that it is TRUE it is enough for the system to fail to prove that it is FALSE, (i.e., it is enough for the system to fail to prove the "NOT" of the predicate with the variable set to ' yes '). To test that it is FALSE, it is enough for the system to fail to prove that it is TRUE, (i.e. it is enough for the system to fail to prove the "NOT" of the predicate with the variable set to ' no ').

For example, suppose that the atomic formula MOTOR(check, x, STARTS) tests whether or not the motor starts.

Then when the predicate STARTS is main, MOTOR(check, yes, STARTS) takes the value TRUE when the motor can be proved to start .
When the predicate STARTS is auxiliary, NOT - MOTOR(check, no, STARTS) takes the value TRUE when the motor cannot be proved not to start.

Exercise 8
****

Find the truth-values of MOTOR(check, no, STARTS) when STARTS is auxiliary, and of NOT - MOTOR(check, yes, STARTS) when it is main.

****

The main/auxiliary distinction is important and must figure in any Expert System. On the other hand, the representation given here is anecdotic. It reflects a way of taking advantage of a detail of PROLOG implementation.

4 ORGANIZATION OF THE PROGRAM FOR THE REPRESENTATION OF ACTIONS

When faced with a problem involving actions, like that of car repair, for example, we do not set ourselves problems in the same sense as when we use a logical knowledge base. Without giving too many details which would be outside the field of ML, we are going to illustrate this problem so as to ensure that the rules presented below will not remain purely abstract.

A typical rule for car repair is to say that
IF the motor does not start, THEN push the starter button.

To be more precise, if we check and find out that the motor does not start, then we must execute the action of pushing the starter button .
This rule can be represented by

IF MOTOR(check, no, START) THEN STARTER(act, yes, PUSH)
which is equivalent to the PROLOG clause form,
STARTER(act, yes, PUSH) :- MOTOR(check, no, START)

The use of this rule is implicitly connected with the fact that problems are not being set here, but facts are being stated. In other words, we are not concerned by actual problem solving (which would lead us to rather use backward chaining), but to looking for some useful information (which leads us to rather use forward chaining).

No user is going to wonder whether he has really pushed the starter button unless he has some special reason to, or unless the motor does not start.
This is reflected in our representation by the fact that the clause
STARTER(act, yes, PUSH) :- MOTOR(check, no, START)
and the clause corresponding to the question whether the motor is not starting:
:- MOTOR(check, no, START)
do not resolve with each other.

However, if the motor does not start, the user will notice and it goes without saying that he will ask what to do.
In our representation, the fact that the motor does not start is stated by
MOTOR(check, no, START) :-
which does indeed resolve with
STARTER(act, yes, PUSH) :- MOTOR(check, no, START)
to propagate the fact
STARTER(act, yes, PUSH) :-
which asks the user to carry out the action of pushing the starter button.

This kind of problem can be represented using PROLOG, but that is not the subject of this book.

However, the reader must think about the clauses of this chapter as resolved by forward chaining (in which the observed facts are propagated), instead of the classical PROLOG backward chaining.

5 THE CASE OF A NEW RULE HAVING THE SAME PREMISE AS AN OLD ONE

As in section 2, let a predicate in the checking mode be written ' A' ' and let the same predicate in the action mode be written ' A '.

Assume that the rule

R_1:   B :- A'

exists in the set of rules already generated.

Assume also that the rule-generating system discovers the new one:

R_2:   C :- A'

Definition.

Let U and V be two predicates in the action mode. Consider the complexity of the actual procedures associated to U and V. Suppose that the procedure associated to U is easier to perform than the procedure associated with V.
We then define the **order on the predicates in the check mode** by U' < V'.

Thus we require a complexity of the actions to define an order on the checkings.

Suppose finally that we are in the case where B' < C' in the two rules R_1 and R_2.

Then we must delete B :- A' from the rule base and replace it by the following two rules

R_1':   B :- NOT - B', A'
$R_2' (= R_2)$:   C :- RETRACT(R_1'), A'

where B and C are in "act" mode, A' and B' are in "check" mode, where NOT is the PROLOG NOT and where RETRACT(x) is the PROLOG system function which eliminates the clause whose "name" is x, as defined in section 1.

Thus, when R_2' is executed, R_1' is deleted from the rule base.

The new set of rules says that R_1 is to be used first, and of course, in order for that to be worthwhile, B' has to evaluate to FALSE, whence the NOT - B' of R_1'. But as it is a simple check, i.e. a auxiliary predicate, we need only check that NOT - B' evaluates to TRUE.

After that, if we want to prove C' then we can apply R_2, but before doing it we delete R_1', which no longer has any purpose.

Suppose we want to learn to repair cars, and that the rule base contains a rule saying that when the motor does not start, then the starter button should be pushed. In our formalism, this will be written

R_1: STARTER(act, yes, PUSH) :- MOTOR(check, no, START).

Suppose, then, that the system generates a new rule

R_2: BATTERY(act, yes, CONNECT-UP) :- MOTOR(check, no, START)

because it has discovered that connecting up the battery is another thing that can be done when the motor does not start.

Suppose also that testing whether the starter button has been pushed is known to be easier than testing whether the battery has been connected up, so that we have

STARTER(check, yes, PUSH) < BATTERY(check, yes, CONNECT-UP)

It would be clumsy to leave R_1 and R_2 as two rules in the rule base.

They have to be definitively deleted and replaced by R_1' and R_2'

R_1': STARTER(act, yes, PUSH) :- NOT - STARTER(check, yes, PUSH), MOTOR(check, no, START)

R_2': BATTERY(act, yes, CONNECT-UP) :- RETRACT(R_1'), MOTOR(check, no, START)

R_1' says that the starter button is pushed after checking that either the starter button is known not to have been pushed or that nothing is known about the state of the starter button.

R_2' says that when the battery is connected up, R_1' is dynamically deleted, because having already checked that the starter there is no point in either doing it again or in testing whether its button has been pushed when the car does not move.

Exercises 9, 10, 11, 12, 13
****

9 - *Suppose that the mechanic is in front of the raised hood of the motor and hence that it is easier to check whether the battery has been connected up than whether the starter button is pushed. Write the new solution.*

10 - *Show that rules of the form*

B :- A *where A and B are in the action mode can be represented in a different way.*

Consider whether they have any point other than being close to the way in which humans organize their knowledge.

11 - *Study the case of rules of the form*

R_1:   B' :- A'

R_2:   C' :- A' *where A', B' and C' are in checking mode and R_1 is the rule initially in the rule base and R_2 is a newly-introduced rule.*

12 - Study the case of rules of the form

$$R_1: \qquad B' :- A'$$
$$R_2: \qquad C :- A' \text{ or}$$
$$R_1: \qquad B :- A'$$
$$R_2: \qquad C' :- A'$$

where A', B' and C' are in checking mode, where B and C are in action mode, R_1 is the rule initially in the rule base and R_2 is a newly-introduced rule.

13 - Reflect on the general problem of temporality without the use of quantifiers of temporality.

****

6 NEW RULE MORE SPECIFIC THAN AN OLD ONE

In this case, generalizing is not enough; we also have to specify the rule 's domain of application. A now famous system exists: LEX [Mitchell, Utgoff & Banerji 1983], which has led to the automated example-based learning of rules of formal integration. Its learning mechanism rests on the judicious use of taxonomies.

This system will be described in the next chapter. In this section we are describing two possible improvements, the possibility of changing the taxonomy and that of using several different taxonomies.

These improvements will be described using the following example.

Suppose that the system is to learn rules concerning the economic relationships between countries.
For example, it will be told that:
If France is a buyer of video recorders, and Japan produces them, then France is a potential buyer of video recorders from Japan.
A formal way of representing this sentence is:

$$E_1: \text{ NEEDS(FRANCE, VIDEOS) \& PRODUCT(JAPAN, VIDEO)} \rightarrow$$
$$\text{POSSBUY(FRANCE, VIDEOS, JAPAN)}$$

Assume that we also have the second example:

$$E_2: \text{NEEDS(BELGIUM, COMPUTERS) \& PRODUCT(USA, COMPUTERS)} \rightarrow$$
$$\text{POSSBUY(BELGIUM, COMPUTERS, USA).}$$

Suppose that the following taxonomies are available:

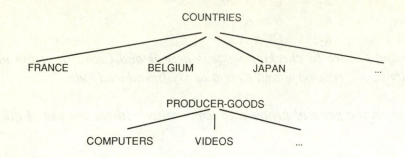

By using an algorithm that will be explained in chapter 7, the following generalization can easily be found

        G: NEEDS(x, u) & PRODUCT(y, u) → POSSBUY(x, u, y).

but the hierarchies give an indication of the nature of x, u and y which must not be ignored. Because of this, the generalization will be a conditional rule.

      IF   COUNTRY(x) & COUNTRY(y) & PRODUCER-GOODS(u) THEN

      NEEDS(x, u) & PRODUCT(y, u) → POSSBUY(x, u, y).

6.1   Use of a finer-grained hierarchy

This will enable us to improve on the fineness of the grain of the description of the domain of the variable ' u '.

Suppose that we now introduce the hierarchy

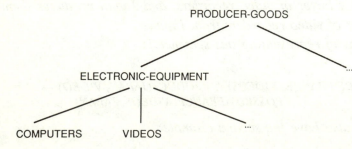

It is immediately apparent that the condition for the application of the rule becomes more precise:

    IF COUNTRY(x) & COUNTRY(y) & ELECTRONIC-EQUIPMENT(u) THEN ...

6.2 Use of several concurrent hierarchies

Suppose we have the two following hierarchies available

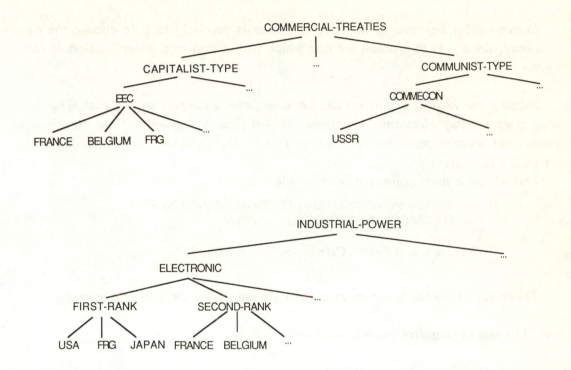

The examples E_1 and E_2 are not enough to decide whether ' x ' belongs to ' EEC ' or to ' SECOND-RANK '.

Supposing we have a farther rule E_3 in which West Germany also buys electronic equipment, this rule will not make a choice between the taxononies possible, but it will enable them to be ordered in terms of their relevance.

In this case (where West Germany also buys electronic equipment), using the first taxonomy would lead to the common parent ' EEC ', whereas using the second would lead to the common grandparent, ' ELECTRONIC '. Thus, the second taxonomy provides less detailed explanations about the use of the rule.

This could be a heuristic for choosing the first taxonomy, but of course it never constitutes a proof that it must be chosen.

There will be some cases where the examples on their own are enough to choose between the taxonomies, but they are quite rare. This occurs when an example contains a descriptor which does not appear in one taxonomy. This taxonomy is then eliminated. Clearly this can only occur very rarely, as these taxonomies are concerned with neighboring concepts.

For example, almost all countries belong to the taxonomies of commercial treaties and those of industrial power at the same time.

6.3 Use of negative examples to choose the right taxonomy

Conversely, a key role of negative examples is precisely to help choose the right taxonomy, since it is to prohibit the one which would lead to a generalization containing it.

Suppose we have a negative rule, i.e. a negative example, saying that West Germany does not buy electronic equipment. It will then be known that the taxonomy of commercial treaties must not be used to qualify the variable ' x ' (the one which designates the buyers).
This allows a finer-grained rule to be inferred:

> IF   *FIRST-RANK-INDUSTRIAL-ELECTRONIC-POWER(y) &*
>   *ELECTRONIC-EQUIPMENT(u)*   *THEN*
>
>   *NEEDS(x, u) & PRODUCT(y, u) → POSSBUY(x, u, y).*

This choice between taxonomies is certainly one of the keys to rule learning.

6.4 The use of negative examples to refine rules

One might almost become afraid of having to refine taxonomies ad infinitum, to the point where a taxonomy would be needed for every rule, which would be an impossible situation.

In order to reduce the application field of the rules, the expert might also be asked for negative examples to enable conditions to be added within the actual rule itself. When a rule like the one above has been found, the human expert is asked for examples of rules saying that the right-hand side of the rule is not to be carried out.

For example, an expert could say that the rule does not apply if another Euro-country produces the particular object ' u ' (rather than just any electronic equipment) at a better price than y. We would have:

> IF   *FIRST-RANK-INDUSTRIAL-ELECTRONIC-POWER(y) &*
>   ¬ *[PRODUCES-BETTER-PRICE(z, u, y) & EURO-COUNTRY(z)] THEN*
>
>   *NEEDS(x, u) & PRODUCT(y, u) → POSSBUY(x, u, y)*

The technique being applied is not a new idea in Expert Systems. Clearly, if we have

> R_1: A → B
> R_2: A & A' → ¬ B then R_1 has to be specialized to

R_1': A & $\neg$ A' $\rightarrow$ B.

What is original is its systematic use in learning, in particular with the aim of limiting the total number of taxonomies. In the above case, if the condition involving the best price were not introduced, there would be a taxonomy of countries for each industrial product, depending on the cost prices in each country. Our suggestion enables this problem to be avoided.

Exercise 14
****

Construct two of the taxonomies needed to replace the negative part of the above rule.

****

7 COMBINATION OF RULES

Suppose the rule base contains rules of the following form

R_{11}: B :- AA'

R_{12}: C :- AA' which means that if AA' is checked, then B and C must be simultaneously executed (otherwise the rule would have a form like that in section 6, and R_{11} and R_{12} would never appear).

Assume, then, that the system generates a new rule of the form

R_2: C :- AAA' and that AA' and AAA' are children of the same parent A'.
Then the rule set R_{11}, R_{12} and R_2 must be converted into the form

R_2': C :- A'

R_2': B :- AA', RETRACT(C)

Example.
The initial rules say that if interference-suppressor2 does not give sparks then cable2 and the contacts need revamping.

R_{11}': *CABLE-2(act, yes, REVAMP) :- SUPPRESSOR-2(check, no, SPARKS)*
R_{12}': *CONTACTS(act, yes, REVAMP) :- SUPPRESSOR-2(check, no, SPARKS)*

Suppose that the system then learns the rule

R_2: *CONTACTS(act, yes, REVAMP) :- SUPPRESSOR-1(check, no, SPARKS)*

and that it knows the taxonomy

SUPPRESSOR

SUPPRESSOR-1   SUPPRESSOR-2

then the rules R_{11} and R_{12} are to be replaced by

R_1': CONTACTS(act, yes, REVAMP) :- SUPPRESSOR(check, no, SPARKS)
R_2': CABLE-2(act, yes, REVAMP) :- SUPPRESSOR-2(check, no, SPARKS),
RETRACT(CONTACTS(act, yes, REVAMP))

This transformation is justified like in section 6 and the same problems arise. Note that a taxonomy of generality has been used.

Exercise 15
****

Show that the transformation is not valid when AA' and AAA' are not children of the same parent.

****

8   GENERALIZATION OF RULES

Generalization can be done either by climbing the taxonomies or by turning constants into variables.

Chapter 5 shows how taxonomies can be climbed validly.

Here is a negative example, given to remove the idea learning from generalization of examples enable taxonomies to be climbed trivially.

Wrong example of the use of taxonomies.
If there are two rules

BB :- AA'
BBB :- AAA'

and the two taxonomies

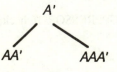   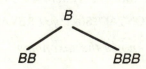

then we cannot infer to B :- A'.

Obviously, for example,

```
                      cable                    suppressor
           cable-1   cable-2    suppressor-1   suppressor-2
```

and from the two rules

> CABLE-1(act, yes, REVAMP) :- SUPPRESSOR-1(check, no, SPARKS)
> CABLE-2(act, yes, REVAMP) :- SUPPRESSOR-2(check, no, SPARKS)

(which say that if suppressor 1 has no spark then cable 1 should be revamped, and similarly for suppressor 2) it would be absurd to induce that

> CABLE(act, yes, REVAMP) :- SUPPRESSOR(check, no, SPARKS)

which says that if a suppressor has no spark then one of the cables should be revamped.

A new predicate would have to be used

> APPROPRIATE-CABLE(act, yes, REVAMP) :- SUPPRESSOR(check, no, SPARKS)

On the other hand, a method of learning in first-order logic, with predicates of variable arity to enable the discovery of new relationships to be taken into account, will solve this problem without difficulty.

This means that when rules of the form

$$A :- B$$

are learned, implication must be considered as a non-commutative function (which it indeed is), and examples must be written in the form $f(A, B)$.

In other words, if there are two examples of the form

$$A :- B, \qquad A' :- B'$$

then A must be generalized with A' simultaneously with B and B', in such a way that common variables can be introduced into the generalization of A and A' and into the generalization of B and B'.

It will be easy to add a variable to the predicates which will become:

> CABLE(act, yes, REVAMP, 1) :- SUPPRESSOR(check, no, SPARKS, 1)
> CABLE(act, yes, REVAMP, 2) :- SUPPRESSOR(check, no, SPARKS, 2)

It can be concluded without any need of taxonomies that their generalization is :

> CABLE(act, yes, REVAMP, x) :- SUPPRESSOR(check, no, SPARKS, x)

where x can have the value 1 or the value 2.

9 RULES FOR INFERENCE CONTROL

Learning to recognize the various independent micro-worlds of a domain has much to do with Learning. We are not going treat this problem in this section.

It can be done at intervals on the whole set of acquired rules, and by processes of automatic symbolic or numerical classification, as chapter 8 shows.

On the other hand, given a hierarchical description of micro-worlds describing the domain of expertise, the problem arises of learning to recognize that we are in a given micro-world and of exploring it.

In a car the micro-world of its ignition and that of its mechanics are kept in relation by the tips of the sparking plugs. But this is only valid from a general functional point of view. From the point of view of the repairer, the sparking plugs belong exclusively to the micro-world of the ignition. This can be represented by the following taxonomy.

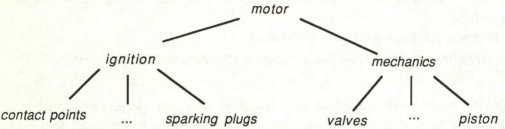

9.1 Learning of meta-rules

We thus need meta-rules of the following form:

$$MICRO\text{-}WORLD_i \text{ :- } C_1, ..., C_n$$

which tells us to go to the i-th micro-world if conditions C_1 and ... and C_n are respected and hence to add the new rule to whichever micro-world if the conditions in question are respected.

It is a research problem to find such rules. Nevertheless, in chapter 9 we shall see an example of such learning.

9.2 Assignment of new rules to the right micro-world

To the extent that the rules are in different micro-worlds, the first problem that arises is to know which micro-world to allocate each new rule to.

Finding out how to do this allocation is a research problem.

In chapter 9, we shall give a more precise idea of the difficulty of this problem. We shall show how logical debugging can become a weapon for learning new rules and assigning them to their micro-world.

5 Learning by Doing

1 THE PROBLEM

This type of learning is known to be typically appropriate when there is a system which is working in a problem-solving situation.

So the learning consists in improving problem-solving performance while it is actually operating.

Several systems of this pattern have been built and it has also been described as Explanation Based Learning (EBL), since one of its essential characteristics is that it uses explanations of its behavior (of its failures or of its successes, depending on the systems) in order to improve itself.

Nevertheless, EBL does not reduce to problem-solving. To demonstrate that the search for explanations is fundamental and not reducible to learning in problem-solving situations, we shall also give some examples involving learning from examples.

A system which learns by doing always contains some initial information which enables it to begin. This information is of two types.

On the one hand, it contains a set of initial operators which are given at the beginning in the form of rules. Starting from these initial operators, it has to generate new and more efficient ones. For learning without a teacher, it even has to generate the initial solutions.

On the other hand, it contains a set of initial heuristics, which control the use of the initial operators, possibly in a clumsy manner at the beginning. The learning has to be able to improve these heuristics too.

Such a system displays four essential characteristics.

1 - the system is capable of modifying its behavior, on the basis either of its mistakes or its successes.

2 - the system possesses a capacity to evaluate its results. It has to be capable of calculating the cost of one solution in relation to another. This constitutes a definition (sometimes implicit) of the efficiency of the system.

3 - in case of failure it has to be capable of identifying the defective operator and in case of success it has to be capable of identifying the operator to assign the credit to. This is the mechanism which enables the behavior to be explained.

4 - it has to be capable of modifying either its operators themselves or the

heuristics for their use to correct its mistakes or chalk up its successes.

Looked at another way, these systems have a mode of functioning which can be described through three phases.

First phase

The solution to a problem (referred to below as the model solution) is supplied to the system, either by making it solve the problem using the initial operators, or by hand if it is not capable of finding this solution on its own.

In any case, the solution must be presented in the form of a series of initial operators.

Second phase

There is an attempt to find the model solution again by applying heuristics for the use of the initial operators.
To enable this model solution to be found again, it is necessary for each operator to be associated with two sets of instances of its application:
a set of positive instances by which the operator has to be triggered,
a set of negative instances by which the operator must not be triggered.

Third phase

The conditions of the rules triggering the operators are to be modified so that in their new form they return TRUE for the positive instances and FALSE for the negative instances. The method consists in searching and modifying the application domain of each operator.

Example

Letting OP_1 and OP_2 be two initial operators, assume that the right solution requires OP_1 to be applied first, but that the heuristics lead to OP_2 being applied first. So we are going to have to modify the heuristics to make them lead to OP_1 being applied first.

P. Brazdil's ELM system [Brazdil 1978] works in algebra, so its aim is to learn to solve equations etc... The basic principle of this system is to detect the order in which to apply the operators. For this it sets up partial orders on the operators.

Suppose we are faced with a conflict situation for actions 1 and 2, that is, in order to accomplish $action_1$, OP_1 has to be applied and not OP_2, whereas to accomplish $action_2$, OP_2 has to be applied and not OP_1. Then the inference from $action_1$ is that $OP_1 > OP_2$, and the inference from $action_2$ is that $OP_2 > OP_1$.

In this contradictory situation, Brazdil introduces two new operators, OP_1' and

OP_2'.

OP_1' is identical to OP_1, except that its premise contains the extra condition enabling OP_1 to be triggered if the action required is $action_1$ and not $action_2$. This extra condition is:

(IF the conditions for accomplishing $action_2$ are FALSE)

Similarly, OP_2' contains, besides the conditions of OP_2:
(IF the conditions for accomplishing $action_1$ are FALSE)

Thus, OP_1' and OP_2' will always be applied before OP_1 and OP_2, so that the calls will be $OP_1' > OP_1$, $OP_1' > OP_2$, $OP_2' > OP_2$, $OP_2' > OP_1$, but OP_2 and OP_1 are considered to be incomparable.

Of course, the limitation of this kind of system is that it accumulates special conditions so that the rules have a tendency to become impracticable. Obviously it would have to be coupled with a system which would generalize when a clear concept began to "emerge" from a series of conditions.

At present this remains an area for research.

Certain limitations of this approach are immediately apparent: the "new" solutions are always a modification of the old ones and there will never be a revolutionary stage in learning.

2 VERSION SPACES [Mitchell 1982] SEEN AS FOCUSSING

This chapter gives an intuitive and incomplete presentation of the version spaces which will be looked at in greater detail, and more formally, in the next chapter.

The notion of version spaces enables generalization to be controlled to exploit the successes and failures of a system. The successes are used to generalize the heuristics for the use of the operators. The failures are used to specialize the heuristics for the use of the operators.

The LEX system [Mitchell, Utgoff & Banerji 1983] was designed for solving formal integrations. The subject itself is interesting, and will be briefly described in the following section.

We are now going to illustrate version spaces with a simpler example involving concept acquisition.

There is a double reason for this choice. For one thing, it is good to illustrate a notion (here, version spaces) by several examples. Mostly systems executing "actions" have been used up to now. For another thing, we want to illustrate the idea that concept learning from examples also uses the idea of version spaces.

A version space is built from a set of taxonomies of descriptors used to describe the initial operators and the initial heuristics.

These taxonomies are in strict accordance with the definition of the word taxonomy:

- the links between concepts are generality links, which means that the child is always a special case of its parent.

- there are no instances in common between the nodes of a given level.

- the child nodes exhaust all the possibilities of their parents.

These last two conditions ensure that a taxonomy is a hierarchy in the strict sense: the instances of the children are a partition of the instances of the parents. For more details on this subject, refer to chapter 8.

It is assumed furthermore that a descriptor can only belong to a single taxonomy.

These restrictions may appear very strong, but the object of research in ML is precisely to study how they can be weakened.

Thus, for example, we are giving the following taxonomies, each of which gives information which is valid only in certain micro-worlds. Assume we have been able to identify the taxonomy to be used.

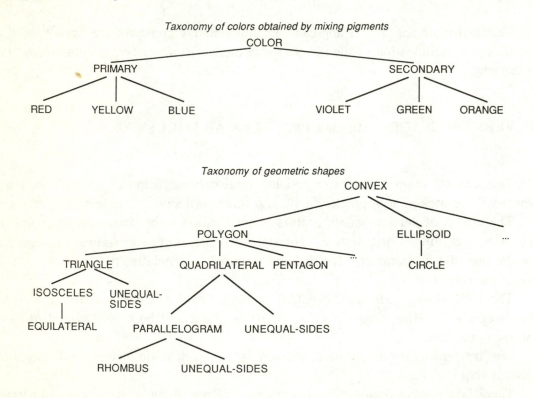

Taxonomy of colors obtained by mixing pigments

Taxonomy of geometric shapes

It will be noticed that if the notion of a right angle were used (i.e. rectangle, square, etc...), then square would be the child both of rectangle (with equal sides) and of rhombus (with right angles).

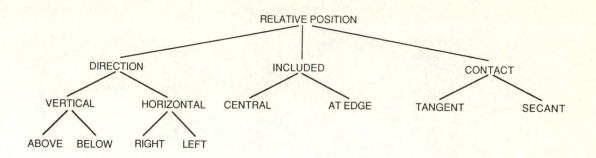

Each of the predicates appearing in the examples will be noted and marked with an upward arrow.

When a node is marked with an upward arrow, that means that it and all its descendants are certainly legal predicates.

Furthermore, nothing is known about predicates which are not ancestors of those marked with an upward arrow.

Downward arrows are also going to be introduced; their meaning is as follows.

When a node is marked with a downward arrow, then it and its descendants are the only legal predicates possible.

So at the beginning, the highest parent in each taxonomy is marked with a downward arrow, since all predicates are legal a priori. On the other hand, no node is marked with an upward arrow, since we cannot be certain of any of them.

Studying the positive and negative examples will enable the assignment of the arrows to be modified.

Consider first the effect of the positive examples.

Each predicate appearing in the positive examples is marked with an upward arrow in the taxonomies.

Here are two positive examples

Suppose that the first says that the concept to be invented is characterized by the presence of a yellow rectangle tangent to a red rhombus. Giving the name ' A ' to the rectangle and ' B ' to the rhombus, this will be written

E_1: *equilateral(A) & yellow(A) & rhombus(B) & red(B) & tangent(A, B)*

Similarly suppose the second is

E_2: *isosceles(C) & yellow(C) & quadrilateral-with-unequal-sides(C) & red(D) & secant(C, D)*

Considering E_1 and E_2, the above taxonomies become

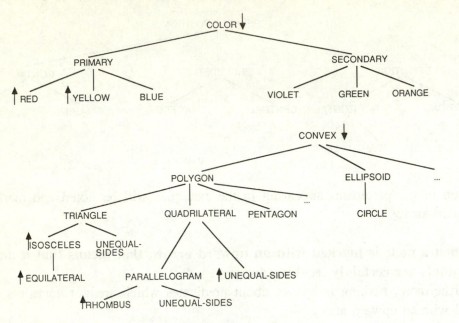

After doing this, the following generalization rule is used.

If all the children are marked with upward arrows, then the father is also marked with an upward arrow.

So it is no longer useful to keep ' CONTACT ' children's upward arrows, and they are removed.

So in our example, the taxonomy of the relative positions become

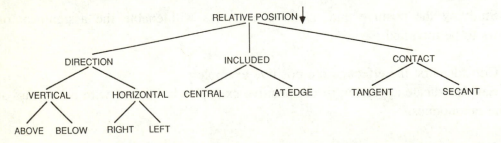

Which means that ' contact ' is a legal predicate (even though it has not occurred in any example), as well as both its children, ' tangent ' and ' secant '.

The negative examples are to be used to lower certain arrows, using the following specialization rule:

If a predicate appears in a negative example and does not appear in any

positive example, then its downward arrow is lowered AS LITTLE AS POSSIBLE, but just enough to exclude the predicate in question. If need be, the downward arrow is duplicated.

Suppose that the predicate ' included ' appears in our negative example. Then the taxonomy of the relative positions would become

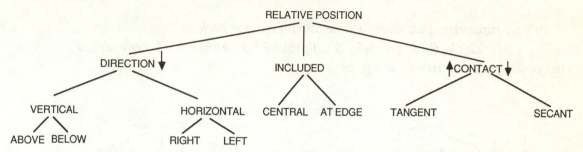

Indeed, in order to prevent ' included ' from appearing as a possible predicate for the positive examples, we need only lower the downward arrow from ' relative position ' to ' direction ' and ' contact '. It will be noted that if, for example, ' central ' or any child of ' subset ' appeared in the negative example, then the effect would be the same.

In this case, note that one predicate is marked with both a downward and an upward arrow. In accordance with the definition for arrowing, it is clear that only this predicate is valid.

When a predicate is marked with both upward and downward arrows, then only it and its descendants are legal, which means to say that it is the greatest generalization possible in this taxonomy.

In practice, it is the ideal generalized expression, taking all the positive and negative examples into account.

This is what we set out to achieve when we use version spaces. If we fail to get it, then there is an inaccuracy about the exact value of the generalization to be found, which remains enclosed between the lowest downward arrow and the highest upward arrow.

Note that we are making the implicit hypothesis that the upward and downward arrows never cross each other. If that ever happened it would indicate either an error in the positive or negative examples, or else an error in the description of the taxonomy. Two boring errors can produce this undesirable effect.

Firstly, there is never any certainty that all the necessary details of the taxonomy have been given, and the "right" node might quite simply not be there. In this case, the domain expert who provided the taxonomies is the person to question again.

Secondly, there is never any guarantee that the "right" taxonomy has been used. In practice, concepts generally belong to several taxonomies at once (Bobi, my dog, is contained in a biological taxonomy marking his belonging among the mammals, in an emotional taxonomy through being my faithful companion, etc ...). In this case, the error has to be analyzed and the process of learning has to be started again with a new taxonomy.

Trapping this kind of error is still a research problem.

Thus, supposing that there is a negative example such as
NE_1*: circle(E) & green(E) & ellipsoid(F) & orange(F) & central(E, F)*
the position of the arrows would be:

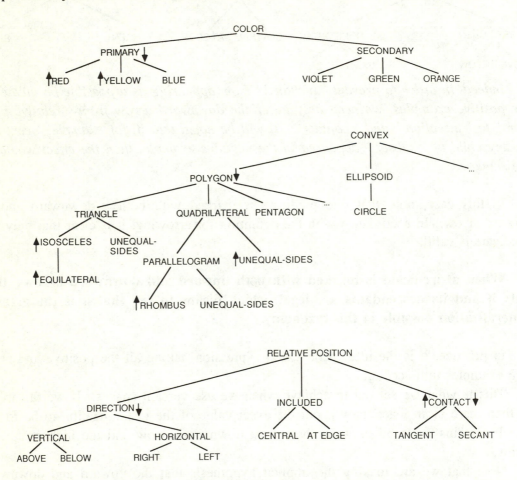

Indeed, it is enough to lower the downward arrow of ' convex ' to ' polygon ' in order to forbid ' ellipsoid ' and ' circle '.

Exercise 16
****

This exercise is designed to create awareness of the notion of an "item". An **item** *is the specific object denoted by a constant appearing in a predicate of arity 1, like,* *for example, the item bearing the name ' A ', which was given above to the yellow equilateral triangle of E_1. By extension, "item" will be used to refer to the members of the set of possible instances of arity 1. So this definition assumes that predicates of arity 1 define items, and that predicates of arity greater than 1 define the relations between items. Associate a set of taxonomies with each item of the scenes E_1, E_2, NE_1 above. Study possible generalizations for each item; for example, generalizing E_1 and E_2, an item ' x ' can be created whose instances will be A in E_1 and C in E_2, or an item ' x ' whose instances will be A in E_1 and D in E_2, etc ... Then study the consequences of each choice for the version space.*

****

From this section, the reader could conclude that the Version Spaces do not use inductive learning at all since they simply keep track of the generalization state of the operators. This is true here because the generalization (how to move the upward arrows) and particularization (how to move the downward arrows) principles are given in a crude form. We leave to the reader to imagine how the generalization rule can be changed in order to allow some inductive reasoning by moving the arrow before one is totally sure that all the children of same level are marked. Symetrically, one could also modify the specialization rule in order to allow some inductive learning from the negative examples.

3   APPLICATION TO RULE ACQUISITION

Rules will be displayed in the form
IF Condition THEN Action
and we shall try to generalize the conditions of several rules which trigger the same action A_1, and to specialize the conditions of rules which are not to trigger action A_1. Note carefully that learning could also modify the actions themselves. This form of learning is particularly sensitive and little studied up to now.

To modify the condition parts of the rules, the procedure will be as we indicated in the previous section, changing the positions of the markers in the version space.

Example
The example above can be used for rule acquisition.
To illustrate this, suppose that we are teaching a game to somebody and that to do this we give him examples of cases where he wins and case where he loses.
So suppose that he "wins" when he is presented with two colored shapes like those described in E_1 and E_2, and that he "loses" if he executes A_1 when NE_1 appears.
Then, assuming that he uses our taxonomies, the process of learning which we have just described by moving the arrows in these taxonomies can be commented on as follows.

Our student has learned that he must execute A_1 when the two figures are in contact without intersecting. He has also learned that the shapes must be polygons, without knowing yet exactly which is the polygon in question. Finally, he must know that the secondary colors are excluded. If he performs an induction which is a little too strong, then he might conclude that the color of the objects has to be primary, although 'BLUE' is still quite possible.

All these conclusions are just a commentary on the information contained in the arrowed taxonomies.

Of course, this illustrates any reward/punishment system, including a system which assesses itself according to the value of its results. In particular, LEX [Mitchell et al. 1983] is a system which notes for itself which are the predicates occurring during a successful session of formal integration. A taxonomy of functions is associated with each action, (integration by parts, extraction of a constant from the scope of the integral, etc ...) and the system is to learn which kind of function which action is to be applied to, depending on its own successes and failures.

To be more precise, the system contains integration operators.
For example, it is given the rule concerning the extraction of a constant from the scope of the integral.

$$OP_1 : \int k\, f(x)\ dx = k \int f(x)\ dx$$

or again, the rule for integration by parts

$$OP_2 : \int u\ dv = u\, v - \int v\ du$$

or yet again, those concerning sines and cosines

$$OP_3 : \int sin(x)\ dx = -cos(x) + C$$

$$OP_4 : \int cos(x)\ dx = sin(x) + C$$

LEX possesses a battery of operators of this type.

Obviously, knowing such rules is not enough to give you the ability to integrate; you also need a set of strategies for using the rules.

OP_2, for example, is not applied always, and when it is, its ' u ' and ' v ' must be carefully chosen in order to succeed. Indeed, in order to integrate
$$3x\ cos(x)\ dx,$$
OP_2 must be applied with $u = 3x$ and $dv = cos(x)\ dx$ and not, say, with $u = cos(x)$ and $dv = 3x\ dx$.
This is the kind of knowledge to which learning will now be applied.
Suppose that at a given moment, the system's knowledge is

R_1: *In order to integrate 3x cos(x) dx, OP$_2$ must be applied with u = 3x and dv = cos(x) dx.*

An additional positive example for the use of OP$_2$ is now to be given by telling the system to integrate 3x sin(x) dx, with u = 3x and dv = sin(x) dx.

LEX has a problem-solving unit which is to control this problem as follows.

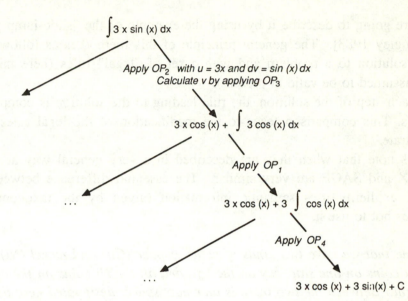

A negative example is now to be suggested to LEX. Assume that the system is told to integrate the same expression as above but with u = sin(x) and dv = 3x dx. You will be able to see that integration by parts does not give any simplification.

So the arrows will be moved upward and downward as we have seen above, but this time in a taxonomy of functions like that described in [Mitchell & Al. 1983] .

This enables the rules concerning the application of integration by parts to be modified.

For example, the system will learn that, if it is asked to integrate by parts

$$\int f(x)\, g(x)\, dx$$

then it can integrate by parts if f(x) is a polynomial and if g(x) is a trigonometric function.

4   LEARNING BY TRIAL AND ERROR

The first to systematically illustrate this approach was Langley, who showed how a relatively simple system could learn sophisticated heuristics from its own experience. This system has shown its effectiveness in several different domains, and so, in spite of the difficulties which we shall emphasize, any criticism must be very cautious.

We are going to describe Langley's SAGE system, to enable us to get used to this type of problem and to properly understand SAGE's limitations.

We are going to describe it by using the example of the "slide-jump puzzle" taken from [Langley 1983]. The general principle of this method is as follows. We begin with the solution to a problem and with a set of "legal" rules (here this means that they are assumed to be valid at present).

For each step of the solution, the rule leading to the solution is compared with the legal rules. This comparison leads to the modification of the legal rules, as we shall now illustrate.

Let us note that when they are described in a very general way as we have just done, LEX and SAGE are very similar. The essential difference between the two is that LEX explicitly uses semantic information (given by the taxonomies) whereas SAGE tries not to use it.

Assume that we have two kinds of coins, copper (Cu) and nickel (Ni). We line up all the Cu coins on one side, say on the left, and all the Ni coins on the other side, say on the right. Between the two there is an empty space, designated here by _.

The Cu coins can only be moved to the right and the Ni coins can only be moved to the left. In the case we are studying, in which there are 2 Cu and 2 Ni, the starting-point is:

$$P_1 : Cu\ Cu\ \_\ Ni\ Ni$$

Now the purpose of the game is to switch the positions of the Ni and the Cu, i.e. to arrive at

$$P_f : Ni\ Ni\ \_\ Cu\ Cu$$

Two moves are possible. The first consists in sliding a coin to the adjacent empty space, so that the empty space and the coin are switched. In this way, for example, starting from P_1, we can reach

$$P_2 : Cu\ \_\ Cu\ Ni\ Ni$$

The second consists in jumping: a coin no matter what its type can jump over another coin (of its own type or the other) to take over the empty space, so that the empty space and the coin are switched. For example, starting from P_1, we can reach

$$P_3 : Cu\ Ni\ Cu\ \_\ Ni$$

Thus the system possesses an initial store of these heuristics, which will not be described, but which corresponds to the use of the rules plus backtracking in case of failure. The system can thus find an initial solution. This initial solution is the starting-point from which learning takes over. This requires the system to be re-run. Two cases are possible.

One is that the system re-plays the same moves as are in the initial solution, and learns nothing.

The other case is that it plays different moves, and each of them is to be compared with those of the initial solution path, to change the rules to force it to follow the path leading to the solution found initially.

Of course, we do not expect this to reveal optimal heuristics at the first attempt, but we rely on improving them progressively.

Before describing how SAGE learns, let us set out clearly what it knows at the start, beginning with the language in which the moves are made. This language contains the variables:

$$coin_1, coin_2, ..., coin_i, position_1, position_2, ..., position_i, direction$$

where $coin_i$ represents one of the pieces in the game, $position_i$ represents one of the positions in the series of positions the coins are put in, and where direction enables the direction of the movement to be noted.

By convention, we write the instances of position in the form POSITION = n where n is the position observed.

For example, the position of the blank in P_1 is POSITION = 3, because the blank is in the third position.

Also, the taxonomies are (implicitly) input by hand

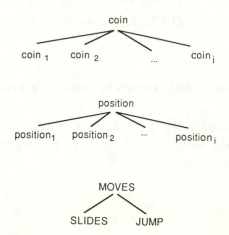

which allow the introduction of a variable representing any coin, of a variable representing any position, and of a variable describing any move.

Three sorts of knowledge are also introduced: predicates of action, predicates of state and rules for actions depending on the states.

For example, the predicate of action
- SLIDES(x, y, z, MOVESSLIDES), which says that the coin ' x ' is to be slid from position ' y ' to position ' z ' by making a MOVEment of SLIDing. The constant MOVESSLIDES is redundant here; the utility of introducing it will become clear later on.

We shall also have the following predicates of state.
- PLACE(x, y), which says that the coin (or the blank) of type ' x ' is at place ' y ', along with its negation, NOT PLACE(x, y).
- DIRECTION(x, y, z), which says that ' z ' is the direction for going from position ' x ' to position ' y ', along with its negation, NOT DIRECTION(x, y, z).
- CANMOVE(x, y), which says that the coin ' x ' can be moved in direction ' y '.
- the predicate PREVIOUSMOVE(x, y, z, t), which says that at the previous move the coin ' x ' moved from ' y ' to ' z ', using the method of transport t.

The constant MOVESSLIDES, which says that the move is carried out by a sliding and not by a jump. This constant could well be left implicit in the predicate SLIDES, but it can appear in other predicates, as for example to instantiate the variable ' t ' of the predicate PREVIOUSMOVE above.

If any of these variables is not defined at the previous move, it will be instantiated in PREVIOUSMOVE by the constant EMPTY.

Besides, an initial rule given to the system which describes how to slide.

R_1 :   *SLIDES(coin, position₁, position₂, MOVESSLIDES) :-*

$$SLIDES(coin, position_1, position_2, MOVESSLIDES) :-$$
$$PLACE(coin, position_1)$$
$$PLACE(blank, position_2)$$
$$CANMOVE(coin, direction)$$
$$DIRECTION(position_1, position_2, direction)$$

Finally
- methods of modifying the already known heuristics are given.

To describe these heuristics, we use the series of rules and states given by the following figure. Note that the suffixes are only there to fix ideas, and have no effect on the generality of the presentation.

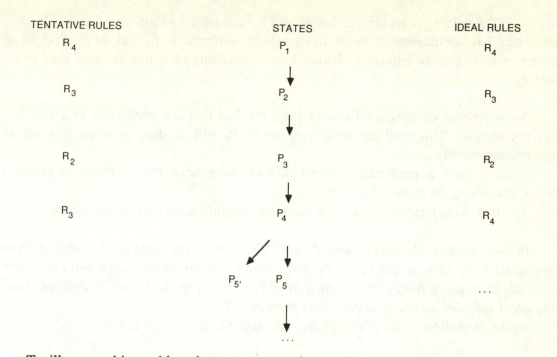

TENTATIVE RULES	STATES	IDEAL RULES
R_4	P_1	R_4
R_3	P_2	R_3
R_2	P_3	R_2
R_3	P_4	R_4
$P_{5'}$	P_5	...

To illustrate this problem better, suppose that, as in the above figure, the solution to the problem goes through the stages P_1, P_2, P_3, P_4, P_5, ... and that P_1 is reached from P_2 by applying R_4, P_2 is reached from P_3 by applying R_3, ..., and P_4 is reached from P_5 by applying R_4. This constitutes the ideal solution which we are attempting to rediscover by beginning to search for the solution to the problem once again.

So suppose that the attempt does indeed go through stages P_1, P_2, P_3, P_4, but that at P_4, instead of applying R_4 as in the ideal solution, R_3 is applied, thus arriving at state P_5'.

The system then backtracks to search for the last successful application of R_3, in this case at P_2.

The rule R_3 is of the form

$$(R_3) \quad ACTION_3 :\text{-} COND_3$$

and, if the system can, it has to modify $COND_3$ to enable it to apply even more specifically in the state P_2 while not applying in the state P_4.

In the states P_2 and P_4, R_3 can be applied, so $COND_3$ is legal in P_2 and P_4.

A predicate TF_{24} is to be sought which is true in P_2 and false in P_4.

So Langley's method consists in transforming R_3 into

$$(R_3') \quad ACTION_3 :\text{-} COND_3, TF_{24}$$

By definition, this new condition is still true in P_2, but false now in P_4.

Similarly, a predicate TF_{42} is sought which is true in P_4 and false in P_2.

Langley's method then consists in transforming R_3 into

$$(R_3'') \quad ACTION_3 :\text{-} COND_3, NOT\ TF_{42}$$

which will clearly no longer apply in P_4, while still applying in P_2.

The rule R_3 is preserved, but R_3' and R_3'' are added to the set of rules. In fact, each rule has coefficients of belief in its validity assigned to it, and the coefficient of belief of R_3 is greatly reduced, whereas high coefficients of belief are attributed to R_3' and R_3''.

An additional complication comes from the fact that the predicates TF_{24} and TF_{42} are not unique. The modification carried out on R_3 will be deepest when they are as general as possible.

Thus, if such a predicate is found, it must be generalized as much as possible while preserving its truth-value in P_2 and P_4.

The following example will show how this generalization can be carried out.

In our example, the succession of states obtained by the method of trial and error begins with the same series P_1, P_2, P_3, given above. Let us assume also that the system now suggests going from P_1 to P_2, then from P_2 to P_3'. This last move is different from the ideal solution, which requires going from P_2 to P_3.

In the formalism of the above figure, this example is represented by

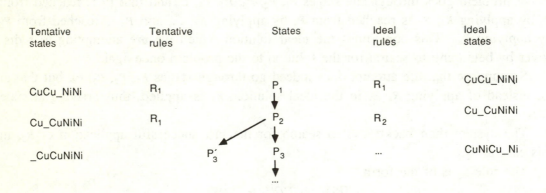

Tentative states	Tentative rules	States	Ideal rules	Ideal states
				CuCu_NiNi
CuCu_NiNi	R_1	P_1	R_1	
				Cu_CuNiNi
Cu_CuNiNi	R_1	P_2	R_2	
				CuNiCu_Ni
_CuCuNiNi	P_3'	P_3	...	
		...		

The application of R_1 at P_2 is incorrect. The last correct application of R_1 is sought, and it turns out to be just the previous move.

To preserve the transition $P_1 \rightarrow P_2$, and to prevent the transition $P_2 \rightarrow P_3'$, the state operators are analyzed and it becomes apparent that PREVIOUSMOVE(EMPTY, EMPTY, EMPTY, EMPTY) is true in P_2 and false in P_3.

So it is added to the conditions for R_1.

This results in

R_1' :   SLIDES(coin, position$_1$, position$_2$, MOVESSLIDES) :-
                        PLACE(coin, position$_1$)
                        PLACE(blank, position$_2$), DIRECTION(position$_1$, position$_2$, direction)
                        CANMOVE(coin, direction)
                        DIRECTION(position$_1$, position$_2$, direction)
                        PREVIOUSMOVE(EMPTY, EMPTY, EMPTY, EMPTY)

Furthermore, it turns out that
        PREVIOUSMOVE(Cu, POSITION = 2, POSITION = 3, MOVESSLIDES)
is true at P_3 and false at P_2.

So its negation has to be added to the condition of R_1 to prohibit the application of R_1 at P_2.

But in fact it is necessary to add a more general condition which is obtained as follows.

Clearly, SLIDES is instantiated by
        Cu, POSITION = 2, POSITION = 3, MOVESSLIDES at P_2 and by
        Cu, POSITION = 1, POSITION = 2, MOVESSLIDES at P_3'.
The variable ' coin ' has the same value at P_2 and at P_3', so let us say that PRE-VIOUSMOVE applies to the same ' coin ' at P_2 as at P_3'. The variable position$_1$ is instantiated by POSITION = 2 and hence has the same value as the variable ' posi-tion$_2$ ' of P_3'. Hence, at the previous move, the value of ' position$_1$ ' is precisely ' position$_2$ '.

On the other hand, the variable ' position$_2$ ' of at P_2 is instantiated by POSITION = 3, which appears nowhere in P_3'. So a new variable, say, ' position$_3$ ', has to be introduced as the second variable of position of PREVIOUSMOVE. Finally, the con-stant MOVESSLIDES is common to both, so it is kept.

So we have
    R_1'' :   SLIDES(coin, position$_1$, position$_2$, MOVESSLIDES) :-
                        PLACE(coin, position$_1$)
                        PLACE(blank, position$_2$)
                        DIRECTION(position$_1$, position$_2$, direction)
                        NOT PREVIOUSMOVE(coin, position$_2$, position$_3$, MOVESSLIDES)
                        CANMOVE(coin, direction)

This kind of transformation is applied systematically and leads to the learning of quite elaborate rules.

Of course, one defect of this system is that it is extremely sensitive to the language used. The right predicates of state and the right rules of generalization have to be introduced to obtain interesting results.

Another defect is the introduction of a tremendous number of rules, some of which can be redundant. It would be fascinating to have a procedure for comparing conditions which eliminated rules whose conditions were too specific. In practice, the less frequently used rules are the ones which get eliminated, by means of the coefficients of belief about their importance. It would be desirable to try to use criteria which enabled better explanations to be given of why one rule is kept and why another is rejected.

6 A Formal Presentation of Version Spaces

The Version Spaces [Mitchell 1982] paradigm is a method that helps to find the exact generalization state in which a descriptor must be used in order to optimize the problem solving efficiency of operators making use of this descriptor. Given a set of positive and negative examples, their "version space" is the set of the consistent formulas, i.e. the set of formulas that are both complete (they recognize all the positive examples) and coherent (they recognize none of the negative examples). From this intuitive definition, we see that the notion of version space depends very much on what is the recognition of an example by a formula. It turns out that this amounts to a definition of what generalization is, this is why we shall first concentrate on a very precise definition of this notion.

It is somewhat surprising to see that Classical Logics do not define the generalization state of an atomic formula. The only existing logical tool is applicable to disjunctive formulas and is called subsumption, while substitution defines the relative generality of terms (i.e., formal functional expressions that are not evaluated). We shall attempt to clarify this situation, up to the point where some of the practical consequences of our theoretical choices can be seen.

In section 1, we study definitions of the generalization of implications and conjunctive formulas, and their differences, we study also the practical consequences of choosing Modus Ponens instead of the Generalization Principle as an inference rule. Another, related, topic of section 1 is the discussion of the use of the properties of the descriptions we want to learn from.

1 DIFFERENT DEFINITIONS OF GENERALIZATION

1.1 Intuitive Definition of Generalization

There exists one definition which is agreed upon by all authors, the most intuitive one. We give it in a simplified form where the formulas depend on one variable only. When there are several variables, one has to take into account the fact that each variable is relative to a given *object*. Object oriented generalization is a rather new topic [Manago 1986], we will not go into it because we would like to stick here to well-known concepts.

Let P(x) and Q(y) be two formulas.

Let us write $\{P_{TRUE}\}$ for the set of the instances of x such that P(x) = TRUE, and similarly for Q.

$$\{P_{TRUE}\} = \{ x / P(x) = TRUE\}$$
$$\{Q_{TRUE}\} = \{ y / Q(y) = TRUE\}$$

Then one says that **P(x) is more general than Q(y)** iff $\{P_{TRUE}\} \supset \{Q_{TRUE}\}$.

This definition is the one actually used when one wants to show that, say, P(x) is not more general than Q(y). In that case it is enough to exhibit an instance of x such that P(x) is FALSE and Q(y) is TRUE.

Let us now present a formalization of this intuitive definition. Let $A \geq$ mean that A is more specific than B. We shall define formally the relation $\geq$ as follows. Let I be the space of the instances, F be the space of the formulas. For each formula x and for each instance i, let M(x, i) be the predicate which is TRUE when i and x match together, that is to say, when i is an instance of x. Then $\geq$ is defined by

$$\forall x \, \forall y \, [(x \in F \, \& \, y \in F) \Rightarrow (x \geq y \Leftrightarrow (\{i \in I \, / M(y, i)\} \supseteq \{i \in I \, / M(x, i)\}))]$$

Let VS be the space of possible formulas (it will be called Version Space later). Then, one is able to define the set of maximally specific consistent formulas S, and the set of maximally general consistent formulas G as follows.

$$S = \{s \in VS / \, (p \in VS \, \& \, s \in S) \Rightarrow s < p\}$$
$$G = \{g \in VS / \, (p \in VS \, \& \, g \in G) \Rightarrow p < g\}$$

The problem, however, is to be able to compute a generalization from its instances, and the above definition gives no way to achieve this goal. This is why alternate definitions, leading to a generalization algorithm, have been developed.

1.2 Vere 's definition of generalization

Let us first consider a conjunction of descriptors. So the formula has the form
$$A = A_1 \, \& \, ... \, \& \, A_n$$
where each A_i is a descriptor.

Let $\{A\}$ be called the set associated to A, defined by
$$\{A\} = \{A_1, ..., A_n\}$$
Then *A* **is more general than** *B* iff there is

- an expression B' such that $\{B'\} \subseteq \{B\}$
- a substitution σ such that $\sigma A = B'$.

Otherwise stated, σA is equal to a subpart of *B*, up to a variable renaming.

For disjunctions of conjunctions, this definition becomes : Let $G_a = g_{a1} \vee ... \vee g_{an}$, $G_b = g_{b1} \vee ... \vee g_{bm}$, then G_a **is more general than** G_b iff $\forall j \, \exists i$ such that g_{ai} is more general than g_{bj}.

The main drawback of this definition is that it gives no control on the way conjuncts are dropped during the generalization process.

1.3 Existential versus Universal quantification

The state of quantification of the variables introduced during the generalization process depends on

　　　　　　1 - the form of the expressions given as example
　　　　　　2 - the use of the generalized expression.

The form of the expressions given as example depends very much on the way the information is represented as we already have seen in chapter 2.

Consider the English sentence "That particular crow, named Jack, is black".
It can be interpreted either as an implication, or as a conjunction. Disputing which is the best would be outside of the scope of this chapter.
In the first case, its first order logic representation will be :
$$CROW(JACK) \Rightarrow BLACK(JACK),$$
in the second case, it will be :
$$CROW(JACK) \& BLACK(JACK).$$

When one is learning from implications (or, more generally, from theorems) the intuitive behavior consists in introducing universally quantified variables [Plotkin 1970].

From the knowledge
$$CROW(JACK) \Rightarrow BLACK(JACK)$$
$$CROW(JOCK) \Rightarrow BLACK(JOCK),$$
one is tempted to infer
$$\forall x \, [CROW(x) \Rightarrow BLACK(x)]$$
because it gives a good representation of the sentence "All crows are black".

When one is learning from conjunctions, it is counter-intuitive to introduce universal quantifiers.

From the knowledge
$$CROW(JACK) \& BLACK(JACK)$$
$$CROW(JOCK) \& BLACK(JOCK),$$

one is not tempted to infer

$$\forall x \ [CROW(x) \ \& \ BLACK(x)]$$

because it represents the sentence "All objects are black crows" which is nowhere in the examples.

Even more convincingly, one cannot learn that

$$\forall x \forall y \ [BLACK(x) \ \& \ WHITE(y)]$$

from

$$BLACK(CROW) \ \& \ WHITE(SWAN)$$
$$BLACK(JAY) \ \ \& \ WHITE(DOVE)$$

since the examples contain no contradiction while $\forall x \forall y \ [BLACK(x) \ \& \ WHITE(y)]$ does.

Nevertheless, it may seem a bit awkward to "infer" from them

$$\exists x \exists y \ [BLACK(x) \ \& \ WHITE(y)]$$

since this existential theorem is nothing but a mere logical deduction from either example.

Suppose that you start from a relation R(A, B) among instances. It is trivial to understand that, most often, the relation $\forall x \forall y \ [R(x, y)]$ is wrong. One has to find a relation of the type

$$\forall x \ \forall y \ [P(x) \ \& \ Q(y) \Rightarrow R(x, y)]$$

where P and Q describe those variables for which R is TRUE, but in general, one has no way to find P and Q.

That explains why some authors define

$$P(A) \ \text{generalizes into} \ \exists x \ P(x) \ \text{iff} \ \exists x \ [P(A) \Rightarrow P(x)]$$

Since this implication is a tautology, this definition is also very much disputable. The idea of generalization conveys some increase in the information content of the generalized formula. Here, on the contrary, generalization would take place, and seemingly decrease the information content of the generalized formula. This last point will be detailed in section 1.3.2.3 below.

Let us now see how these problems are handled in each particular case.

1.3.1   Theorem Learning

When one is learning from example theorems, one will introduce universally quantified variables. This gives rise to two different difficulties. Both of them are extremely deep problems and their answer belong to long term research. Nevertheless, we shall now describe them briefly.

Firstly, there exist indeed theorems that contain existential quantifiers, and the recognition of this existential quantifier is very difficult problem which amounts to function synthesis.

Secondly, the examples usually do not specify what is the domain of validity of the theorem (i.e., one usually learns false theorems from examples) and the determination of this domain amounts to predicate synthesis.

1.3.1.1 Inventing Skolem Functions

When some variables are existentially quantified, there is always a hidden function which will be extremely difficult to reveal.

Suppose that one is learning from set of examples like : $0 + 1 = 1$, $0 + 2 = 2$, ..., $1 + 0 = 1$, ..., $1 + 1 = 2$, etc ..., where + is an unknown symbol. From this set, it would be wrong to infer formulas whose variables are all universally quantified like : $\forall x \forall y \forall z$ [x + y = z].

Let us now suppose that it has been possible, say by using suitable counter-examples, to guess that one possible formula is $\forall x \forall y \exists z$ [x + y = z].
Obviously, this last theorem, although true, does not solve the learning problem implicitly stated by the above sequence of examples : "invent a definition of a function + that fits with this set of input-output examples".

When a theorem contains existential quantifiers, the first goal is, of course, to recognize which are the variables under their scope. In general, as the example shows, this is not the ultimate goal which is rather : "remove those existentially quantified variables by synthesizing a suitable Skolem function that fits with the examples".

Instead of $\forall x \forall y \exists z$ [x + y = z], one rather wants to find a function f such that $\forall x \forall y$ [x + y = f(x, y)], and f realizes the operation +.

Several methodologies that propose an approach to the solution of this problem can be found in [Biermann & al. 1984]. Recently, an original approach has been developed and implemented in our group [Franova 1985, 1986, 1988].

1.3.1.2 Finding Domain Definitions

Let us suppose now that we are in the simpler case where all quantifications are universal ones. It does not mean that the theorem is true in all possible interpretations : one must also find the domain of definition of the variables.

Suppose that the system is to learn rules concerning the economic relationships between countries.
For example, it will be told that :
If France is a buyer of video recorders, and Japan produces them, then France is a potential buyer of video recorder from Japan.
A formal way of representing this sentence is :

E_1 : *NEEDS(FRANCE, VIDEOS) & PRODUCES(JAPAN, VIDEOS)* →
POSSBUY(FRANCE, VIDEOS, JAPAN).

Assume that we also have the second example :
E_2 : *NEEDS(BELGIUM, COMPUTERS) & PRODUCES(USA, COMPUTERS)* →
POSSBUY(BELGIUM, COMPUTERS, USA).

It is then easy to find the following generalization :
G : $\forall x \forall y \forall u$ *NEEDS(x, u) & PRODUCES(y, u)* → *POSSBUY(x, u, y).*
*This generalization is still not correct since, for instance, it would allow x and u to be
instantiated by the same value.*

In this simple case, suppose that the following taxonomies are available :

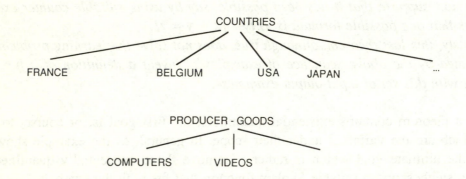

*Since these hierarchies describe the possible domains of the variables, this informa-
tion can be introduced as a condition to the application of the rule :*
$\forall x \forall y \forall u$ *[IF COUNTRY(x) & COUNTRY(y) & PRODUCER-GOODS(u)*
       THEN { NEEDS(x, u) & PRODUCES(y, u) → *POSSBUY(x, u, y) }].*

A greater refinement is of course possible when we have more detailed information
than that given in the two above taxonomies [Kodratoff 1985], [Kodratoff 1986a].

1.3.2 Concept Learning or Different Ways to Use a Recognition Function

In this section, let us assume that we are not learning rules or theorems, but conjunctions of atoms.
This kind of learning aims at obtaining a formula, called a **recognition function**, that
characterizes the micro-world to which the examples belong.

When quantifiers are introduced, the recognition process will work by using a deduc-
tive principle.
In our example, we shall use refutation and represent the recognition as deduction in a
PROLOG program, using Edinburgh notation [Clocksin & Mellish 1981]

Suppose that we start from
$$E_1 : \text{"This scene contains KOKO who is a white swan",}$$
$$E_2 : \text{"This scene contains KIKI who is a white swan".}$$

These examples are interpreted as a description of some scene "This scene".
They are then given the form :
$$E_1' : SWAN(KOKO) \ \& \ WHITE(KOKO)$$
$$E_2' : SWAN(KIKI) \ \& \ WHITE(KIKI).$$

Obviously, one aims here at recognizing scenes that contain a white swan.
This example has been chosen on purpose to be contrasted with the "black crow" one since not all swans are white.

1.3.2.1 Universal quantification

All variables are universally quantified, the recognition "function" has therefore the form : $\forall x \ [P(x)]$.
It will be used as a recognition function of a scene, say S_1, as defined as follows :
$$\forall x \ [P(x)] \textbf{ recognizes } S_1 \textbf{ when one can prove } \forall x \ [P(x)] \Rightarrow S_1.$$

Using refutation for the proof of $(\forall x \ [P(x)]) \Rightarrow S_1$ amounts to proving that its negation leads to a contradiction, i.e. that
$$(\forall x \ [P(x)]) \ \& \ \neg S_1$$
leads to a contradiction.

E_1' *and* E_2' *will generalize to*
$$\forall x \ [P(x)] = \forall x \ [SWAN(x) \ \& \ WHITE(x)]$$
which will be used to recognize a scene made of a white swan.
Suppose that we want to check that
$$S_1 = [SWAN(JACKO) \ \& \ WHITE(JACKO)]$$
is recognized.
One has to prove that
$$SWAN(x) \ :\text{-}$$
$$WHITE(x) \ :\text{-}$$
$$:\text{- } SWAN(JACKO), WHITE(JACKO)$$
leads to a contradiction, which is of course the case.
Therefore, the scene is recognized by this recognition function.

This kind of generalization has the property (in some cases it is a drawback, in some others it may be an advantage) that it will fail to recognize a scene with additional details.

Considering a scene with a white swan and a Peugeot car, one will have to find a contradiction in the set:

$$SWAN(x) \; :\text{-}$$
$$WHITE(x) \; :\text{-}$$
$$:\text{-} \; SWAN(JACKO), \; WHITE(JACKO), \; CAR(PEUGEOT\text{-}405)$$
and this will not be possible.

In conclusion, one must use universally quantified variables when one looks for a recognition function that recognizes whole scenes. One must not use them when the recognition function is supposed to recognize sub-parts of a scene.

1.3.2.2 Existential quantification

All variables are existentially quantified, the recognition "function" has therefore the form : $\exists x \; [P(x)]$.
It will be used as a recognition function of a scene, say S_1, as defined :
One says that

$$\exists x \; [P(x)] \; \textbf{recognizes} \; S_1 \; \textbf{when} \; S_1 \vdash \exists x \; [P(x)],$$

i.e., when one can deduce $\exists x \; [P(x)]$ from S_1.
Using refutation for the proof of $S_1 \vdash \exists x \; [P(x)]$ amounts to proving that deducing the negation of $\exists x \; [P(x)]$ from S_1 leads to a contradiction, i.e. that

$$S_1 \; \& \; \neg \; \exists x \; [P(x)]$$

leads to a contradiction.

E_1' and E_2' will generalize to
$$\exists x \; [P(x)] = \exists x \; [SWAN(x) \; \& \; WHITE(x)],$$
therefore one has :
$$\neg \; \exists x \; [P(x)] = \forall x \; \neg P(x) = \forall x \; \neg[SWAN(x) \; \& \; WHITE(x)]$$

Suppose that we want to check that
$$S_1 = [SWAN(JACKO) \; \& \; WHITE(JACKO)]$$
is recognized.
One has to prove that
$$SWAN(JACKO) \; :\text{-}$$
$$WHITE(JACKO) :\text{-}$$
$$:\text{-} \; SWAN(x), \; WHITE(x)$$
leads to a contradiction, which is of course the case.
Therefore, the scene is recognized by this recognition function.

1.3.2.3 Conclusion

Existential quantification might have been felt as counter-intuitive because "nothing is learned" from it. This is not true for the following reasons.

- The existential theorem $\exists x \; [P(x)]$ learned from a set of examples $\{E_1, ..., E_n\}$ must be deducible from **each** E_i. It therefore catches some of the common features of the examples, as it should be.

It will recognize a scene by its sub-parts.

Considering again a scene with a white swan and a Peugeot car, one will have to find now a contradiction in the set :

$$SWAN(JACKO) :-$$
$$WHITE(JACKO) :-$$
$$CAR(PEUGEOT-405) :-$$
$$:- SWAN(x), WHITE(x)$$

and the presence of a car is no longer harmful. It follows that we have made the inductive step as small as possible. Induction itself lies in the way we choose P(x) among the infinity of formulas that can be deduced from a set of examples. This phenomenon is quite usual when we are automatizing induction, as in ML. Choosing from finite (nevertheless large) sets of possibilities is already a form of induction, while the fullest induction we practise is a choice from an infinite, even though well-defined, set of possibilities.

- This definition is actually very near to the intuitive one. In particular, it contains Michalski's generalization rules [Michalski 1983, 1984]. For instance, the example of section 1.3.2.2 shows how it contains the "dropping condition" rule.

- This approach has been used in [Kodratoff 1985] for the specific case of counter-examples. It has been generalized by Nicolas [Nicolas 1986a, 1986b, 1988] who uses a theorem prover in order to perform inductive learning, which may seem surprising at first sight.

We have developed another way to define generalization, by extending the classical definition of term generalization, as seen in the next section.

In order to prove the necessity of introducing these new concepts, let us consider the following counter-example to the methods derived from Modus Ponens, as presented in sections 1.3.1 and 1.3.2.

1.3.3 A Counter-example

Let us now give a "counter-example" to deductive definition, in the sense that a best generalization is not found by it.

1.3.3.1 A definition of "best generalization" derived from Modus Ponens

There is an obvious way to define a best generalization when one quantifies the variables existentially.

The best generalization is the one which is the "nearest" to all the examples, but contains the information they have in common.

Let $\{E_i\}$ be a set of examples, and $\{G_j\}$ be a set of possible generalizations, i.e., $\forall i$, one must be able to prove that $E_i \vdash G_k$, for each of the G_k's.

Since one infers the generalizations from the examples, it is obvious that one must define the **best generalization** among the G_k's as being the most specific one, i.e. the one, if it exists, from which all others can be inferred.

1.3.3.2 The counter-example

Suppose that one starts from the two examples
$$E_1 : ON(A, B) \text{ \& } NEAR(B, C)$$
$$E_2 : ON(D, E)$$
with the theorems
$$\forall x \, \forall y \, [ON(x, y) \Rightarrow NEAR(x, y)]$$
$$\forall x \, \forall y \, [NEAR(x, y) \Leftrightarrow NEAR(y, x)]$$

Using these theorems, one can show that the two following Potential Generalizations
$$G_1 : \exists x \, \exists y \, [ON(x, y)]$$
$$G_2 : \exists x \, \exists y \, \exists z \, [ON(x, y) \text{ \& } NEAR(y, z)]$$
are equivalent relative to our definition, since $G_1 \Leftrightarrow G_2$.

Nevertheless, the associated generalizations obtained by substitution techniques, as seen below, are :
$$f_1 : ON(x, y)$$
$$f_2 : ON(x, y) \text{ \& } NEAR(y, z)$$
These are not equivalent since, using the theorems, one can show that f_1 is equivalent to
$$f_1' : ON(x, y) \text{ \& } NEAR(y, x).$$
f_2 is clearly (from definition 1.5.2 below) more general than f_1 since the substitution $\sigma = \{x \leftarrow x, y \leftarrow y, z \leftarrow x\}$ is such that $\sigma f_2 = f_1'$.

1.4 Term generalization

1.4.1 Terms

Let V be a countable set of variables and F a family of functions indexed by the natural numbers. When a function f belongs to F_n, one says that the arity of f is n. The set F_0 of functions of arity zero is called the set of the constants.

The set of terms on V and T, is defined by
(i) $v \in V$ is a term
(ii) $f(t_1, ..., t_n)$ is a term iff $f \in F_n$ and $t_1, ..., t_n$ are terms.

Intuitively, the set of terms is a set of expressions built with functions of some arity, constants and variables.

1.4.2 Generalization

The term t_1 **is more general than the term** t_2, denoted by $t_1 \leq t_2$, iff there exists a substitution $\sigma t_1 = t_2$.

This definition does not take into account the properties of the functions. One describes these properties by a "theory" ε, and one defines a generalization modulo this theory.

1.4.3 ε - generalization

Let ε be a set of axioms which express the properties of the functions.

When one needs to use these axioms in order to recognize the equality of two terms, one says that they are **ε-equal**

For instance, the two terms $t_1 = (2 + 3)$ *and* $t_2 = (3 + 2)$ *are not considered as "equal" but as "ε-equal" because one needs to use the axiom of + commutativity :*

$$\forall x \, \forall y \, [(x + y) = (y + x)],$$

in order to recognize that $t_1 =_\varepsilon t_2$.

This definition may seem counter-intuitive but is it necessary to single out the use of axioms in the context of an automatic generation of generalizations because their use may lead to infinite computation loops (using the axiom in one direction and then in the other one). This kind of problems have been very much studied, see for instance [Stickel 1981], [Hsiang 1982].

Let $=_\varepsilon$ denote ε-equality.

A term t_1 **is more general than a term** t_2 in the theory ε iff **there exist** $t_1' =_\varepsilon t_1$ **and** $t_2' =_\varepsilon t_2$ **and a** σ **such that** $\sigma t_1' = t_2'$.

Depending on ε, it may be that the above definition of ε-generalization is not consistent with its implicit future use for defining an (at least partial) order. Using some of the properties one may find t_1' and t_2' such that $t_1 =_\varepsilon t_1'$ and $t_2 =_\varepsilon t_2'$ and there is a σ such that $\sigma_1 t_1' = t_2'$.

Nevertheless, it may well also be that, using other properties, one can find t_1'' and t_2'' such that $t_1 =_\varepsilon t_1''$ and $t_2 =_\varepsilon t_2''$, and there exists σ_2 such that $\sigma_2 t_2'' = t_1''$ even when $t_1' \neq_\varepsilon t_2''$ [Kodratoff & Ganascia 1986].

Since we want to use the properties of the functions, and further define the generality of formulas (therefore using the properties of our connectors) it is necessary to find a definition of ε - generalization that avoids this difficulty.

1.4.4 Example of ε - generalization (where atomic formulas are treated like terms)

Let us suppose that we are working in a world of objects which have a color and the the following knowledge is available

$$\forall x \; \exists y \; COLOR(y, x)$$

It states that each object x has a color named y. In addition, RED is a kind of COLOR and this information is supposed to be also known. This knowledge allows us to transform any atomic formula like

RED(x) into an instance of the more general atomic formula COLOR(RED, x).
Let us compare the generality of the concept "red square" C_1 and "square" C_2.

$$C_1 = SQUARE(x) \; \& \; RED(x)$$
$$C_2 = SQUARE(x)$$

Applying the above theorem, one knows that for any x of C_2 , it has an unknown color , say y. Therefore C_2 is equivalent to $C_2' = SQUARE(x) \; \& \; COLOR(y, x)$. Based on the fact that RED is more particular than COLOR, one can find $C_1' =_\varepsilon C_1$, $C_1' = SQUARE(x) \; \& \; COLOR(RED, x)$. Now the usual term definition of generality can be applied since $\sigma C_2' = C_1'$ with $\sigma = (y \leftarrow RED)$. Therefore C_2 is more general than C_1 in the theory which contains the above information.

1.5   Definition of Formula Generalization modulo a theory

Let E_1 and E_2 be two formulas and ε an equational theory.

1.5.1   Generalized formula

We say that formula E_1 is a **generalization** of formula E_2 if Condition 1 is fulfilled.

Condition 1 : there exists E_1' such that $E_1' =_\varepsilon E_1$ and there is σ_2 such that $\sigma_2 E_1' =_\varepsilon E_2$.

This condition states that there exists E_1', equivalent to E_1 and that E_1', considered as a term, is more general than E_2 considered as a term.
The next definition gives another condition which ensures that formula generality is a partial ordering.

1.5.2   Generality relation between two formulas.

We shall say that E_1 **is more general than** E_2 when Condition 1 and Condition 2 are fulfilled. Condition 1 is as above and

Condition 2 : For all E_2' such that $E_2' =_\varepsilon E_2$, if there exists σ_1, such that $\sigma_1 E_2' =_\varepsilon E_1$, then $E_2' =_\varepsilon E_1$.

This second condition states that the first condition can actually be used for ordering the formulas.

It says that if there is a E_2' which is equivalent to E_2 and which is more general (as a term) than E_1, then all three of E_1, E_2, E_2' must be equivalent.

Some theoretical consequences of condition 2 have been studied in [Kodratoff & Ganascia 1986] under the name of *i-implication*.

Here we shall explain how one can make an algorithm out of definition 1.5.2.

One needs to find out the transformed E_1 and E_2, called E_1' and E_2' in the above definition. We have called this work : **Structural Matching** [Kodratoff 1983].

1.6 Structural Matching (SM)

1.6.1 Definition

Two formulas structurally match if they are identical except for the constants and the variables that instantiate their predicates.

More formally :
Let E_1 and E_2 be two formulas,
E_1 **structurally matches** E_2 iff there exists a C and there exist σ_1 and σ_2 such that
1- $\sigma_1 C = E_1$ and $\sigma_2 C = E_2$.
2- σ_1 and σ_2 never substitute a variable by a formula or a function.

It must be understood that SM may be difficult up to undecidable. Nevertheless, in most cases, one can use the information coming from the other examples, in order to know how to orientate the proofs necessary to the application of this definition.

1.6.2 SMatching two formulas

SM may well fail, but nevertheless the effects of the attempt to put into SM may still be interesting.

We say that two formula have been **SMatched** when every possible property has been used in order to put them into SM.

When the SM is a success, then SMatching is identical to putting into SM.

When the SM is a failure, SMatching keeps the best possible result in the direction of matching formulas.

1.6.3 A simple example of (successful) Structural Matching

Consider the two following examples.

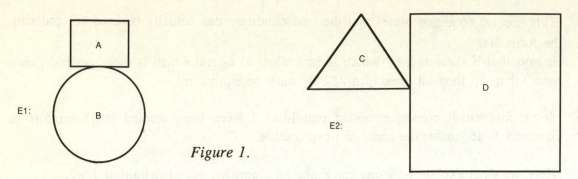

Figure 1.

Using his intuition, the reader may notice that he can find two different generalizations from these examples. He will see that either
  - there are two different objects touching each other, and a small polygon

  - there are two different objects touching each other, one of them is a square.

Both generalizations are true and there is no reason why one of them should be chosen rather than the other. We shall now see that one of the interesting features of SM is that it keeps all the available information, and therefore constructs a formula containing both the above two "concepts".

The examples can be described by the following formulas

E_1 = SQUARE(A) & CIRCLE(B) & ON(A, B) & SMALL(A) & BIG(B)
E_2 = TRIANGLE(C) & SQUARE(D) & TOUCH(C, D) & SMALL(C) & BIG(D)

Let us suppose that the following hierarchy is given to the system.

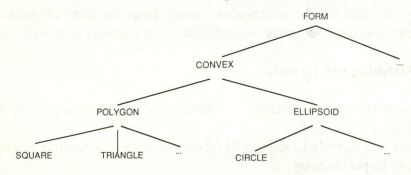

together with the theorems

$$\forall x \, \forall y \, [ON(x, y) \Rightarrow TOUCH(x, y)]$$
$$\forall x \, \forall y \, [TOUCH(x, y) \Leftrightarrow TOUCH(y, x)]$$

This taxonomy and the theorems represent our semantical knowledge about the micro-world in which learning is taking place.

The SM of E_1 and E_2 proceeds by transforming them into equivalent formulas E_1' and E_2', such that E_1' is equivalent to E_1, and E_2' is equivalent to E_2 in this micro-world (i.e., taking into account its semantics).

When the process is completed, E_1' and E_2' are made of two parts.

One is a variablized version of E_1 and E_2. It is called the **body** of the SMatched formulas. When SM succeeds, the bodies of E_1' and E_2' are identical.

The other part, called the **bindings** (of the variables), gives all the conditions necessary for the body of each E_i' to be identical to the corresponding E_i.

The algorithm that constructs E_1' and E_2' is explained in [Kodratoff 1983, Kodratoff & Ganascia 1986]. It has been implemented several times in our research group.

In our example, it would find
Body of E_1' =
POLYGON(u, y) & SQUARE(x) & CONVEX(v_1, v_2, z) & ON(y, z) & TOUCH(y, z) & SMALL(y) & BIG(z)
Bindings of E_1' =
((x = y) & (y ≠ z) & (x ≠ z) & (v_1 = ELLIPSOID) & (v_2 = CIRCLE) & (u = SQUARE) & (x = A) & (z = B))

Body of E_2' =
POLYGON(u, y) & SQUARE(x) & CONVEX(v_1, v_2, z) & TOUCH(y, z) & SMALL(y) & BIG(z)
Bindings of E_2' =
((x ≠ y) & (y ≠ z) & (x = z) & (v_1 = POLYGON) & (v_2 = SQUARE) & (u = TRIANGLE) & (x = D) & (y = C))

The reader can check that E_1' and E_2' are equivalent to E_1 and E_2.

E_1' and E_2' contain exactly the information extracted from the hierarchy and the theorems which is necessary to put the examples into SM.

For instance, in E_1', the expression ' (POLYGON(u, y) ' means that there is a polygon in E_1, and since we have the binding (u = SQUARE), it says that this polygon is a square, which is redundant in view of the fact that SQUARE(x) & (x= y) says that x is a square and is the same as y. This redundancy is not artificial when one considers the polygon in E_2 which is a TRIANGLE.

This example shows well that, once this SM step has been performed, the generalization step itself becomes trivial : we keep in the generalization all the bindings common to the SMatched formulas and drop all those not in common.

In other words, this SM technique enables us to reduce the well-known generalization rules [Michalski 1983, 1984] just to the "dropping condition rule" which becomes legal on SMatched formulas. All the induction power is in the dropping condition rule, all other rules are purely deductive. We must admit that formal proof of the above statement is still under research.

The generalization of E_1 and E_2 is therefore

E_g :   POLYGON(u, y) & SQUARE(x) & CONVEX(v_1, v_2, z) & TOUCH(y, z) & SMALL(y) & BIG(z)
with bindings (y ≠ z).

In "English", this formula means that there are two different objects (named y and z), y and z touch each other, y is a small polygon, z is big and convex, and there is a square (named x) which may be identical to y or z.

 It can be easily guessed that using theorems can lead to many difficulties, since one enters the realm of Theorem Proving, which is well-known for being a good source of yet unsolved problems.
In the case of SM, one is driven by the need to put the examples into a similar form, and the usual difficulties of Therorem Proving are somewhat smoothed out.
We cannot formally prove this point, but the following example, taken from [Vrain 1986] can at least illustrate our claim.

1.7   Using theorems to improve generalization

Starting from two examples that have no common predicates, we show that they nevertheless have a common generalization, found by using theorems that link the predicates.

Let the examples be
    E_1 = MAMMALIAN(A) & BRED_ANIMAL(A)
    E_2 = TAME(B) & VIVIPAROUS(B)

to which the following theorems are added
    R_1: ∀x [MAMMALIAN(x) & BRED_ANIMAL(x) ⇒ TAME(x)]
    R_2: ∀x [TAME(x) & VIVIPAROUS(x) ⇒ MAMMALIAN(x)]
    R_3: ∀x [TAME(x) ⇒ HARMLESS(x)]

The first step of SM is here trivial : we replace the constants by a variable x, and obtain the equivalent examples :

    E_1' = MAMMALIAN(x) & BRED_ANIMAL(x) [EQ(x, A)]
    E_2' = TAME(x) & VIVIPAROUS(x) [EQ(x, B)]

Since the predicates have no common occurrence, we consider the first (this ordering is not significant, and just follows the one in which the examples are given) predicate of E_1' : MAMMALIAN. We see that we can deduce this predicate from E_2, using the rule R_2. We get:

$$E_1'' = MAMMALIAN^*(x) \text{ \& } BRED\_ANIMAL(x) \text{ } [EQ(x, A)]$$
$$E_2'' = TAME(x) \text{ \& } VIVIPAROUS(x) \text{ \& } MAMMALIAN^{**}(x) \text{ } [EQ(x, B)]$$

The MAMMALIAN of E_1' has been treated, this why it is marked by an * in E_1''. The one of E_2'' is derived from the use of theorems, this is why it is marked by **.

Using again the order in which the examples are given, the next non-marked predicate is BRED_ANIMAL.
-- No rule can be applied to E_2'' to make explicit the presence of BRED_ANIMAL in it.
*-- Nevertheless, we remark that applying the rule R_1 to E_1'' uses the predicate concerned: BRED_ANIMAL. Checking the effect of this application, we see that it generates the atomic formula TAME(x) and that there is an occurrence of x in E_2'' which matches this occurrence. Therefore, we conclude that we **must** apply R_1 to E_1''.*
We obtain

$$E_1''' = MAMMALIAN^*(x) \text{ \& } BRED\_ANIMAL^*(x) \text{ \& } TAME^{**}(x) \text{ } [EQ(x, A)]$$
$$E_2''': TAME^*(x) \text{ \& } VIVIPAROUS(x) \text{ \& } MAMMALIAN^{**}(x) \text{ } [EQ(x, B)]$$

Now the only unmatched predicate is VIVIPAROUS in E_2'''.
-- No rules can be applied to E_1''' to make its presence explicit.
-- The only rule which can be applied in E_2''', relative to VIVIPAROUS is R_1. But it would introduce the atomic formula MAMMALIAN(x), which is already matched since its instances are starred.

No other rule can be applied, we star the predicate VIVIPAROUS to remember that it has already been dealt with, obtaining :

$$E_1'''' = MAMMALIAN^*(x) \text{ \& } BRED\_ANIMAL^*(x) \text{ \& } TAME^{**}(x) \text{ } [EQ(x, A)]$$
$$E_2'''' = TAME^*(x) \text{ \& } VIVIPAROUS^*(x) \text{ \& } MAMMALIAN^{**}(x) \text{ } [EQ(x, B)]$$

All possible occurrences have been dealt with, a complete SM is not possible, therefore the SMatching operation stops here.

Now, the generalization step is trivial : one drops the non-common occurrences, obtaining the generalization

$$G = TAME(x) \text{ \& } MAMMALIAN(x)$$

This example shows well how potential infinite proof loops can be easily avoided, simply because they do not improve the SMatching state of the examples.

More generally, one can use theorem proving techniques in order to improve the degree of similarity detected among the examples.

Such a system is under development in our group [Vrain 1987]. It is not the concatenation of a classical theorem prover and of generalization algorithms, but instead is rigorously adapted to the kind of proofs required by Machine Learning.

As an instance of its peculiarity (and of its incompleteness), it will not allow the same theorem to be used twice during a given derivation. This is of course a crude way to avoid infinite loops but, as the above example shows, the corresponding incompleteness is not so wide as one could fear.

2   VERSION SPACES

Definition.
Given:
 - consistency criteria,
 - criteria for choosing maximally specific (Inf) and maximally general (Sup) formulas,
 - a definition of generalization,
 - a set of positive and negative examples
Define:
their Version Space as the set of consistent formulas between Inf and Sup.

Notations.
We shall suppose here that the domain in which learning is taking place is described by a theory T, often called background knowledge in the literature. We know a set of positive examples P, and of negative ones, N. The typical element of P is denoted by P_i, and the typical element of N is denoted by N_j. Let F, R and S be any logic formulas. We shall presently use the following definition of "more general than": F is more general than R, noted F≤R, iff T, R ⊢ F.

2.1   Consistency criteria

2.1.1   First definition

F is said to be consistent for the theory T and the sets of positive and negative examples P and N if

$$\forall i \; T, P_i \vdash F$$
$$\&$$
$$\forall j \; T, N_j \vdash \neg F$$

This definition says that, given T, P, and N, one considers all the formulas that can be deduced from each of the P_i but that cannot be deduced from any N_j, for each P_i. The intersection of all those formulas is the set of consistent generalizations.

Example.
T =

    {square :- rectangle, equal-sides
    rectangle :- square
    equal-sides :- square
              :- rectangle, circle }

P =

    { square :-
    rectangle :- }

N =

    { circle :- }

Let us suppose that our deduction system is able to avoid infinite loops, we then deduce from P1 = square, by doing all the possible deductions from T & P1:

    square :-
    equal-sides :-
    rectangle :-

that is to say, we deduce "square, rectangle, equal-sides".
From P2 = rectangle, we similarly deduce "rectangle, ¬circle".
The intersection of these two deductions is "rectangle".

Let us consider now the negative example N1 = "circle", from which we deduce "¬rectangle, ¬square, ¬(rectangle & equal-sides), ¬(square & equal-sides)".

It follows from the above definition that we have been able to deduce the generalization "rectangle" from T, P and N.

Let us see now an example where this definition fails to find the right generalization. Let T, P and N be as follows.
T =

    { square :-   rectangle, equal-sides
    rectangle :- square
    equal-sides   :- square
              :- rectangle, circle }

P =

    { square :-
    square :- }

N =

    { circle :-
    rectangle :- }

From P1 = square, we deduce "square, rectangle, equal-sides" as above.
From N1 = "circle", we deduce "¬rectangle".
From N2 = "rectangle", we deduce "¬circle" as above.

The intersection is empty, which shows that the first definition does not lead to any generalization for this example, while intuition tells us that "equal-sides" is a valid generalization.

This is why one may be tempted to introduce a

2.1.2 Second definition

F is said to be consistent for the theory T and the sets of positive and negative examples P and N if

$$\forall i \; T, P_i \vdash F$$
$$\&$$
$$\forall j \; T, N_j \, (\neg \vdash) \, F$$

Using again the above example, we see that we can deduce "square & equal-sides" from the positive examples, and that we cannot deduce "square" from the negative ones. Therefore, we obtain the generalization "square & equal-sides".

Unfortunately, this second generalization can also be shown to be imperfect.

Suppose that P=rectangle and N=square. Then, from P we shall deduce "rectangle" as above. From N we shall also deduce "square, rectangle, equal-sides". Since we deduce "rectangle" also from the negative example, this generalization is not valid for our second definition, for which there is no possible generalization.
On the other hand, using the first definition, we deduce "square & equal-sides", i.e. ¬square & ¬equal-sides plays the role of "¬F" in the definition. This is not yet the best possible result, nevertheless, in this case, the first definition is nearer the mark than the second one.

This is why we propose the following third definition which takes into account the drawbacks of the preceding ones.

2.1.3 Third definition [Nicolas 1986]

F is said to be consistent for the theory T and the sets of positive and negative examples P and N if

$$\forall i \; T, P_i \vdash F$$
$$\&$$
$$\forall j \; T, N_j \, (\neg \vdash) \, F$$
$$OR$$
$$\forall i \; T, P_i \, (\neg \vdash) \, \neg F$$
$$\&$$
$$\forall j \; T, N_j \vdash \neg F$$

Exercise 17
****

Show that this definition finds the intuitively correct generalization for T as above, and for P=rectangle and N=square.
****

2.2 Choice criterion

2.2.1 First definition (Version Space à la Mitchell)

Set of the most specific formulas:
Let R be any formula, let S belong to {S}, the set of the most specific formulas. Then S is consistent and R is such that

$$\forall R\ [[R \text{ is consistent and } T, R \vdash S] \Rightarrow [T \vdash [R \Leftrightarrow S]]]$$

Intuitively, this definition tells that T, R ⊢ S means that R is more specific than S. {S} is the set of most specific formulas since any R which is more particular than a formula of {S}, is itself a formula of {S}.

Set of the most general formulas:
Let R be any formula, let G belong to {G} the set of the most general formulas. Then G is consistent and R is such that

$$\forall R\ [[R \text{ is consistent and } T, G \vdash R] \Rightarrow [T \vdash [R \Leftrightarrow G]]]$$

Intuitively, this definition says that T, G ⊢ R means that R is more general than G. {G} is the set of most general formulas since any R more general than a formula of {G}, is itself a formula of {G}.

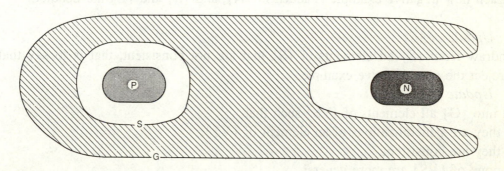

Figure 2. The version space is the striped part between the set S and the set G.

Our definition formalizes Mitchell's, who defines the S and G sets as follows [Mitchell 1982, pp 210-212] :

S = {s/ s is a generalization that is consistent with the observed instances, and there is no generalization which is both more specific than s, and consistent with the observed instances}

G = {g/ g is a generalization that is consistent with the observed instances, and there is no generalization which is both more general than g, and consistent with the instances}.

Recall that "the generalization is consistent with the observed instances" means that it covers all the observed positive examples and rejects all the observed negative examples.

Given these definitions, it is implicitly assumed that a conjunctive description of the target concept exists. Otherwise, if disjunctions were allowed, the S set would always be reduced to a trivial set containing a single element: the disjunction of the positive examples. This statement is only true if the negation connective is not allowed.

Mitchell's candidate elimination algorithm can be at once deduced from this definition.

One starts with empty sets of positive and negative examples {P} and {N}. The version space {VS} contains all the valid formulas and the set {G} . The set {S} is empty.

1 - Each new positive example is added to {P}, and {S} and {G} are *updated* as follows.

Update of {S}
Add into {S} all elements of {VS} such that
 1 - they are specializations of an element of {G},
 2 - they are consistent,
 3 - none of {VS} are more specific.
Update of {G}
Withdraw from {G} all elements of {G} that are not consistent.

2 - Each new negative example is added in {N}, and {S} and {G} are updated.

Update of {S}
Withdraw from {S} all elements of {S} that are not consistent, that is to say that do not reject the new negative example.
Update of {G}
Add into {G} all elements of {VS} such that
 1 - they are generalizations of an element of {VS},
 2 - they are consistent,
 3 - none of {VS} are more general.

2.2.2 Second definition (Version Space à la Manago)

It may become necessary to introduce disjunctive generalizations, especially when a pure conjunctive generalization recognizes some negative examples. We shall then say that a formula is **minimally disjunctive** when it is consistent and, following a given **quality criterion**, there are no other formula that contain less many disjuncts and that optimize the quality criterion.

2.2.2.1 Disjunctive generalizations

If any kind of disjunction is allowed, then S will reduce trivially to a disjunction of the examples. This would define an extentional generalization which we are supposed to avoid since we look for intentional generalizations. In this case, one is tempted to simply forbid any disjunct in a generalization. Nevertheless, it happens that conjunctive generalizations (even minimal ones) are sometimes inconsistent (i.e. over-general). In this case, a disjunctive generalization rejecting every counter-example is needed. Consider the following: Let E_1, E_2 and E_3 be 3 positive examples, and NE a negative example:

E_1:[x: <INSTANCE-OF FRUIT> <COLOR RED> <SIZE VERY-BIG> <TEXTURE SOFT>]
E_2:[x: <INSTANCE-OF FRUIT> <COLOR GREEN> <SIZE BIG> <TEXTURE HARD>]
E_3:[x: <INSTANCE-OF FRUIT> <COLOR GREEN> <SIZE VERY-BIG> <TEXTURE HARD>]
NE:[x: <INSTANCE-OF FRUIT> <COLOR RED> <SIZE BIG> <TEXTURE HARD>]

A conjunctive generalization of the positive examples is:

G:[x: <INSTANCE-OF FRUIT> <COLOR ANY> <SIZE LARGE> <TEXTURE ANY>]

It is intuitively clear that it is minimal but it covers NE as well. A less general expression (which necessarily contains one or several disjunctions) must be found. There are three possibilities (Gen is the generalization operator [Michalski & Stepp 1983]):

solution 1 $Gen(E_1, E_2) \lor E_3$
solution 2 $Gen(E_1, E_3) \lor E_2$
solution 3 $Gen(E_2, E_3) \lor E_1$

Let us suppose that we dispose of the following generalization taxonomies

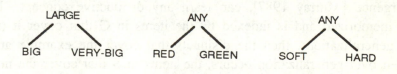

Figure 3.

The first solution is inconsistent with the training data ($Gen(E_1, E_2) = G$) and to lift the inconsistency we would have to specialize $Gen(E_1, E_2)$ finding "$E_1 \lor E_2 \lor E_3$" which is the most trivial characteristic generalization.

The other two generalizations are consistent disjunctive generalizations.

In solution 2, the discriminant features are:

$Gen(E_1, E_3)$ (first cluster)   :   <SIZE VERY-BIG>
E_2 (second cluster)   :   <COLOR GREEN>

In solution 3, the discriminant features are:

Gen(E_2, E_3) (first cluster) : <COLOR GREEN>
E_1 (second cluster) : <SIZE VERY-BIG> & <TEXTURE SOFT>

Depending on the heuristics of generalization/specialization, one of the two will be found.

2.2.2.2 State-of-the-art about disjunctive version spaces

The original version space strategy has been extended to learn disjunctive concepts [Mitchell 1978, p. 127]. The algorithm is stated as follows: "At each step, select the version space consistent with all negative instances and the largest possible number of positive instances". By requiring that the version space be consistent with the largest number of positive instances, Mitchell informally introduces a notion of "quality" of the disjunctions. Before discussing this in more details, let us first criticize the method. This extended candidate elimination algorithm fails to produce a target concept for the example we have shown previously when the training data is presented in the order E_1, E_2, E_3, NE. When it encounters NE, the algorithm has already produced a S set that is too general (all the items in S cover NE). To find a consistent generalization, the S set must be specialized (this is what has been called the inconsistency condition in [Murray 1987]). If the examples previously encountered are totally forgotten ([Mitchell 1978, p. 24]), it is impossible to select the S set that will produce a version space consistent with the largest possible number of positive instances. The algorithm would therefore fail to find a solution.

At the moment the S set becomes too general (or the G set becomes too specific), disjunctions are introduced in S and/or G. One can show that due to this, the algorithm lacks the ability to obtain results independently of the order in which the training instances are presented (the original candidate elimination algorithm was able to do so [Mitchell 1978, p. 24]). Another improved candidate elimination algorithm, called multiple convergence [Murray 1987], can learn any disjunctive concept. Each positive example is memorized and is indexed by the items in G that cover it (if G contains disjunctive generalizations, then the disjuncts that cover the example are used as an index). When over-generalization occurs, the items in S that cover the negative example are "minimally" specialized by introducing disjunctions. This specialization is done in all possible directions and all the disjuncts are retained even when they do not cover any positive examples. There are several advantages to multiple convergence. It can always produce a concept consistent with the training data, the incrementality of the candidate elimination algorithm is more or less preserved (depending on the definition of incrementality, one might consider that the algorithm is not incremental since the positive instances are memorized) and, according to the author, the final concept is independent of the order in which the training instances are presented to the system. However, the method is computationally expensive (the complexity is exponential) and the generation of the disjuncts is data-driven. The latest implies that when the data is not perfect, the algorithm will produce concepts with too many disjuncts and that pre-pruning based on statistical significance cannot take place. Furthermore, for the example discussed in the last section, multiple convergence does not find one of the consistent generalizations with two disjuncts: $Gen(E_2, E_3) \vee E_1$ and $Gen(E_1, E_3) \vee E_2$. It finds a generalization with three disjuncts (note however that each of these is simpler than the $E_1 \vee E_2 \vee E_3$).

As a conclusion, let us also recall that there are other learning systems that can learn disjunctive concepts as well. They are described in chapters 8 and 10.

2.2.2.3 Definition of a quality criterion

As we have mentioned, if we want to learn characteristic descriptions of a disjunctive concept, we must add constraints on the kind of generalizations we want to obtain. The lower and upper bounds of the version space of all the complete and consistent concepts are :

$$S = S_1 \cup S_2 \cup ... \cup S_n$$
$$G = G_1 \cup G_2 \cup ... \cup G_n$$

Where S_i ($1 \leq i \leq n$) is the set of most specific complete and consistent generalizations with exactly i disjuncts, G_i the set of most general complete and consistent generalizations with i disjuncts and n is the number of positive training examples. (Note that if there is no complete and consistent generalizations with i disjuncts, S_i is empty.) S_n is a singleton that contains the disjunction of the positive examples and G_n is a set containing each positive example generalized against the negative examples in all possible ways. If we are interested in minimally disjunctive generalizations, the learning task can be stated as finding S_i and G_i such that $\forall j$, $1 \leq j < i$, $S_j = \varnothing$. (Whenever there is a non empty set S_j, then G_j is also non empty. Otherwise, if G_j was empty, it would mean that there is no complete and consistent generalizations with j disjuncts and therefore S_j would also be empty.)

The modified definition of S and G for minimally disjunctive concepts can be stated the following way.

S = {s/ s is a generalization that is complete and consistent, there is no complete and consistent generalization containing fewer disjuncts than s, and there is no complete and consistent generalization containing the same number of disjuncts that is more specific than s}.

G = {g/ g is a generalization that is complete and consistent, there is no complete and consistent generalization which contains fewer disjunct than g, and there is no complete and consistent generalization containing the same number of disjuncts that is more general than g}.

Recall that "is consistent" means that the generalization must reject all the negative example, and "is complete" means that it must cover all the positive examples.

Given these definitions, it is clear that if there exists a conjunctive description of the target concept (a "one disjunct" solution), then we obtain the same S and G sets as originally.

However, we are not always interested in minimally disjunctive concepts. These will minimize the total number of recognition rules since disjunctive rules of the form "A ∨ B ⇒ C" are interpreted as the two recognition rules "A ⇒ C" and "B ⇒ C". We could prefer, for instance, a generalization which contains more disjuncts but where the disjuncts are smaller on the average. This will minimize the average size of the recognition rules. We could also prefer concepts that are more reliable and resilient to noise during consultation (see [Manago and Kodratoff 1987]). In our previous example, we would favor concepts that do not rely on the difference between Big and Very-big to be identified since these two low level concepts are polymorphic and are a potential source of error at consultation time. We might prefer concepts that are "cheaper" to identify in some sense.

For example, in the medical domain, we would like to minimize pain inflicted to a patient, or the actual cost of performing the tests etc. Intuitively, in our applications we are interested in finding generalizations with a fixed number of disjunct such they satisfy all the criteria mentioned previously. There is usually a trade-off between these and we aim to reach the appropriate equilibrium.

In the present case, let us suppose that we have noticed that GREEN and RED are easy to differentiate, while BIG and VERY-BIG are very polymorphic, i.e. symbolic noise is lower for GREEN and RED than for the BIG and VERY-BIG. The system will favor solution 3.

We can now see how knowledge about the environment (the relative reliability of the descriptors) can be used to generate clusters that are resilient to noise and thus rules which are more reliable. This is one way to symbolically deal with noise without using any numerical uncertainty.

In the following, we shall call "quality criterion" a criterion such as the above, that favors the disjunctive generalizations which put more emphasis on descriptors that are considered of better quality. The quality criterion is used together with the minimization of the number of disjunction in order to select the generalizations that will be put in the S-set. It is used as follows. Among consistent generalizations choose those that optimize the quality criterion and then chose those that contain a minimum of disjunctions.

The following definition will capture the essence of the above.

Set of the most specific formulas:
Let R be any formula, let S belong to {S} the set of the most specific formulas. Then S is consistent **and minimally disjunctive**, and R is such that

$$\forall R \ [[R \text{ is consistent, and } T, R \vdash S] \Rightarrow [T \vdash [R \Leftrightarrow S]]]$$

Set of the most general formulas:

Let R be any formula, let G belong to {G} the set of the most general formulas. Then G is consistent **and minimally disjunctive**, and R is such that

$$\forall R [[R \text{ is consistent, and } T, G \vdash R] \Rightarrow [T \vdash [R \Leftrightarrow G]]]$$

2.2.3 Third definition (Version Space à la Nicolas)

Suppose that we have been able to define consistency relative to the positive examples, called P-consistency. A formula is P-consistent when it recognizes all {P} and it rejects all {N}.

We are now able to define consistency relative to negative examples, called N-consistency. A formula is N-consistent when its negation recognizes all negative examples and rejects all positive examples.

Let us now define the two sets {SP} and {GP} maximally particular and general for the positive examples, and the sets {SN} and {GN} maximally particular and general for the negative examples.

Set of the the most P-particular (N-particular) formulas:

Let R be a formula, let S belong to {S}, then S is said to be P- consistent (N-consistent) and minimally disjunctive, if R is such that

$$\forall R [[R \text{ is P-consistent (N-consistent), and } T, R \vdash S] \Rightarrow [T \vdash [R \Leftrightarrow S]]]$$

Set of the the most P-general (N-general) formulas:

Let R be a formula, let G belong to {G}, then G is said to be P-consistent (N-consistent) and minimally disjunctive, if R is such that

$$\forall R [[R \text{ is P-consistent (N-consistent), and } T, G \vdash R] \Rightarrow [T \vdash [R \Leftrightarrow G]]]$$

Exercise 18
****

Apply the above third definition to the following examples.

$T = \{$

square	*:-*	*rectangle, equal-sides*
rectangle	*:-*	*square*
equal-sides	*:-*	*square*
stripes	*:-*	
stripes	*:-*	
small	*:-*	
small	*:-*	
small	*:-*	
mean	*:-*	
mean	*:-*	
mean	*:-*	
mean	*:-*	

big   :-
big   :-
big   :-

For your solution, think of the following.
If pure conjunctive formula are looked for then {S} and {G} are

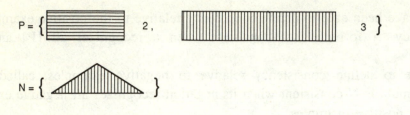

S = { MEAN STRIPED RECTANGLE, SMALL STRIPED RECANGLE}

G = { MEAN, RECTANGLE}

If disjunctive formulas are allowed, they become

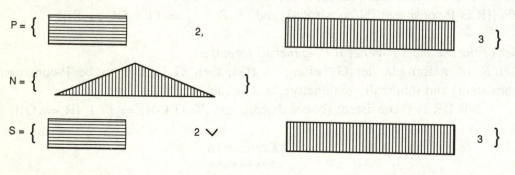

G = { MEAN, RECTANGLE }

7 Explanation-Based Learning

In recent years, the main body of Machine Learning has been inductive learning, as shown by the taxonomy below, which is taken from the books "Machine Learning, volumes 1 and 2".

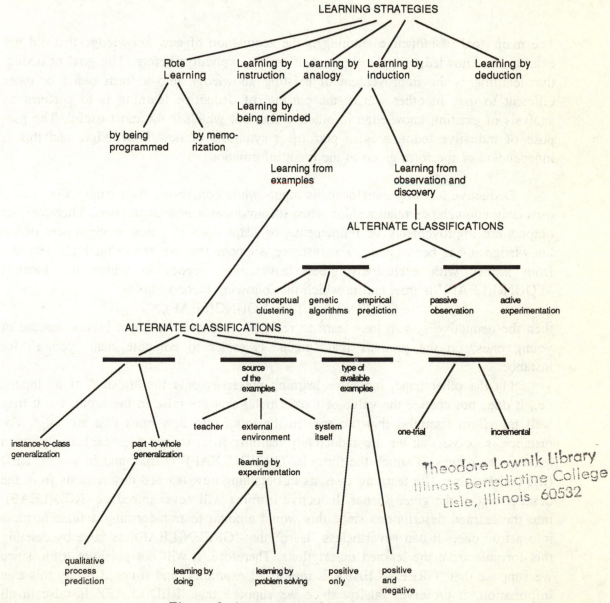

Figure 1. A taxonomy of ML topics

These volumes gave the state-of-the-art up to 1986. But a new volume, 'Machine Learning 3' is presently under preparation, and the way it will describe the field puts deductive and inductive learning on an equal footing. This reflects the recent evolution of EBL the growth of which has been explosive since 1985.

This chapter tries to give a comprehensive description of results that, even though recent, managed to become classics almost as soon as they have been published in the research literature.

1 INDUCTIVE VERSUS DEDUCTIVE LEARNING

The main goal of inductive learning is the acquisition of new knowledge that did not exist in the knowledge implicitly (and of course explicitly) before. The goal of deductive learning is the improvement of existing knowledge into a form easier or more efficient to use. In other words, the purpose of deductive learning is to perform an analysis of existing knowledge in order to find out which is the most useful. The purpose of inductive learning is to perform a synthesis of new knowledge, and this is independent of the form given to the input information.

Deductive learning transforms its inputs while conserving their truth value, i.e., it uses only equivalence relationships when it introduces a new expression. Therefore, its outputs are improvements, or refinements, or adaptations to a new environment of the knowledge it has been given. For instance, suppose that we are deductively learning from scenes with exclusively green leaves, i.e., scenes in which the formula 'YOUNG(LEAF)' is true, and in which the following theorem holds:

$$GREEN(LEAF) \Leftrightarrow YOUNG(LEAF),$$

then the deductive system may learn to recognize scenes with green leaves, instead of young ones, on the grounds that 'green' is easier to compute than 'young', for instance.

On the other hand, inductive learning preserves only the "falsity" of its inputs, i.e., it does not change the value of the formulas that are false in the input, but it may well transform formulas that are true in the input into new ones that are false. For instance, suppose that we are inductively learning from scenes with exclusively green leaves, i.e., scenes in which the formula 'GREEN(LEAF)' is true, and in which 'RED (LEAF)' is false. The learning consists in obtaining new learned descriptions from the descriptions of the given scenes. Inductive learning will never introduce 'RED(LEAF)' into the learned descriptions since this would amount to transforming a false formula into a true one. It can nevertheless "learn" that 'GREEN(LEAF)' is false by deleting this formula from the learned descriptions. Therefore, it will not preserve truth, since we suppose that 'GREEN(LEAF)' is true in all examples, and it could forget this true information. It preserves falsity, since we suppose that 'RED(LEAF)' is false in all examples, and it would never introduce this false information.

2 INTUITIVE PRESENTATION OF EBL

Depending on the type of the source of experience, deductive learning can have two sub-fields. When the source of experience is a specification of relations that should be preserved, and the deductive process transforms these relations into an algorithm that actualizes the relations, one can speak of specification-guided learning. A typical example of this approach is the synthesis of programs from their specifications in which a deductive (in spite of its name) process is used, namely mathematical induction. This approach is briefly described in appendix 2 of this book. When the deduction is example-guided, then the example is used in order to show which new rules are interesting to derive from the existing knowledge base.

The knowledge base may be given as schemes or semantic nets that do not need to be not so rigorous as the logical representation. It can also represented as a logical knowledge base, therefore supposed to be coherent and complete.

In the first class, the explanations are provided by a knowledge base or the system's user. The work of the program is then to retrieve them, to adapt them to the problem it is working on, to combine them when new explanations are needed. This approach primarily asks for a good knowledge representation of the explanations. Work done by Roger Shank shows the need to adapt stored explanations, and work done by Bruce Porter (see their chapters in the forthcoming 'Machine Learning 3') shows how to combine stored explanations. Both are typical illustrations of the use of pre-stored explanations. In their case, the justifications are stored in a case library and retrieved when needed. These justifications are then combined and transformed to become explanations. The nature of the explanations differs from the way the user has classified them. For instance, when explaining why a 'car' has a 'motor', one can be provided with strange explanations if the semantic net has been built with indications that a PART-OF link is an explanation. The system could then answer "Because 'motor' is PART-OF 'car'". However, if the semantic net is built so that some goal has to be achieved to get an explanation, the system will have to find "goal-achieving" links in the semantic net to answer, for instance "Because 'motor' is the means by which 'car' achieves its 'movement' which is the goal of all vehicles, of which 'car' is an instance". The ultimate decision on the kind of explanations to be provided is in the hands of the semantic net builder. Notice that the system will probably find several such goal-achieving links and that one will have to choose, or to ask the user, which one is the best one.

In the second class, the explanations are "invented" from examples and background knowledge. The first step of these methods is always to obtain a proof trace of the validity of the training example or examples. Actually, this proof trace is a simple justification of the training example. The pruning, generalization or particularization of this justification transforms it into an explanation. As an example of the latter, suppose that we want to learn more about suicide. Suppose that we know about John's suicide, and that we have a whole set of background knowledge about depressive persons, fire-arms, murders, etc ... From this background knowledge, we prove that John achieved the goal of committing a suicide (by murdering himself). Suppose also that we have defined the trace of this proof as being the justification of John's suicide. Notice that this simple justification may have some explanatory content. Nevertheless, transforming this justification into a real explanation is done in three steps.

- step 1. Some additional background knowledge is contained in an operationality criterion that tells at which level details become insignificant. For instance, suppose that our proof makes use of the trademark of the used fire-arms, and that we have the rule: 'makers of the tools are insignificant'. In that case, the part of the proof trace which contains this information is pruned.

- step 2. One applies then a process called goal regression (see [Waldinger 1977], and section 3 of this chapter) by regressing the goal 'John's suicide ' through the pruned proof trace. One will thus obtain the most general expression that preserves the proof of John's suicide and that uses the same operators as the proof. For instance, one will obtain an expression identical to the proof trace except that the constant 'John' is replaced by a variable 'x' , meaning that any 'x' can commit suicide in the same way.

- step 3. The generalized pruned trace is compared to stored schemes of action. If it is "recognized" by some of them, i.e. if it partially matches them within some threshold (see more details on partial matching in chapter 12), then the generalizations known as safe in the scheme are applied to the trace. For instance, suppose that we dispose of the scheme 'crime of x against y' in which it is known that the crime can be achieved not only with a 'fire-arm' but with any 'weapon'. Suppose also that the trace matches this scheme enough to be recognized as an instance of the scheme. Then the 'fire-arm' of the trace will be generalized into a 'weapon', thereby increasing its explanatory value.

In the following chapters, we shall study the second approach, in which an explanation is built up from background knowledge.

3 GOAL REGRESSION

The idea of goal-regression stems from the study of how a robot may perform changes in an environment.

3.1 A classical representation of robots' actions

We first recall a knowledge representation made classical by the system STRIPS (see [Nilsson 1980] for instance). Given a robot, and a set of basic moves it can be ordered to perform, the problem is to describe a sequence of such actions achieving a goal by starting from a given initial situation. The figure below illustrates such an action

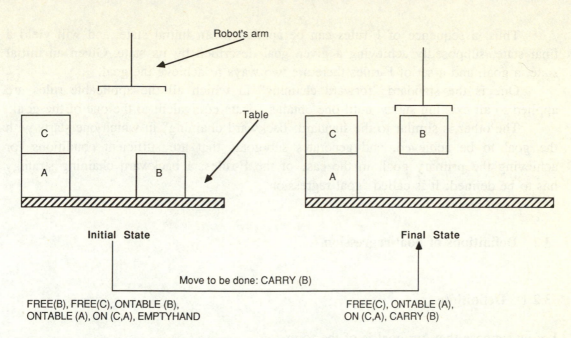

Initial State   Final State

Move to be done: CARRY (B)

FREE(B), FREE(C), ONTABLE (B),   FREE(C), ONTABLE (A),
ONTABLE (A), ON (C,A), EMPTYHAND   ON (C,A), CARRY (B)

Figure 2. The goal to be achieved is 'CARRY(B)'

Let us suppose that the states of the robot the can be described by conjuncts of completely instantiated atoms, in other words all the variables of the descriptors are replaced by constants, and the state is described by a conjunction of such instantiated descriptors.

In figure 2 the initial state is described by

    FREE(B), FREE(C), ONTABLE(B), ONTABLE(A), ON(C, A), EMPTY-HAND

and the final state is described by

    FREE(C), ONTABLE(A), ON(C, A), CARRY(B)

as figure 2 shows.

In order to describe how the initial is transformed into the final state, we shall use rules, called F-rules that contain three components. A F-rule is made of

- a list of preconditions, the P-list, for applying the F-rule.

- a list of the atoms that take the value FALSE during the action, they must be deleted from the F-rule once the action has been performed. This is called the D-list as a mnemonic for Delete-list.

- a list of the atoms that must be added to reach the final state, it is called the A-list as a mnemonic for Add-list.

For instance, the F-rule that describes how carrying a block 'x' lying on the table can be as follows.

    DO-CARRY(x):

        P-list(x) = ONTABLE(x), FREE(x), EMPTY-HAND

        D-list(x) = ONTABLE(x), FREE(x), EMPTY-HAND

        A-list(x) = CARRY(x)

It can be easily seen that applying the above F-rule to the initial state of figure 2, i.e. substituting 'x' by 'B', deleting [x ← B]*D-LIST(x), and adding [x ← B]*A-LIST(x) to the initial state, yields the final state of figure 1.

Thus, a sequence of F-rules can be applied to an initial state, and will yield a final state, supposedly achieving a given goal described by its state. Given an initial state, a goal, and a set of F-rules there are two ways to achieve the goal.

One is the standard "forward chaining" in which all the applicable rules are applied to all existing states, until one obtains a state equivalent to the one of the goal.

The other is similar to the standard "backward chaining" in which one starts with the goal to be achieved, and generates sub-goals that are sufficient conditions for achieving the primary goal. In the case of the F-rules, a backward chaining strategy has to be defined: It is called "goal regression".

3.2 Definitions of goal-regression

3.2.1 Definitions

Let us suppose that our goal is of the form
$$G = L, G1, ..., Gn$$
where each ',' symbolizes a logical AND. Let us suppose that the A-list of the F-rule through which we want to regress G contains an atom L' which unifies with L. Let σ be the most general unifier of this unification. We thus have:
$$\sigma L = \sigma L'$$

For instance, in the above example, if we want to regress 'FREE(C), ONTABLE(A), ON(C, A), CARRY(B)' through 'DO-CARRY(x)', then 'CARRY(B)' in the goal unifies with 'CARRY(x)' in the A-list of 'DO-CARRY(x)', with the unification [x ← B] since
$$[x ← B] \, CARRY(B) = [x ← B] \, CARRY(x)$$

Suppose that our F-rule depends on a set of variables symbolized by 'x', i.e., F-rule(x) is made of P-list(x), D-list(x), A-list(x).

Definition

We say that the sub-goals of the goal regression of goal G (supposed to be of the form G = L, G1, ..., Gn) are the atoms contained in {σ P-list(x), G1', ..., Gn'} where each Gi' is the regression of Gi through G.

This definition needs to be completed by a definition of the regression of an atom through a formula, which is given in the following.

3.2.2 Regression of an atom AT through an instantiated rule

The atom has the form σAT. There are three cases.

1 - σAT is contained in σA-list. Then, the regression of AT has the value: TRUE.

2 - σAT is contained in σD-list. Then, the regression of AT has the value: FALSE.

3 - σAT is not contained in σA-list or in σD-list. Then, the regression of AT has the value: σAT.

Example 1.
Let the F-rule be
      STACK(x, y):
               P-list(x, y) = CARRY(x), FREE(y)
               D-list(x, y) = CARRY(x), FREE(y)
               A-list(x, y) = FREE(x), EMPTY-HAND, ON(x, y)
Suppose that the goal to be regressed is
                        ON(A, B), ON (B, C)
There are obviously two ways to regress this goal through STACK(x, y). Let us choose to study the result obtained when 'ON(A, B)' is unified to 'ON(x, y)' with the substitution σ = [x ← A, y ← B]. This substitution instantiates the F-rule completely. Our definition tells us that the sub-goals resulting from the regression of 'ON(A, B), ON (B, C)' through STACK(x, y) are the conjunction of the regression of 'ON(A, B)' through STACK(x, y) and the regression of the other, here 'ON(B, C)', through the instantiated 'STACK(A, B)'.
It has a σ P-list = CARRY(A), FREE(B). Regressing 'ON(B, C)' through 'STACK(A, B)' yields therefore ON(B, C) itself since it can unify with none of the σA-list or the σD-list.
Therefore, the result is
                    CARRY(A), FREE(B), ON(B, C).

3.2.3 Regression through a rule containing variables

Let AT be the atom to be regressed through F-rule(x). One must first consider three cases.

1 - AT can be unified with one of the atoms of the D-list(x). Then, the regression of AT has the value: FALSE.

2 - AT can be unified with none of the atoms of A-list(x) nor of D-list(x). Then, the regression of AT has the value: AT.

3 - AT can be unified with one of the atoms of A-list(x) with the substitution σ. Then, the regression of AT has the value:
      IF   σ = TRUE   THEN   σA-list(x)

The result of the regression of AT through F-rule(x) is the conjunction of the results of the three above cases.

Example 2.
Let us suppose that we want to regress a formula containing the atom 'CARRY(B)' through
      UNSTACK(x, y):

P-list(x, y) = FREE(x), EMPTY-HAND, ON(x, y)

   D-list(x, y) = FREE(x), EMPTY-HAND, ON(x, y)

   A-list(x, y) = CARRY(x), FREE(y)

This goal unifies to 'CARRY(x)' in the A-list, we shall thus have to regress through the F-rule

   UNSTACK(B, y):

   P-list(B, y) = FREE(B), EMPTY-HAND, ON(B, y)

   D-list(B, y) = FREE(B), EMPTY-HAND, ON(B, y)

   A-list(B, y) = CARRY(B), FREE(y)

   Example 2.1

Suppose the formula to regress is 'CARRY(B), EMPTY-HAND'. Then its regression through UNSTACK(x, y) is FALSE since the regression of 'EMPTY-HAND' through UNSTACK(B, y) is FALSE.

   Example 2.2.

Suppose the formula to regress is 'CARRY(B), FREE(C)'. Then its regression through UNSTACK(x, y) is the regression of FREE(C) through UNSTACK(B, y) which TRUE if y=C, and FREE(C) if y≠C. The regression is therefore

   (IF y=C THEN TRUE) & (IF y≠C THEN FREE(C))

   ((y=C)⟹ TRUE) & (y≠C⟹FREE(C))

   (¬(y=C)∨ TRUE) & (¬(y≠C∨FREE(C))

   TRUE & (y=C) & FREE(C)

Let us suppose that we want to regress 'FREE(C)' through

   UNSTACK(x, B):

   P-list(x, B) = FREE(x), EMPTY-HAND, ON(x, B)

   D-list(x, B) = FREE(x), EMPTY-HAND, ON(x, B)

   A-list(x, B) = CARRY(x), FREE(B)

We obtain

   (IF x=C THEN FALSE) & (IF x≠C THEN FREE(C))

   ((x=C)⟹ FALSE) & (x≠C⟹FREE(C))

   (¬(x=C)∨ FALSE) & (¬(x≠C∨FREE(C))

   (¬(x=C) & ((x=C) ∨ FREE(C))

   TRUE ∨ (¬(x=C) & FREE(C))

   (x ≠ C) & FREE(C)

4   EXPLANATION-BASED GENERALIZATION

EBG is essentially the regression of a goal through the proof of the validity of this goal. When the proof uses ordinary rules, like PROLOG clauses, of the form
' H :- B ', there is no D-list, the A-list is the head of the clause, ' H ', the P-list is the body of the clause, ' B '.

4.1 EBG: An intuitive presentation

We shall use here a PROLOG version of the "safe-to-stack" example, taken from [Mitchell and al. 1986]. Several versions of EBG have been implemented as for instance in [Kedar-Cabelli 1987, Siqueira and Puget 1988].

The "safe-to-stack" example shows how to learn a more efficient rule to stack given
- a definition a theory of stacking
- and an example of a particular box 'BOX_1' stacked on a particular table '$ENDTABLE_1$'. In this very particular example it happens that one needs to know the default value of the type 'ENDTABLE'.

The **first kind of information** is the one relative to the specific box, 'BOX_1', and the specific table '$ENDTABLE_1$'.

C_1	ON(BOX_1, $ENDTABLE_1$)	:-
C_2	COLOR(BOX_1, RED)	:-
C_3	COLOR($ENDTABLE_1$, BLUE)	:-
C_4	VOLUME(BOX_1, 10)	:-
C_5	DENSITY(BOX_1, 1)	:-
C_6	FRAGILE($ENDTABLE_1$)	:-
C_7	OWNER($ENDTABLE_1$, CLYDE)	:-
C_8	OWNER(BOX_1, BONNIE)	:-

The **second kind of information** is the one relative to the background knowledge about stacking things, also called the theory of the domain.

C_9	SAFE-TO-STACK(x, y)	:-	NOT FRAGILE(y)
C_{10}	SAFE-TO-STACK(x, y)	:-	LIGHTER(x, y)
C_{11}	WEIGHT(x, w)	:-	VOLUME(x, v), DENSITY(x, d), w is $v*d$
C_{12}	WEIGHT($ENDTABLE_1$, 50)	:-	
C_{13}	LIGHTER(x, y)	:-	WEIGHT(x, w_1), WEIGHT(y, w_2), LESS(w_1, w_2)
C_{14}	LESS(x, y)	:-	$x < y$

The reader may be surprised to find C_{12} placed in the background knowledge. This is due to a PROLOG difficulty with expressing default values. In new versions of PROLOG that include data typing, it would be possible to declare that '$ENDTABLE_1$' is of type 'ENDTABLE' in the above first kind of information and to declare in the second one that the default value of the weight of the type ENDTABLE is 50. Since our aim is not the illustration of typed PROLOGs that would require a paper by itself, let us go on with a standard PROLOG language and notice that there is no real contradiction to put C_{12} in the background knowledge.

The **third kind of information** is the one expressing that one can safely stack 'BOX_1' on '$ENDTABLE_1$'. Since we want to prove that by PROLOG, i.e. by a refutation procedure, this knowledge will be given as question to the PROLOG interpreter. It reads

C_{15}	:-	SAFE-TO-STACK(BOX_1, $ENDTABLE_1$)

Most clauses are a straightforward rewritings of those in [Mitchell and al. 1986], but two differences must be pointed out.

The first difference is that we use integers, therefore we multiply by ten the values given in [Mitchell et al., 1986].

The second difference is that the "ISA" links are dropped. This would have to be expressed as types in a typed PROLOG, as already pointed at, typing PROLOG is not our present topic.

The proof proceeds as shown by the following trace. This trace is provided by most PROLOG interpreters. The comment 'Call' means that the predicate has been used as a question to the system. The comment 'Exit' means that the the predicate (with the instances in the 'Exit') has been proven TRUE. The comment 'Fail' means that the predicate has been proven FALSE. The comment 'Back to' means that back-tracking is taking place. The numbers to the left are those provided by the compiler, we have put on the right the level of embedding they actually represent.

For instance, call 'NOT FRAGILE($ENDTABLE_1$)' is indexed by '2' and call LIGHTER(BOX_1, $ENDTABLE_1$) is indexed by '4' in the computer output. Actually, they are at the same level of embedding and are labelled respectively 2_1 and 2_2 on the right.

1	Call:	SAFE-TO-STACK (BOX1, ENDTABLE1)	
2	Call:	NOT FRAGILE (ENTDABLE1)	2_1
3	Call:	FRAGILE (ENDTABLE1)	
3	Exit:	FRAGILE (ENDTABLE1)	
2	Back to:	NOT FRAGILE (ENDTABLE1)	
2	Fail:	NOT FRAGILE (ENDTABLE1)	
4	Call:	LIGHTER (BOX1, ENDTABLE1)	2_2
5	Call:	WEIGHT (BOX1, w1)	
6	Call:	VOLUME (BOX1, v1)	4_1
6	Exit:	VOLUME (BOX1, 10)	
6	Call:	DENSITY (BOX1, d1)	4_2 3_1
6	Exit:	DENSITY (BOX1, 1)	
6	Call:	w1 is 10*1	4_3
6	Exit:	10 is 10*1	
5	Exit:	WEIGHT (BOX1, 10)	
5	Call:	WEIGHT (ENDTABLE1, w2)	
6	Call:	VOLUME (ENDTABLE1, v2)	3_2
6	Fail:	VOLUME (ENDTABLE1, v2)	
5	Back to:	WEIGHT (ENDTABLE1, w2)	
5	Exit:	WEIGHT (ENDTABLE1, 50)	
5	Call:	less (10, 50)	
6	Call:	10<50	4_4 3_3
6	Exit:	10<50	
5	Exit:	less (10, 50)	
4	Exit:	lighter (BOX1, ENDTABLE1)	
1	Exit:	SAFE-TO-STACK (BOX1, ENDTABLE1)	1

Figure 3. An execution trace directly provided by an interpreter

Let us now analyze the above proof and show that it actually gives a set of explanations of why it is safe to stack BOX_1 on $ENDTABLE_1$, which, in the rest of this section will be abbreviated to 'expl.stack'. A level always begins with a question, labelled as a 'Call'. When it succeeds, it ends with an 'Exit'. The exit contains the reason why the call succeeded. This is why one can say that each level provides an 'expl.stack', that becomes more and more refined as one goes down the levels.

Level 1 is the outermost. In a sense it says

"it is safe to stack BOX_1 on $ENDTABLE_1$ because I have proven it just now".

It is the most superficial level of explanations. Children use it quite often !

Level 2 contains sub-level 2_1 and sub-level 2_2.

Sub-level 2_1 is a failure sub-level : it says that "NOT FRAGILE" has nothing to do with 'expl.stack'. We disregard it here, but one must be aware that, when explanations for negative features are looked for, then only failure sub-levels can provide an explanation of the negative feature.

Sub-level 2_2 provides the 'expl.stack' :

"it is safe to stack BOX_1 on $ENDTABLE_1$" because BOX_1 is lighter than $ENDTABLE_1$".

Level 3 contains three sub-levels 3_1, 3_2, and 3_3. The explanations obtained from each one must be conjuncted to obtain the explanation. They provide the 'expl.stack' :

"it is safe to stack BOX_1 on $ENDTABLE_1$" because

the weight of BOX_1 is 10, the weight of $ENDTABLE_1$ is 50, and 10 is less than 50.

One can be tempted to generalize at once by saying that the weight of BOX_1 is w_1, the weight of $ENDTABLE_1$ is w_2, and w_1 is less than w_2. This is not allowed by EBG, which says that one can generalize further only if the numerical values come from example data. If some numerical value is derived from theory data, then this value should be kept as such. In this case, the default value : the weight of $ENDTABLE_1 = 50$, is part of the theory data, not of the example data. Another way to look at this is to say that one must keep them when there is no deeper explanation of the numerical values. In this case, there is no deeper explanation of the fact that the weight of $ENDTABLE_1 = 50$, since sub-level 3_2 contains no inner sub-level. Therefore, this value will be kept in the final result.

Sub-level 3_1 says that the weight of BOX_1 is 10 because its volume is 10, its density is 1, and because $10*1 = 10$. In this case, the numerical values are derived from the example and can be generalized. The value of the volume is called v_1, the value of the density is called d_1, which gives the partial 'expl.stack' :

"The weight of BOX_1 is $w_1 = v_1*d_1$".

Sub-level 3_3 contains an explanation given by 4_4. This explanation is disregarded because it uses a function, like $<$, of low level. Deciding what is at "low level" is a strategic decision that must always be taken beforehand. In EBG this decision is taken by the choice of an *operationality criterion* given by the user, as explained above.

Applying this generalization into the explanation of level 3 (which is the last 'expl.stack' found) leads to the final 'expl.stack' :

"it is safe to stack BOX_1 on $ENDTABLE_1$" because

the weight of BOX_1 is $w_1 = v_1 * d_1$, the weight of $ENDTABLE_1$" is 50, and w_1 is less than 50. The process we describe here is nothing but a paraphrasing of EBG, with two differences from the original paper. Firstly, our presentation has a stronger theorem-proving orientation. Secondly, instead of forcing the variables down to elementary facts, we force the constants up to some level where they can be generalized.

In the next section we shall present an implementation of genuine EBG.

4.2 EBG: An implementation

Let us consider again the safe-to-stack example. The proof trace is

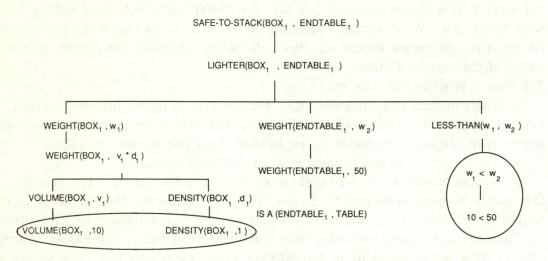

Figure 4.

in which the non-operational descriptors are circled. By pruning the non-operational descriptors and generalizing, we obtain the following explanation structure.

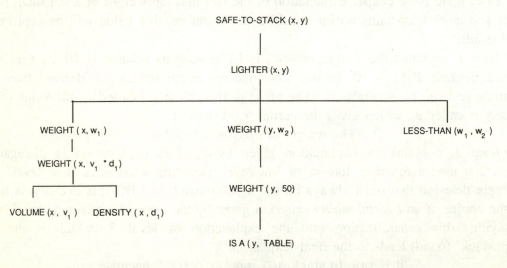

Figure 5.

EBG then regresses a general goal through the explanation structure, and propagates the obtained instantiations through the whole set of regressed sub-goals. The final set of sub-goals become the new conditions for the achievement of the general goal. The figure below shows the explanation structure for safe-to-stack.

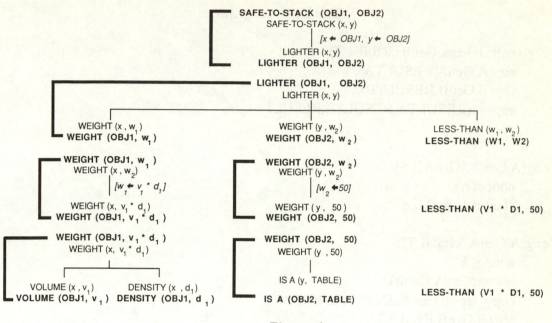

Figure 6.

Around each part of the explanation structure are the goals and their regressions indicated in bold font. At each level of regression, the substitutions are transmitted in all the sub-goals. The last line of sub-goals is the regression of "SAFE-TO-STACK (OBJ1, OBJ2)" through the explanation structure. The learned rule is therefore

```
SAFE-TO-STACK(OBJ1, OBJ2) :-
      VOLUME(OBJ1, v1),
      DENSITY(OBJ1, d1),
      LESS-THAN(v1 * d1, 50),
      ISA(OBJ2, TABLE)
```

Here is a PROLOG program that is able to perform this kind of job.

This program is written in QUINTUS PROLOG which provides, for instance, for a function 'copy-term' copying a term with a change of its variable names.
The predicate 'CLAUSE(A, B)' takes the value TRUE if it finds a clause A :- B. Once found, this clause will be active only if its head A is marked as "dynamic". This is

why the predicate 'nonop' below says which are the predicates that are not operational. Here "operational" means that the learned clause must be made of operational predicates. This meaning is much more restricted than the one given in the preceding section.

The EBG program

```
ebg((A,B),(GenA,GenB),RESULT) :-!,
    ebg(A,GenA,RESULTA),
    ebg(B,GenB,RESULTB),
    append(RESULTA,RESULTB,RESULT).


ebg(A,GenA,[GenA]) :-
    nonop(A),
    clause(A,true),!.

ebg(A,GenA,RESULT):-
    nonop(A),
    clause(GenA,GenB),
    copy_term((GenA:-GenB),(A:-B)),
    ebg(B,GenB,RESULT).

ebg(A,GenA,[GenA]) :-
    call(A).


nonop(A):-predicate_property(A,(dynamic)).
```

Stating the operationality criterion

```
:- dynamic safe_to_stack/2, lighter/2, weight/2, weight1/2.
```

The background knowledge

```
safe_to_stack(X,Y):- lighter(X,Y).

lighter(P1,P2):-
            weight(P1,W1),
            weight(P2,W2),
            W1<W2.

weight(P,W):-    weight1(P,W),!.

weight(P,5):-    isa(P,endtable).
```

```
weight1(P,W):-
          volume(P,V),
          density(P,D),
          W is V*D.
```

The training example

```
on(obj1,obj2).
isa(obj1,box).
isa(obj2,endtable).
color(obj1,red).
color(obj2,blue).
volume(obj1,1).
volume(obj2,4).
density(obj1,1).
```

The call to EBG

```
? ebg(safe_to_stack(obj1, obj2), safe_to_stack(O1, O2), Result).
```

Obtained result

```
O1 = _1,
O2 = _4,
[volume(O1,_451),density(O1,_454),_199 is _451*_454,!,isa(O2,endtable),_199<5]
```

5   EXPLANATION-BASED LEARNING

EBG is certainly the main method for learning from explanation but, as pointed at by DeJong and Mooney [DeJong and Mooney 1986] other ways for learning from explanations are possible. In particular, EBG will keep the descriptors it starts from, while it may be useful to generalize them in order to obtain a true explanation.

Suppose that we start from the knowledge
MORTAL(x) :- MAN(x)
MAN(SOCRATES) and that we ask the question
? MORTAL(SOCRATES)
we hope that it is now clear to our reader that EBG of this proof will simply give back what we started from: MORTAL(x) :- HUMAN(x).
One would like nevertheless to be able to learn something like: Socrates is mortal because he is a human, or because he is a living being. Notice that adding clauses

like
HUMAN(x) :- MAN(x)
LIVING(x) :- HUMAN(x)
would not improve EBG.

The solution proposed by DeJong is the use of background knowledge as general schemes that are instantiated by the training example. These schemes contain causal relationships that are used to generalize non-causal events of the training example.

Suppose that the knowledge about mortality is contained in the following clauses.
MORTAL(x) :- MAN(x)
MAN(SOCRATES)
HUMAN(x) :- MAN(x)
LIVING(x) :- HUMAN(x)
CAUSE(MORTAL(x)) :- LIVING(x)
The last clause is a possible representation of causality in a logic knowledge base. The reader will find other examples of the use of clauses for expressing causality in the chapter 12.
Asking the question
? MORTAL(SOCRATES)
will yield no new information as before, but asking the question
? CAUSE(MORTAL(SOCRATES))
would generate
? LIVING(SOCRATES)
? HUMAN(SOCRATES)
? MAN(SOCRATES)
Depending on the operationality criterion, we can obtain a different explanation of why Socrates is mortal.

The above over-simplified example gives an over-simplified idea on how we can handle causality, and possibly generalize descriptors from an example of their use. In order to show the real complexity of this problem, let us comment on the 'kidnapping' example found in the Mooney and DeJong paper referred to above.

In this example, the training example is a story of a kidnapping, and the background knowledge is a set of schemes about threatening, bargaining, telephoning etc ... In the story, the kidnapper telephones the kidnappeé s father to demand money. Instantiating the scheme for bargaining by this particular story, we find that the 'telephone ' is a particular means for 'communication' between the threatening and the threatened person. The causal relationship lies in the communication and not in the telephoning. It follows that we can learn about kidnapping that the threatening person has to communicate to the threatened person, and that any means of communication is allowable. Once one reduces the Universe to the world of threatening, there is little difficulty on how we should proceed to represent this learning by clauses.

Exercise 19
****

Write a kidnapping story and the scheme for threatening as clauses. Introduce a causal clause in order to show how it can be learned that the threatening and threatened persons have to communicate with each other.
****

In reality, a particular story can instantiate many different schemes and the generalizations performed in one scheme are not always valid in other schemes. The difficulty, when dealing with more realistic problems will be to recognize which schemes are validly instantiated, and in taking the intersection of the possible generalizations in all possibly instantiated schemes. For instance, in the case of kidnapping, a scheme of bargaining should also be instantiated, and this would again point at any means of communication. A scheme of 'illegal action' could also be instantiated, restricting the possible means of communication to discrete and hasty ones, therefore making the telephone much more probable than before.

As a conclusion to this chapter, the reader should notice that new methodologies have been developed that can bring real help during the learning process. An EBG algorithm has been implemented by all my graduate students with seemingly little difficulty. The elegant version given here is due to a PhD student in my group, Jean-François Puget. The "trick" which consists in performing the regression by a simple "copy" is due to Smadar Kedar-Cabelli.

This approach was essentially developed by Michalski and his team, who were the first to show how a system could learn rules not known by the experts on the basis of samples of their decisions.

This approach can be described as empirical in the sense that the generalizations made are "inductive inferences"; you always take a certain risk when you generalize because the generalization may not be valid. After all, the rules of generalization are justified by empirical arguments. Remember that learning by deducing explanations is perfectly rational, which partly explains its success. On the other hand, learning by similarity detection is an empirical process which is always prone to uncertainty, yet is a necessary step in the creation of new knowledge.

The following chapter will present an approach, in which the inductive inference is made as late as possible. It shows that the element of chance which guides learning by similarity detection can be reduced, but can never be eliminated. It is in the spirit of Michalski's approach that stresses the role of background knowledge in the process of empirical formation of hypotheses.

We shall say nothing in this book about the increasingly rational approaches which are now emerging, and which use techniques of automatic theorem-proving to carry out learning by similarity detection. (For this see [Kodratoff 1985, Nicolas 1986].)

Another characteristic of Michalski's approach is that it produces an original method of conceptual classification. Thus clustering and generalization are intimately connected, to such an extent that we have preferred to present them together in this chapter. More details on methods of classification and their importance in ML can be found in chapter 8.

1 GENERAL DEFINITIONS

Learning by Similarity Detection is designed for concept acquisition. In chapter 1 we have already described how concept acquisition can be useful for rule acquisition.

This chapter illustrates this point perfectly since the first application of the system which we are going to present was nothing other than the generation of rules designed for the treatment of soybean diseases.

The aim of concept acquisition is to find a characteristic description of a class of objects.

Let us say that a description recognizes an example when the example is an instance of the description. We shall give an even more precise definition of "recognition" farther on.

Let us say that a description is **consistent** when it does not recognize any negative example.

Let us say that a description is **complete** when it recognizes all the positive examples.

In this chapter we shall require the description obtained to be consistent and complete. You will be well aware of the importance of the concepts of consistency and completeness, which have played a key role so far.

By way of an aside, however, let us point out, that the requirement of complete and consistent descriptions could be a view which oversimplifies reality. One could perfectly well admit, for example, that one could use two sorts of descriptions, some designed to recognize concepts when they are mixed with other concepts, and others designed to describe an already recognized concept.

In these conditions, "descriptions for recognizing" must be consistent but need not be complete, and one can require them to be efficient or suitable for immediate needs, such as dealing with descriptors which are measured well by the available measuring instruments, for example.

"Descriptions for describing" must be complete but they do not have to be consistent, and one can require them to recognize well the details which make up the concept, for example.

This subject is still a research issue and we shall not say any more about it here.

Variables can be of three kinds: nominal, linear or structured.

Variables of **nominal type** belong to a non-hierarchical domain and the only relations which exist between them are given with the help of theorems. For example, there are no relations between eye colors, even though if we combine this domain with that of parental relations, we know that blue is recessive. This is not translated by a taxonomy but by the theorem:

$$\forall x \, \forall y \, \forall z \, [eyes(blue, x) \, \& \, eyes(blue, y) \, \& \, parents(x, y, z) \Rightarrow eyes(blue, z)]$$

Only this type of relation is authorized for talking of variables as being of nominal type.

Variables of **linear type** belong to a totally ordered whole, like the natural integers, for example. For such variables the notions of interval, of the beginning of an interval, etc... can be defined. Linear variables can also exhibit features expressed by theorems. Once again, the example of the integers illustrates this well.

Variables of **structured type** belong to a universe where taxonomic relations exist between concepts. In other words, generic relations between descriptors are already known and are used during the learning process. It can happen that these "taxonomies" are in reality tangled taxonomies like the one described by the variable X_2 below (and represented by several taxonomies). Furthermore, a structured variable can also be ordered, as the variable X_3 below shows. Furthermore, quite obviously, theorems which are valid in this universe can exist.

We are now going to describe the principles which enabled Michalski's group to construct an algorithm to obtain complete and consistent descriptions.

For this we shall first give an example which presents the difficulties which can be met in this kind of problem. Let us remember that we are not trying to give a research report or a historically exact presentation of Michalski's work: we are giving our interpretation of it. We hope that this presentation gives an accurate account of the original articles, but turn to them if you are curious or want more details. In any case, we guarantee that you will be able to read these articles easily after understanding our presentation.

Next we shall define the basic notions that we shall eventually need to present the learning algorithms which are deduced from them.

2 DESCRIPTION OF THE WHOLE EXAMPLE

We start from ten examples described by means of four variables. The values associated with each variable (or, generally, the descriptors) are considered as strictly independent.

For example, farther on, the "teenager" of X_2 and that of X_3 do not represent the same reality.

Let X_1 be the variable describing the values of weight. They are linear and ordered in the sequence

$$\{light < medium\text{-}weight < heavy\}$$

Let X_2 be the variable describing the social roles whose relations are given by the descriptors structured by the following taxonomies.

It will be noticed that we have represented a tangled taxonomy (as defined in chapter 8) by two taxonomies having values in common.

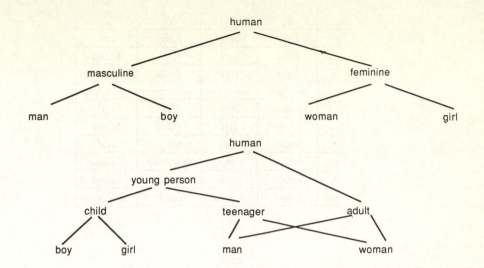

In these "taxonomies", we have assumed that children are not yet fully either men or women, whereas teenagers are. Adults are no longer young people, whereas teenagers and children are. Men and boys belong to the masculine gender and women and girls to the feminine gender.

It is possible for these relations to be even more complex and to take the form of a graph.

Then, in practice, it may be replaced by a series of equivalent theorems and instead of "climbing the generalization tree" we can "climb" the successive implications using theorems of the form: [man ⟹ adult], or [man ⟹ masculine], etc ...

Let X_3 be the variable describing the relations of age given by values ordered according to:

$$\{baby < child < teenager < adult\} \text{ and structured by:}$$

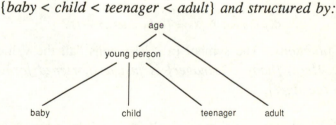

It will be noticed that certain values of X_3 are shared by X_2. This has been done deliberately to show clearly that when two values are attached to two different variables, then they are totally independent. For example, the ' child ' of X_2 has nothing to do with the ' child ' of X_3.

Let X_4 be a variable describing hair color, given by three nominal values
$$\{blond, red, chestnut\}$$
This means that there are no relations among these values.

Let us assume now that we have ten examples we wish to classify and which are given by

	X_1	X_2	X_3	X_4
e_1	light	boy	baby	red
e_2	light	girl	baby	blond
e_3	light	boy	child	chestnut
e_4	medium	woman	teenager	chestnut
e_5	medium	boy	child	red
e_6	heavy	girl	child	blond
e_7	heavy	man	teenager	red
e_8	heavy	woman	teenager	chestnut
e_9	heavy	man	adult	blond
e_{10}	heavy	woman	adult	chestnut

3   RECOGNITION

We are going to have to recognize subsets of $\{e_1, ..., e_{10}\}$ and this will be done with the help of recognition functions defined as follows: A recognition function R is an expression of the form

$$(X_i = V_i) \ \& \ ... \ \& \ (X_k = V_k)$$

where each of the X_j are variables (*in the example they belong to* $\{X_1, ..., X_4\}$) and where V_j are possible values of these variables, disjunctions of possible values, or else sets of possible values.

For instance,

$$X_2 = man$$
$$X_2 = man \ \lor \ woman \ \lor \ boy$$
$$X_3 = [baby \ .. \ teenager]$$
$$(X_2 = man) \ \& \ (X_3 = [baby \ .. \ teenager])$$

are recognition functions. The symbol [a .. b] means "all the values contained in the interval [a, b]". *Here, [baby .. teenager] is just a shortened form of the disjunction [baby $\lor$ child $\lor$ teenager].*

By convention, when a variable takes all its possible values in a recognition function, then it can be omitted (we do not omit them in the following, when we feel that they can usefully be recalled to the reader).

The expression $X_2 = man$ is in fact an abbreviation for $X_1 = (light \lor medium \lor heavy) \ \& \ (X_2 = man) \ \& \ (X_3 = baby \lor child \lor teenager \lor adult) \ \& \ (X_4 = red \lor blond \lor chestnut)

A recognition function takes the value TRUE for any example E_i where the values of the variables of E_i are one of those of the function.

We then say that the recognition function **recognizes** the example.

Otherwise, it takes the value FALSE.

When a function does not recognize an example, we say that it **rejects** this example.

The recognition function $X_2 = man \lor woman \lor boy$ takes the value TRUE for the examples e_1, e_3, e_4, e_5, e_7, e_8, e_9, e_{10} since only e_2 and e_6 have the value ' girl ' for X_2.

The recognition function $X_3 = [baby .. teenager]$ takes the value FALSE for e_9 and e_{10}.

When a recognition function R recognizes more than one example, we call the subset of values for which it takes the value TRUE the **subset recognized by R.**

The recognition function $X_2 = man \lor woman \lor boy$ recognizes the subset $\{e_1, e_3, e_4, e_5, e_7, e_8, e_9, e_{10}\}$.

Conversely, given a subset of examples, one can create a **recognition function generated by this subset** by taking the disjunction of the values of their variables.

Note carefully that a subset can be recognized by a function R_1 and generate a function which is not always R_1.

The recognition function R_1: $X_2 = man \lor woman \lor boy$ recognizes the subset $\{e_1, e_3, e_4, e_5, e_7, e_8, e_9, e_{10}\}$. This subset can be used to generate R_1 again.

Let us check that the function generated by $\{e_1, e_3, e_4, e_5, e_7, e_8, e_9, e_{10}\}$ really is R_1.

The values taken by X_1 in the subset $\{e_1, e_3, e_4, e_5, e_7, e_8, e_9, e_{10}\}$ are ' light ' (for $\{e_1$ and e_3), ' medium ' (for e_4 and e_5), and ' heavy ' (for e_7, e_8, e_9 and e_{10}). So for X_1 the recognition function generated by the subset $\{e_1, e_3, e_4, e_5, e_7, e_8, e_9, e_{10}\}$ is $X_1 = light \lor medium \lor heavy$. In other words, X_1 can take all the values possible and so it will be omitted from the function generated by $\{e_1, e_3, e_4, e_5, e_7, e_8, e_9, e_{10}\}$.

You will see in the same way that the values taken by X_2 are of course $X_2 = man \lor woman \lor boy$, so that is part of the function generated by $\{e_1, e_3, e_4, e_5, e_7, e_8, e_9, e_{10}\}$.

You will see that X_3 and X_4 take all the values possible for this subset.

Conversely, consider the recognition function

    R_1: $(X_1 = heavy \lor light)$ & $(X_4 = red \lor chestnut)$

The subset recognized by R_1 is $\{e_1, e_3, e_7, e_8, e_{10}\}$, indeed, for example, e_2 is not recognized by R_1, since, for e_2, the value of X_4 is ' blond ', which gives the value FALSE to R_1 for e_2.

The function generated by $\{e_1, e_3, e_7, e_8, e_{10}\}$ is the same as R_1 for X_1 and X_4, obviously. For X_3, you can see that it takes all the values possible. On the other hand, X_2 only takes the values ' boy ' (for e_1 and e_3), ' man ' (for e_7) and ' woman ' (for e_8 and e_{10}). So the function generated by $\{e_1, e_3, e_7, e_8, e_{10}\}$ is

    R_2: $(X_1 = light \lor heavy)$ & $(X_2 = boy \lor man \lor woman)$ & $(X_4 = red \lor chestnut)$ or else

        R_2: R_1 & $(X_2 = boy \lor man \lor woman)$

R_2 is a specialization of R_1.

It is clear that the function generated by a subset is either the same as or more specialized than the function which recognizes this subset.

4 SPARSENESS AND THE SELECTION CRITERIA FOR A "GOOD" FUNCTION

Let there be a recognition function R. The total number of items able to give it the value TRUE can be calculated: it is the product of the number of values of each variable, where the variables able to take all values are no longer kept implicit.

The function R_2 above can take two values for X_1 and X_4, and three for X_2, as its expression shows. Furthermore, we know that the values of X_3 are not indicated because X_3 can take all the values possible, i.e. four values. So the total number of items able to give it the value TRUE is 2 * 3 * 4 * 2 = 48.

Furthermore, examples recognized by this function can be found and their number can be counted, as we have done already.

The function R_2 recognizes $\{e_1, e_3, e_7, e_8, e_{10}\}$, i.e. five examples.

Let the **sparseness of a recognition function** be the difference between the total number of different items it can potentially recognize and the number of items (in the actual examples) which have been observed.

The sparseness of R_2 is 48 - 5 = 43.

If there is a choice among several recognition functions, the one with the least sparseness will be chosen.

The reason for this rule is that sparseness estimates a "degree of generalization" achieved in the recognition function. The less the sparseness the more compactly described is the information.

One interesting special case is that of recognition functions which partition a set.

Let there be two recognition functions R_1 and R_2 and a set E of examples. Let E_1 be the subset of E recognized by R_1 and let E_2 be the subset of E recognized by R_2.

We say that the two recognition functions R_1 and R_2 **partition** E when E_1 and E_2 partition E, that is:
$$E_1 \cup E_2 = E \text{ and } E_1 \cap E_2 = \varnothing.$$
The notion of sparseness is thus extended to a partition by two recognition functions R_1 and R_2 by saying that the **sparseness of the partition** by R_1 and R_2 is the sum of the sparseness of R_1 and that of R_2.

It can thus be said that a partition by two recognition functions (R_1, R_2) is **better**

from the point of view of sparseness than a partition by (R_1', R_2') if the sparseness of (R_1, R_2) is less than that of (R_1', R_2').

There are other notions used to classify the recognition functions obtained. In particular, various **simplicity criteria** can be defined. Since they can be ad hoc, we shall not take the trouble to describe them precisely but here are two examples.

A function may be said to be simple when it contains fewer descriptors or disjuncts etc... than some number that has been fixed in advance.

A function may be said to be more simple than another if it contains fewer descriptors, disjuncts etc...

5   THE PROCEDURE OF "EMPTYING THE INTERSECTIONS"

Let there be a set of examples E and two recognition functions R_1 and R_2. Let E_1 and E_2 be the two subsets recognized by R_1 and R_2. Let us suppose that E_1 and E_2 are intersecting subsets.

We are going to define a procedure to attempt to transform them into a partition. In fact, this procedure certainly leads to disjoint subsets, but we may possibly have to add subsets containing a very small number of examples, or even a single one.

So let E be a set of examples covered by two subsets E_1 and E_2, whose recognition functions are R_1 and R_2.

We then have $E_1 \cap E_2 \neq \varnothing$.

We then define

$$E_1' = E_1 - E_1 \cap E_2$$
$$E_2' = E_2 - E_1 \cap E_2$$

Let R_1' and R_2' be the recognition functions generated by E_1' and E_2'.

Let $\{e_1, ..., e_n\} = E_1 \cap E_2$. Then the examples e_i are those common to E_1 and E_2. For each e_i of $\{e_i\}$, we attempt the following procedure.

Define $E_1' \cup e_i$ and calculate the recognition function R_1'' generated by $E_1' \cup e_i$.

As we have said, we are not sure that $E_1' \cup e_i$ is the subset recognized by R_1''.

Define $E_2' \cup e_i$ and calculate the recognition function R_2'' generated by $E_2' \cup e_i$.

We then attempt to see whether (R_1'', R_2') and (R_1', R_2'') are partitions of E.

If they are, then we choose the best one from the point of view of sparseness and begin again with it as the starting-point, trying to incorporate another element of $E_1 \cap E_2$ into it.

If they are not, then we begin again with another element of $E_1 \cap E_2$.

Thus it is possible for certain examples never to be incorporated into either of the two subsets if a partition is not obtained by adding them to one or other of the subsets.

Example.

Let us consider the (disjoint) starting sets $\{e_1, e_2, e_3, e_4\}$ and $\{e_5, e_6, e_7, e_8, e_9, e_{10}\}$
The recognition function generated by $\{e_1, e_2, e_3, e_4\}$ *is*

R_1 :

$X_1 = light \lor medium$
$X_2 = boy \lor girl \lor woman$
$X_3 = baby \lor child \lor teenager$
$X_4 = red \lor blond \lor chestnut$

The recognition function generated by $\{e_5, e_6, e_7, e_8, e_9, e_{10}\}$ *is*

R_2:

$X_1 = heavy \lor medium$
$X_2 = boy \lor girl \lor woman \lor man$
$X_3 = child \lor teenager \lor adult$
$X_4 = red \lor blond \lor chestnut$

Thus, R_1 *recognizes* $E_1 = \{e_1, e_2, e_3, e_4, e_5\}$ *and* R_2 *recognizes* $E_2 = \{e_4, e_5, e_6, e_7, e_8, e_9, e_{10}\}$.

We therefore have $E_1 \cap E_2 = \{e_4, e_5\}$ *and* $E_1' = E_1 - \{e_4, e_5\} = \{e_1, e_2, e_3\}$ *and* $E_2' = E_2 - \{e_4, e_5\} = \{e_6, e_7, e_8, e_9, e_{10}\}$. *These two subsets generate two recognition functions* R_1' *and* R_2'.

R_1':

$X_1 = light$
$X_2 = boy \lor girl$
$X_3 = baby \lor child$
$X_4 = red \lor blond \lor chestnut$

R_2':

$X_1 = heavy$
$X_2 = girl \lor woman \lor man$
$X_3 = child \lor teenager \lor adult$
$X_4 = red \lor blond \lor chestnut$

It will be noted that R_1' *only recognizes* E_1' *and that* R_2' *only recognizes* E_2'.

During the first stage, we try to incorporate e_4 into E_1' and E_2', to obtain two partition starts (hereafter, following Michalski, called "seeds"), the one recognized by (R_1'', R_2') and the other recognized by (R_1', R_2'')

During the second stage, we try to incorporate e_5 into these seeds to complete them.

The recognition function R_1'' generated by $\{\{e_1, e_2, e_3\} \cup \{e_4\}\}$ is of course equal to R_1. We know that it recognizes e_5 and does not recognize E_2'.

The recognition function R_2'' generated by $\{\{e_6, e_7, e_8, e_9, e_{10}\} \cup \{e_4\}\}$ is

R_2'':
$$X_1 = heavy \lor medium$$
$$X_2 = girl \lor woman \lor man$$
$$X_3 = child \lor teenager \lor adult$$
$$X_4 = red \lor blond \lor chestnut$$

which recognizes $\{e_4, e_6, e_7, e_8, e_9, e_{10}\}$.

You may have the impression that our work is finished since $R_1 = R_1''$ recognizes $\{e_1, e_2, e_3, e_4, e_5\}$ and R_2' only recognizes $\{e_6, e_7, e_8, e_9, e_{10}\}$, so that we have a partition. But in fact this is not the only a priori possibility and, as we have said, the sparseness of the possible partitions must be compared before taking a decision.

We have two possible seeds; the one recognized by (R_1'', R_2') and the one recognized by (R_1', R_2''), whose sparseness we are now going to calculate.

Sparseness of $R_1'' = R_1$:
$$(2 * 3 * 3 * 3) - 5 = 49.$$

Sparseness of R_2':
$$(1 * 3 * 3 * 3) - 5 = 22.$$

Total for the partition started by (R_1'', R_2'): $49 + 22 = 71$.

Sparseness of R_1':
$$(1 * 2 * 2 * 3) - 3 = 9.$$

Sparseness of R_2'':
$$(2 * 3 * 3 * 3) - 6 = 48.$$

Total for the partition started by (R_1', R_2''): $49 + 9 = 57$.

So we shall use this partition, in spite of what we would have done if we had immediately followed our intuitions. We shall try to finish the partitioning process by attempting to incorporate e_5 either into the subset recognized by R_1' or into the subset recognized by R_2''.

Let us call the subsets and functions of the new iteration E_{11}', E_{12}', R_{11}', R_{12}':
$$E_{11}' = \{\{e_1, e_2, e_3\} \cup \{e_5\}\}, \quad E_{12}' = \{\{e_4, e_6, e_7, e_8, e_9, e_{10}\} \cup \{e_5\}\}$$

The function generated by E_{11}' is

R_{11}':
$$X_1 = light \lor medium$$
$$X_2 = girl \lor boy$$
$$X_3 = child \lor baby$$
$$X_4 = red \lor blond \lor chestnut$$

which recognizes $\{e_1, e_2, e_3, e_5\}$.

The function generated by E_{12}' is

R_{12}':

$$X_1 = \text{heavy} \vee \text{medium}$$
$$X_2 = \text{girl} \vee \text{boy} \vee \text{woman} \vee \text{man}$$
$$X_3 = \text{child} \vee \text{teenager} \vee \text{adult}$$
$$X_4 = \text{red} \vee \text{blond} \vee \text{chestnut}$$

which recognizes $\{e_4, e_5, e_6, e_7, e_8, e_9, e_{10}\}$

So we then try the "possible partitions" which are the subsets recognized by (R_{11}', R_2'') and by (R_1', R_{12}').

We check carefully that each of them is indeed a partition of E, and we then choose the best, first using sparseness criteria and then using simplicity criteria.

Exercise 20
****

Choose between the partitions made from the subsets recognized by (R_{11}', R_2'') and by (R_1', R_{12}').

****

6 CREATION OF RECOGNITION FUNCTIONS

6.1 Case where there are two examples

This requires a procedure for creating the most general recognition function which recognizes the example e_i and rejects the example e_j. We shall denote it by:

$$G(e_i/e_j)$$

This function is obtained very simply by comparing the values of the variables in e_i and e_j.

If the variable X_i has the same value in e_i and in e_j, then X_i does not occur in $G(e_i/e_j)$.

If the variable X_i does not have the same value in e_i and e_j, then letting V_j be the value of X_i in e_j, then we add the disjunct $\vee$ $(X_i \neq V_j)$ to $G(e_i/e_j)$. Of course, it follows from this definition that $G(e_i/e_j) \neq G(e_j/e_i)$.

The examples e_1 and e_2 differ by the variables X_2 and X_4 and, in e_2, we have $X_2 = $ girl and $X_4 = $ blond.

Thus, $G(e_1/e_2) = (X_2 \neq \text{girl}) \vee (X_4 \neq \text{blond})$.

Similarly, $G(e_1/e_4) = (X_1 \neq \text{medium}) \vee (X_2 \neq \text{woman}) \vee (X_3 \neq \text{teenager}) \vee (X_4 \neq \text{chestnut})$.

The reason why G(e_i/e_j) is the most general expression recognizing e_i and not recognizing e_j is quite obvious: we choose a recognition function with the sole constraint that it must not recognize e_j.

6.2 Case of an example compared with a set

This is a procedure for creating the most general recognition function which recognizes the example e_i and rejects the set of examples $\{e_j\}$.

It will be denoted by

$$G(e_i/\{e_j\}).$$

For each e_k in $\{e_j\}$, we calculate G(e_i/e_k). The conjunction of all the G obtained is the most general recognition function which recognizes the example e_i and rejects the set of examples $\{e_j\}$.

$$G(e_i/\{e_j\}) = \&_k \, G(e_i/e_k) \text{ for all } e_k \in \{e_j\}$$

Of course, this function is going to reject every e_k of $\{e_j\}$ since it is the conjunction of functions which reject each e_k. Once again, the fact that it is the most general function rejecting each e_k and recognizing the e_i is due to the fact that it requires nothing but the rejection of the e_k.

We thus obtain a conjunction of disjunctions of the form
$$(A_1 \lor \dots \lor A_n) \, \& \, \dots \, \& \, (F_1 \lor \dots \lor F_m)$$
where all the expressions $A_1, \dots A_n, F_1, \dots F_m$ are of the form $(X_i \neq V_j)$.

We have G(e_1/e_2) = ($X_2 \neq girl$) $\lor$ ($X_4 \neq blond$)
and B(e_1/e_4) = ($X_1 \neq medium$) $\lor$ ($X_2 \neq woman$) $\lor$ ($X_3 \neq teenager$) $\lor$ ($X_4 \neq chestnut$).
Thus G($e_1/\{e_2, e_4\}$) = G(e_1/e_2) & G(e_1/e_4) =
(($X_2 \neq girl$) $\lor$ ($X_4 \neq blond$)) & (($X_1 \neq medium$) $\lor$ ($X_2 \neq woman$) $\lor$ ($X_3 \neq teenager$) $\lor$ ($X_4 \neq chestnut$))   =
(($X_2 \neq girl$) & ($X_1 \neq medium$)) $\lor$ (($X_2 \neq girl$) & ($X_2 \neq woman$)) $\lor$ (($X_2 \neq girl$) & ($X_3 \neq teenager$)) $\lor$ (($X_2 \neq girl$) & ($X_4 \neq chestnut$)) $\lor$ (($X_4 \neq blond$) & ($X_1 \neq medium$)) $\lor$ (($X_4 \neq blond$) & ($X_2 \neq woman$)) $\lor$ (($X_4 \neq blond$) & ($X_3 \neq teenager$)) $\lor$ (($X_4 \neq blond$) & ($X_4 \neq chestnut$))

By exploiting the fact that the number of possible values of the variables is finite, let us transform each of the $\neq$ into a disjunction.

We shall thus obtain a disjunction of recognition functions.

G($e_1/\{e_2, e_4\}$) =
(($X_2 = man \lor woman \lor boy$) & ($X_1 = light \lor heavy$)) $\lor$
(($X_2 = man \lor woman \lor boy$) & ($X_2 = man \lor girl \lor boy$)) $\lor$

$((X_2 = man \lor woman \lor boy)$ & $(X_3 = baby \lor child \lor adult)) \lor$
$((X_2 = man \lor woman \lor boy)$ & $(X_4 = red \lor blond)) \lor$
$((X_4 = red \lor chestnut)$ & $(X_1 = light \lor heavy)) \lor$
$((X_4 = red \lor chestnut)$ & $(X_2 = man \lor girl \lor boy)) \lor$
$((X_4 = red \lor chestnut)$ & $(X_3 = baby \lor child \lor adult)) \lor$
$((X_4 = red \lor chestnut)$ & $(X_4 = red \lor blond))$

This is the disjunction of 8 recognition functions.

6.3   Optimization of the functions

Under this heading we consider a procedure for creating the "best" recognition function which recognizes the example e_i and rejects the set of examples $\{e_j\}$. It will be denoted by

$$G_{opt}(e_i/\{e_j\}).$$

We have obtained $G(e_i/\{e_j\})$ in the form of a disjunction, so each of the terms of the disjunction is capable of carrying out the desired operation, which consists of recognizing e_i and rejecting $\{e_j\}$.

Check that, for example
$(X_2 = man \lor woman \lor boy)$ & $(X_1 = light \lor heavy)$,
which is the first term of the disjunction expressing $G(e_1/\{e_2, e_4\})$, *takes the value TRUE for* e_1 *and FALSE for* e_2 *and* e_4.

Let us call one of these recognition functions R_i. We are going to improve the sparseness of each of them as much as possible by proceeding as follows.

For each R_i, we calculate the subset $\{e_i\}$ of examples which it recognizes. After that we calculate the recognition function R_i' generated by each $\{e_i\}$.

We then use the elementary laws of combination for expressions involving & and $\lor$ on the one hand, and any knowledge available about the domain (taxonomies, theorems) on the other hand, in order to simplify the formulation of R_i' as much as possible.

Finally, we define $G_{opt}(e_i/\{e_j\})$ as being the **least sparse** R_i' at the start, **and** after that the **simplest possible**.

We have
$R_1 = ((X_2 = man \lor woman \lor boy)$ & $(X_1 = light \lor heavy))$
$R_2 = ((X_2 = man \lor woman \lor boy)$ & $(X_2 = man \lor girl \lor boy))$
$R_3 = ((X_2 = man \lor woman \lor boy)$ & $(X_3 = baby \lor child \lor adult))$
$R_4 = ((X_2 = man \lor woman \lor boy)$ & $(X_4 = red \lor blond))$
$R_5 = ((X_4 = red \lor chestnut)$ & $(X_1 = light \lor heavy))$

$R_6 = ((X_4 = red \lor chestnut) \& (X_2 = man \lor girl \lor boy))$

$R_7 = ((X_4 = red \lor chestnut) \& (X_3 = baby \lor child \lor adult))$

$R_8 = ((X_4 = red \lor chestnut) \& (X_4 = red \lor blond))$.

Let us study R_1.

It recognizes $\{e_1, e_3, e_7, e_8, e_9, e_{10}\}$. The recognition function generated by this subset is $R_1' = R_1$ itself.

The total number of items which R_1 can recognize is $2 * 3 * 4 * 3 = 72$. The number of examples it recognizes is six, so its sparseness is $72 - 6 = 66$.

The theorems about the values of X_2 can be used in two different ways to obtain

$$(man \lor woman) \Leftrightarrow adult$$
$$(man \lor boy) \Leftrightarrow masculine$$

So, finally, we are going to re-write R_1 in the simple form:

R_1': $(X_2 = adult \lor masculine) \& (X_1 = light \lor heavy)$

Knowledge about the domain has made it possible to make the written form of R_1' simpler than that of R_1.

On the other hand, a study of R_2, R_3 and R_4 makes it apparent that they cannot be greatly modified.

Let us now examine $R_5 = ((X_4 = red \lor chestnut) \& (X_1 = light \lor heavy))$. The subset it recognizes is $\{e_1, e_3, e_7, e_8, e_{10}\}$. The recognition function generated by this subset is

$R_5 \& (X_2 = boy \lor man \lor woman)$.

By following the kind of simplification that we applied to R_1, we obtain

$R_5' = ((X_4 = red \lor chestnut) \& (X_1 = light \lor heavy)) \& (X_2 = adult \lor masculine)$

The total number of items which R_5' can recognize is $2 * 3 * 4 * 2 = 48$. The number of examples it actually recognizes here is five, so its sparseness is $48 - 5 = 43$.

To compare R_1' and R_5', we first compare their sparseness. On this comparison, R_5' is better than R_1', even though the formula expressing it is longer.

7 RULES OF GENERALIZATION

We shall only give the main rules of generalization here. The reader will find others in [Michalski 1983, 1984] and an in-depth discussion in [Kodratoff and Ganascia 1986]. The reader should note that the first two rules preserve logical truth value, whereas the remainder do not.

- the dropping condition rule.

For any expression, A & B is more specific than A.

Thus, starting from an expression of the form A & B, we achieve a generalization by transforming it into A (or else B).

It is more general to talk of going to the cinema rather than of going to the cinema and eating ice lollies.

Nevertheless, beware of the semantics of the predicates that you use.

In an expression the occurrence of two different variables means that the instances of these variables can be different, but they can also be the same.

For example, if we know that we are in a universe where

$$E_1: RED(x) \ \& \ SQUARE(y) = TRUE$$

then this expression means that there are always red items and square items, but also that in principle there can be red squares when the square item and the red item are the same. So this expression implicitly contains the disjunction

$$(RED(x) \ \& \ SQUARE(y) \ \& \ DIFFERENT(x, y)) \lor (RED(x) \ \& \ SQUARE(x)) = TRUE$$

Hence it is not surprising that

$$RED(x) \ \& \ SQUARE(y) = TRUE$$

should be more general than

$$E_1': (RED(x) \ \& \ SQUARE(y) \ \& \ DIFFERENT(x, y)) = TRUE.$$

Let us now give a counter-example to the dropping rule.

Suppose that we change the semantics of the representation of the variables and that we decide, conversely, that when two variables have different names, then all their instances must be different.

Then, $E_2: RED(x) \ \& \ SQUARE(y) = TRUE$ means that there is always a square item and a red item different from the square.

In sum, we have now implicitly given the meaning of E_1' to E_2.

If we add the conjunct & MAYBETHESAME(x, y) to E_2, it is quite obvious that

$E_2': (RED(x) \ \& \ SQUARE(y) \ \& \ MAYBETHESAME(x, y)) = TRUE$ is more general than E_2, even though an unthinking application of the dropping rule would say the opposite.

This rule is certainly the best known and the most used of the rules of generalization. It is also one of the most dangerous to use, since it removes information which might be needed later.

In chapter 7 we shall show an algorithm which tries to minimize the use of this rule.

- the adding disjuncts rule.

This is a rule which is symmetrical to the dropping rule: A $\lor$ B is always more general than A.

152

The same remarks apply as for the dropping rule.

- the turning constants into variables rule.

If A is a predicate of arity greater than zero, for example one, and if CT is a constant then $A(x)$ is more general than $A(CT)$.

For example, an operator which recognizes a class of items is more general than an operator which only recognizes a single one of the elements of the class.

- the adding names of variables rule.

When a variable has several occurrences, for example, in $A(x, x)$, then one can generalize by giving a different value to one of the occurrences.

$A(x, y)$ is more general than $A(x, x)$.

- the extending domain rule.

This is a special and interesting case of the adding disjuncts rule. If a predicate is true for a known domain, for example if we have

$$A(x) \ \& \ x \in \{x_1, ..., x_n\}.$$

This expression is equivalent to

$$E_1: A(x_1) \lor ... \lor A(x_n).$$

Hence adding a possible value, x_{n+1}, to the domain of x amounts to transforming E_1 into

$$E_1': A(x_1) \lor ... \lor A(x_{n+1}) \text{ and hence to generalizing it.}$$

Another special case of this rule occurs in linear domains. If we have

$$E_2: A(x) \ \& \ x \in [a .. b] \text{ which means that x belongs to the interval (a,}$$

b) of the linear domain, then if b' > b, E_2' is more general than E_2.

$$E_2': A(x) \ \& \ x \in [a .. b']$$

In the integers, another example can be expressed as follows.
Let A(x) be true for the values x = 1, 2, 3, 5, 6.
This is written

$$E_3: A(x) \ \& \ ((x = 1) \lor (x = 2) \lor (x = 3) \lor (x = 5) \lor (x = 6))$$

By adding 4 as a possible value we complete the interval and E_3 is less general than $E_3' : A(x) \ \& \ x \in [1 .. 6]$

We can justify this kind of generalization by not allowing any extensions to the domain which are too great.

- the climbing generalization tree rule

If the domain is structured then we can generalize by replacing a child by one of its ancestors.

It is more general to say that Medor is a mammal than to say that he is a dog. Here "mammal" is an ancestor of "dog".

In Chapter 5, we saw that version space was designed to master this type of generalization.

- the rule of suppressing the antecedents of implications

If the domain contains a theorem of conditional form like A $\Rightarrow$ B, then any expression containing A can be generalized by turning one or several occurrences of A into B.

In reality, this rule is an instance of the dropping condition rule. In fact, if A $\Rightarrow$ B then we know that A & B is equivalent to A, so that by applying the dropping condition rule to the ' A ' of A & B, we get B.

At the beginning of this chapter we gave the theorem
$\forall x \, \forall y \, \forall z$ [eyes(blue, x) & eyes(blue, y) & parents(x, y, z) $\Rightarrow$ eyes(blue, z)]
We can apply it to the particular case
eyes(blue, Marie) & eyes(blue, Pierre) & parents(Marie, Pierre, Jacques)
which is hence equivalent to
eyes(blue, Marie) & eyes(blue, Pierre) & parents(Marie, Pierre, Jacques) & eyes(blue, Jacques)
So the rule of generalization that we are illustrating says that
eyes(blue, Jacques)
is a generalization of
eyes(blue, Marie) & eyes(blue, Pierre) & parents(Marie, Pierre, Jacques)
which is obviously wrong, in our familiar every-day micro-world.

The example above clearly shows that this kind of generalization is extremely risky and that there must be good reasons for doing it. For example, you could check that carrying out this generalization does not modify the set of examples that the formula recognizes. Of course, it does have the advantage of simplifying the formulae.

8 GENERATION OF RECOGNITION FUNCTIONS

We are going to study an algorithm for the generation of complete and discriminating recognition functions on the basis of positive and negative examples.

Let POS be the set of positive examples and let NEG be the set of negative examples (counter-examples). Let e_i be the current member of POS.

We calculate $G_{opt}(e_i/\text{NEG}) = R_{ei}$. By construction, R_{ei} is consistent.

If R_{ei} recognizes all of POS, then we have found a complete and consistent function. We repeat with another member of POS to look for another.

If R_{ei} does not recognize the whole of POS, we add $\vee \, R_{ei}$ to the current function and test whether $R_{ei-p} \vee ... \vee R_{ei}$ is complete.

If it is, we have found a complete and consistent function in the form of a disjunction. We repeat with another member of POS to look for farther examples.

If it is not, we repeat with another member of POS to try to construct another member to add to the disjunction already obtained.

9 APPLICATION TO SOYBEAN PATHOLOGY

The aim is to automatically synthesize rules for the treatment of soybean plants. Details concerning these results will be found in [Michalski & Chilausky 1980].

When an Expert System is built using methods of direct interrogation, (which one might call "learning rules by heart"), the expert may occasionally give up because of limitations due to the language of the system.

For example, a perfectly obvious limitation of systems based on EMYCIN is that the control of the coefficients of probability is not accessible to the user. Another example: to express yourself in PROLOG you use Horn clauses; this is another kind of limitation imposed on the user.

At the University of Illinois computer scientists and biologists have pooled their knowledge to create an expert system for soybean pathology, and the constraints on its expressions were modelled on the desires of the experts [Michalski & al. 1982]. We shall call it the standard expert system. In parallel fashion, another expert system was built starting from a set of diagnoses used as a set of examples. Some rules were thus learned automatically, constituting a expert system obtained by ML.

We are now going to describe these two systems briefly.

9.1 The standard expert system

Without entering into all the details, let us say that this is a standard expert system, because it is made up simply of actions and of conditions for executing these actions.

The descriptors can be assigned a weight whose dependence on other selectors can be stated explicitly. This is the essential difference between this system and those that can be called "standard" - because they founded the entire subject of expert systems.

Many details on how the beliefs were evaluated can be found in [Michalski et al. 1982].

For example, in a certain rule the belief that pustules have appeared on the leaves may very well not be absolute but may depend on the month when the observation was made. There is a way to express such a dependence. It will be written by an expression of the type:

$$PUSTULE(x) \ \& \ OCCURRENCE(x, f(x, t))$$

where f(x) is an indicator of the behavior of x as a function of the time t which can be, for example

$$f(x, t) =$$

$$IF \ t = July \ THEN \ 0.1 \ ELSE$$
$$IF \ t = [1st \ August \ ... \ 15 \ September] \ THEN \ 0.2 \ ELSE$$
$$0.01$$

This enables us to express descriptors of the type : "If precipitation was above normal in August and below normal in September then ..." using an appropriate f(x, t).

Exercise 21
****

Express the above descriptor using IF ... THEN ... ELSE, as we have done, then translate into PROLOG.

****

9.2   The expert system obtained by ML

The initial knowledge base is made out of several hundred diagnoses given by experts.

Each diagnosis is presented as a questionnaire in which all the possible values of the descriptors are indicated. For example, there will be a line with:

> leaf malformation: yes - no

another with

> stem: normal - abnormal

Beneath the descriptors there is a list of possible diseases.

For a given case, the expert keeps a tally of the disease he diagnoses and the correct values of the descriptors.

Thus a set of several hundred case descriptions is obtained. Each set of cases where a given disease was diagnosed is considered as a set of examples for this disease, and the others as negative examples to the disease.

Let us arbitrarily choose a disease at the beginning (call it *disease$_1$*) and let us calculate, using the method described here, a recognition function which is complete for the examples of this disease and consistent for the examples of other diseases. Let F_1 be this recognition function. It then becomes the recognition condition for *disease$_1$*.

We have thus generated the rule:

$$IF \ F_1 \ THEN \ disease_1.$$

The process is repeated over the set of cases, removing the cases describing *disease*₁.

In this way we obtain a set of rules which enables us to diagnose illnesses given as examples.

9.3 Comparison of results

They can be compared from two points of view: the form of the rules obtained and their efficiency.

A striking point about the form of the rules obtained by learning is that they do not use all the descriptors that the experts needed. For example, the rules obtained do not include probability coefficients, nor, of course, the complicated functions associated with their variation in value as a function of another descriptor.

Another point is that the quality of the rules learned deteriorates in the order in which the diseases are studied. The rules about the first diseases studied are clear and short. Those about the last are complicated and include many disjunctions which make them incomprehensible.

This method therefore requires improvement to enable us to take account of all the diseases at once, so that the order in which they are studied has less influence on the result.

One quite obvious cause of this defect is that all the diseases are considered as independent and a formula distinguishing each of them from all the others is demanded right away. In other words, the recognition tree only has one level.

We could envisage constructing recognition trees with several levels, where the intermediate concepts introduced would cluster several diseases. These trees could then be constructed to make it easier to understand the rules which will finally diagnose the diseases. We shall say no more about this topic; it remains a research issue.

10 APPLICATION TO AN ALGORITHM FOR CONCEPTUAL CLUSTERING

Let E be a set of examples.

We start with a certain number of examples called seeds, on the basis of which we are to carry out the clustering.

This requires us to know a priori the number of groups we want to obtain. So, in practice, we need an additional repetition of the algorithm which progressively increases the number of seeds and tests the result obtained, as in the previous examples, by sparseness and simplicity.

To begin, let us assume a given number k, of seeds. For each one of them, g_i, we calculate $G_{opt}(g_i/\{g_j\})$ where $\{g_j\}$ is the set of the other seeds.

We thus obtain k better recognition functions which in principle do not define a partition of E. We apply to them the procedure for emptying intersections seen above.

We have thus obtained a partition of E.

By sparseness and simplicity we measure the value of this partition.

If it is better than that obtained in the previous repetition, we keep it and use the new better partition to choose new seeds which will be the most "central" points of members of the new partition.

If it is not better than that obtained in the previous repetition, we choose as seeds the points that look the most like "boundary" instances from the members of the partition from before.

The definition of "central" and "boundary" is ad hoc and will not be given here.

In chapter 8 we shall see other methods of partitioning and we shall show the importance of the availability of good methods for partitioning in ML.

9 Learning by Similarity Detection
The 'Rational' Approach

In the last chapter, an "empirical" approach was described.

We use the label of "rational" approach to make it clear that in this approach we adopt a certain number of laws of generalization, some of which do not preserve logical equivalence between a formula and its generalization. These laws are used, and only afterwards are the consequences of their application analyzed.

In the approach described as "rational" (because it is a little more deductive than the previous one), even before applying the laws of generalization we first try to bring to the fore the reasons for applying them. Thus, before generalizing, we subject the examples to an analysis which must be as exhaustive as possible in order to convert them into the most suitable form possible for the impending generalization.

This operation is well-known when used as a strategy; we then call it "converting the examples into their internal form", or alternatively "looking for the most suitable representation". No methods exist right now that would enable these problems to be solved on a systematic basis.

We are now going to describe a method we have developed which, in the case where not all the descriptors in the examples correspond to each other, it gives a solution to a sub-problem of those pointed out above.

For example, supposing that one example contains the descriptor ' GREY ' and another the descriptor ' BEIGE ', then the type of problem we want to solve is that of finding how to generalize them to ' CLEAR-COLOR '.

The reader should know, looking at the history of this kind of problem, that it was already partly solved in the empirical approach we have attributed to Michalski. It is mainly for pedagogical reasons that we separate them here so sharply.

Our method has already been briefly described in chapter 7 where we called it "Structural Matching". This chapter will present it in full detail. Let us start by showing how to represent the knowledge needed to describe the features of the domain in which the generalizing is done.

1 KNOWLEDGE REPRESENTATION

In order to work, an algorithm for generalization by similarity detection has to be supplied with a list containing examples to generalize, taxonomies of generality, theorems and rules of representation for the language. It then produces the right generalization for the list of examples.

1.1 The expressions to generalize

The examples to be generalized are set out in the form of expressions in first-order predicate logic. Each predicate is a descriptor describing one of the features of the example.

Example 1.
Let E_1, E_2 and E_3 be three expressions for which a generalization is sought:

E_1: *WHALE(MOBY-DICK) & WHITE(MOBY-DICK)*
E_2: *DOLPHIN(FLIPPER) & GREY(FLIPPER)*
E_3: *CETACEAN(OUM)*

Thus, in E_1, ' MOBY-DICK ' is the object of the example, whereas ' WHALE ' is a predicate with one argument, describing one of the features of ' MOBY-DICK '.

So these expressions are a representation of "Moby Dick is a white whale", "Flipper is a grey dolphin" and "Oum is a cetacean".
' MOBY-DICK ', ' FLIPPER ' and ' OUM ' are constants representing objects (or individuals) whereas ' WHALE ', ' DOLPHIN ', ' CETACEAN ', ' WHITE ' and ' GREY ' are predicates applicable to these objects.

1.2 Taxonomies

A set of taxonomies of generality has to be supplied to the generalization algorithm by the user. These taxonomies are n-ary trees of predicates whose generality diminishes toward the leaves.

In other words, these taxonomies are hierarchies in which the children inherit all the features of their parents.

In this chapter, we only consider taxonomies where the children are mutually exclusive.

Also, another restriction is that we do not consider any hierarchies other than those describing relations of generality.

Here are some examples of taxonomies, and an example of a hierarchy which is not a taxonomy.

In example 1, one possible taxonomy is the following.

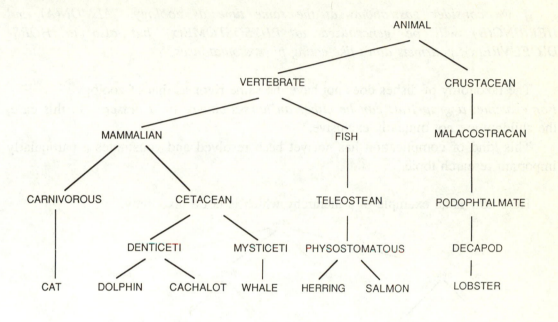

Taxonomy T_1.

We cannot have ' MAMMAL(A) ' and ' FISH(A) ' at the same time, but we can have ' MAMMAL(A) ' and ' CETACEAN(A) '.

Taxonomies are neither unique nor universal. If we generalize WHALE(A) and SALMON(B) on the basis of T_1, then we shall get the same result as by generalizing CAT(C) and SALMON(B) (the generalization being VERTEBRATE(x)). We might wish to have another classification in which ' WHALE ' and ' SALMON ' will be closer than ' CAT ' and ' SALMON '. We would then have to modify T_1 by creating, for example, a ' MARINE-ANIMAL ' predicate as a common ancestor of ' WHALE ' and ' SALMON '.

Thus the generalization obtained depends entirely on the taxonomies supplied to the system. The taxonomies enable the features of the universe we are generalizing in to be described. The user him/herself is responsible for constructing his/her own taxonomies.

In the version of the generalization algorithm described here, the same predicate can only appear once in a single taxonomy. There are, however, cases where this restriction is too stringent. We have just noted that there can be more than one possible taxonomy, and so we may want to consider several of them at the same time. Ways of tackling this problem will not be discussed here. In the context of *object-oriented languages*, this is called "multiple inheritance", so that it is part of certain commercial systems.

If we consider gastronomy at the same time as zoology, SALMON(A) and HERRING(B) will be generalized to PHYSOSTOME(x) but also to HORS-D'OEUVRE(x); gourmets don't like eating physostomatouses.

The taxonomy of dishes does not have the same rigor as that of zoology
For example, a grapefruit can be either an hors-d'oeuvre or a dessert. In this case, the children are not mutually exclusive.

This kind of complication has not yet been resolved and constitutes a particularly important research topic.

Here now is an example of a hierarchy which is not a taxonomy.

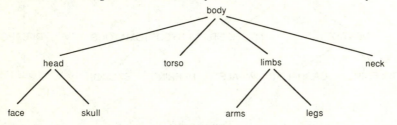

In this type of hierarchy, features are not transmitted like they are in taxonomies. For example, if some animal is hairy, it can indeed be said that it has hairs on its body, but not that its body is hairy.

Solving this kind of problem as it applies to learning is also a research topic.

It will be noted that the various hierarchies are nothing but an abbreviated representation of a set of theorems. For example, the fact that ' CAT ' is a child of ' CARNIVORE ' tells us that all the theorems which are true for ' CARNIVORE ' are true for ' CAT '. This can become an intolerable over-simplification, because classifications are obviously always arbitrary to a certain extent. The existence of vegetarian cats is an example.

A standard solution to this problem is that the children inherit the properties of their parents unless there is some indication to the contrary; this is inheritance by default.

1.3   Axioms

A set of axioms must also be supplied to the generalization algorithm. Like taxonomies, axioms describe the features of the relevant universe.

In example 1, one set of axioms could be:
Ax_1: $\forall x\ \forall y[EATS(x, y) \Leftrightarrow IS\text{-}EATEN\text{-}BY(y, x)]$
Ax_2: $\forall x\ [ANIMAL(x) \Rightarrow COLORED(x)]$
These axioms mean respectively: "if an individual ' x ' eats an individual ' y ' then ' y ' is eaten by ' x ' and vice versa" and "every animal has a color".

All axioms are used in the form of equivalences, which will be justified below. Implications are transformed by means of the property: "A $\Rightarrow$ B is logically equivalent to A $\Leftrightarrow$ A & B".

So Ax_2 will become $\forall x\ [ANIMAL(x) \Leftrightarrow ANIMAL(x)\ \&\ COLORED(x)]$

1.4 The rules of representation for the language

This information describes the properties of the connectives in the expressions. The only connective we shall talk about here is logical conjunction, which possesses the properties of commutativity, associativity, the neutral element (TRUE) (A $\Leftrightarrow$ A & TRUE). and idempotence (A $\Leftrightarrow$ A & A).

1.5   Result of the generalization algorithm

The generalization algorithm produces an expression in the form of conjunctions of predicates and preserving as much information as possible.

The generalization of DOLPHIN(FLIPPER) and WHALE(MOBY-DICK) found by using T_1 is CETACEAN(x) where ' x ' is a generalization variable.

In the real world, the generalizations to be found are much more complex. The following example illustrates a traditional problem.

Example 2.

E_1: *WHALE(MOBY-DICK) & DOLPHIN(FLIPPER) & BIGGER-THAN(MOBY- DICK, FLIPPER)*
E_2: *CAT(MIMI) & DOLPHIN(OUM) & BIGGER-THAN(OUM, MIMI)*

In spite of being very simple, E_1 and E_2 can intuitively be generalized in at least two different ways:

- There is a mammal and a cetacean, and the bigger of them is a cetacean.
- There is a mammal and a dolphin, and one of them is bigger than the other.

These generalizations are both correct and there is no reason to prefer one of them rather than the other.

When descriptions are complex, a considerable number of possible generalizations exist which usually cannot be compared with each other. One of the interesting things about the generalization algorithm presented here is that bringing examples into structural correspondence can often lead us toward an expression which covers several generalizations, as will now be described.

By using the idempotence of the logical &, it will yield the expression "There is a mammal and a cetacean, one of them is a dolphin, and the bigger of them is a cetacean".

This covers both the generalizations seen above.

2 DESCRIPTION OF A RATIONAL GENERALIZATION ALGORITHM

The algorithm consists of four distinct stages: Structural Matching, the introduction of links between the variables of an expression, the suppression of everything that differs between one expression and another and, finally, simplification.

One of the characteristics of this algorithm is the clear separation between deductive processes (carried out by successive equivalences) and inductive processes (carried out by generalization).

2.1 Structural Matching

2.1.1 Tentative Generalization Variables

The aim of structural matching is to make expressions correspond with respect to their structures.

Definition

We say that n expressions $E_1, ..., E_n$ are in **structural correspondence** or **match structurally** if there is a formula F and n substitutions σ_i such that for all i, $\sigma_i(F) = E_i$.

In order to bring expressions into structural correspondence, we introduce what we have called Tentative Generalization Variables in the places where the expressions differ.

By the device of Tentative Generalization Variables the differences which exist between the expressions are to be rubbed out little by little until they are all equal (except for the instances of the Tentative Generalization Variables).

Writing WHALE(MOBY-DICK) is equivalent to writing WHALE(x)[(x = MOBY-DICK)], where x is a Tentative Generalization Variable and where the expression between square brackets contains the instances of the Tentative Generalization Variables.

We shall distinguish two sorts of Tentative Generalization Variables:

- The Tentative Generalization Variables which occur in the arguments of predicates and which can therefore be instantiated by logical terms (constants representing objects, variables, functions, compound functions etc ...). These Tentative Generalization Variables will be called Predicate-Argument Variables (PAV).

In WHALE(x), the Tentative Generalization Variable ' x ' is a PAV.

- The Tentative Generalization Variables which can be instantiated by constants representing predicates. These Tentative Generalization Variables are typed and have a finite number of possible instantiations. When one of them is instantiated, it is a specialization of its parents in the taxonomy associated with it. These Tentative Generalization Variables will be called Predicate-Specialization Variables (PSV).

In example 2, MOBY-DICK is not only a whale but also a cetacean. So we can write
$$(CETACEAN\ u\ v)(MOBY\text{-}DICK)[(u = MYSTICETE)\ (v = WHALE)]$$
the syntax of which is explained below and where ' u ' and ' v ' are PSVs.

Note that ' u ' can only be instantiated by ' DENTICETE ' or ' MYSTICETE ', and ' v ' by ' DOLPHIN ', ' WHALE ' or ' CACHALOT '. Furthermore, ' v ' can only be instantiated by the children of ' u '.

We adopt the following conventions for writing:

Convention 1: $A_1(O_1 \dots O_n) \Leftrightarrow (A_2\ A_1)\ (O_1 \dots O_n)$
where the n-ary predicate A_2 is the parent of the n-ary predicate A_1 in the taxonomy they both belong to.

CETACEAN(FLIPPER) can be represented by (ANIMAL VERTEBRATE MAMMAL CETACEAN)(FLIPPER) as needed.

Convention 2a: $(A_2\ A_1)(O_1\ ...\ O_n) \Leftrightarrow (A_2\ u)\ (O_1\ ...\ O_n)\ [(u = A_1)]$ where the variable ' u ' is a PSV.

Thus we shall be able to rewrite (MAMMAL CETACEAN)(FLIPPER) to (MAMMAL u)(FLIPPER) [(u = CETACEAN)]

Convention 2b: $A(O_1\ ...\ O_n) \Leftrightarrow (O_1\ ...\ O_j - 1\ x\ O_j + 1\ ...\ O_n)\ [(x = O_j)]$ where the variable ' x ' is a PAV.

For example, BIGGER-THAN(MOBY-DICK, FLIPPER) can be transformed into BIGGER-THAN(x, FLIPPER) [(x = MOBY-DICK)].

Convention 3: $A(O_1\ ...\ O_n) \Leftrightarrow (A\ u)(O_1\ ...\ O_n)$ where the variable ' u ' is an uninstantiated PSV and A is an n-ary predicate which is not a leaf in a taxonomy.

So we can have (MAMMAL u)(FLIPPER) resulting from MAMMAL(FLIPPER).

2.1.2 Using Tentative Generalization Variables in the expressions to be generalized

To bring several expressions into structural matching, the generalization algorithm at each stage chooses a constant in each of the expressions, making sure that these constants play similar roles in each of these expressions.

In order to do this, it takes an expression E_i to generalize and chooses a constant in it which is to be replaced by a Tentative Generalization Variable.

For each occurrence in a predicate P_{ij} where this Tentative Generalization Variable appears, the algorithm proceeds to the other expressions E_k (k $\neq$ i), and seeks in them the occurrences in the predicates Q_{kl} which can be brought into structural correspondence with P_{ij}. These occurrences belong to predicates which have the same associated taxonomy as the occurrences of P_{ij}.

Note that in order to determine the occurrences of the predicates Q_{kl} which can be matched with P_{ij}, the system must take into account the axioms (as we shall see in section 2.3). By using heuristics which will not be spelled out here, a constant is chosen in each of the other examples. The choice criteria taken into account are bound up with the number of occurrences shared by the predicates, or with the number of occurrences which are structurally identical with those of the constant that has just been variablized. Once these constants have been chosen, the algorithm variablizes them in each of the examples which have the same Tentative Generalization Variable.

After that, it eliminates the structural differences between the atoms in each of the examples where the Tentative Generalization Variable appears.

Example 3.

E_1: *DOLPHIN(FLIPPER) & MAMMAL(MOBY-DICK) & BIGGER-THAN(MOBY-DICK, FLIPPER)*
E_2: *WHALE(JONAS) & WHALE(MOBY-DICK) & BIGGER-THAN(MOBY-DICK, KIKI)*

Suppose that, in E_1, the generalization algorithm decides to replace the constant ' FLIPPER ' appearing in DOLPHIN(FLIPPER) by a PAV, ' x '.
We shall then have:

E_{1a}: *DOLPHIN(x) & MAMMAL(MOBY-DICK) & BIGGER-THAN(MOBY-DICK, x)*
  [(x = FLIPPER)]

The algorithm now searches for all the elements which can be matched with DOLPHIN(x). These elements are WHALE(JONAS) and WHALE(MOBY-DICK), since WHALE has the same associated taxonomy and the same arity as ' DOLPHIN ' . Even by using the axioms no other elements can be made to appear in E_2 which are matchable with DOLPHIN(x).

Using heuristics, the algorithm decides to match DOLPHIN(x) with WHALE(JONAS). So the constant ' JONAS ' is replaced by the PAV ' x ' in E_2, which is rewritten:

E_{2a}: *WHALE(x) & WHALE(MOBY-DICK) & BIGGER-THAN(MOBY-DICK, KIKI)*
  [(x = JONAS)]

The algorithm now has to wipe out the structural difference between DOLPHIN and WHALE, by showing up their common ancestor and then by variablizing all that distinguishes them. This mechanism has already been explained in chapter 6, section 7 under the name of "climbing the generalization tree".

E_{1b}: *(CETACEAN u_2 u_1)(x) & MAMMAL(MOBY-DICK) & BIGGER-THAN(MOBY-DICK, x)*
  [(x = FLIPPER) (u_1 = DOLPHIN) (u_2 = DENTICETE)]
E_{2b}: *(CETACEAN u_2 u_1)(x) & WHALE(MOBY-DICK) & BIGGER-THAN(MOBY-DICK, KIKI)*
  [(x = JONAS) (u_1 = WHALE) (u_2 = MYSTICETE)]

The first element is the same in E_{1b} and E_{2b} (apart from the instances of the Tentative Generalization Variables). Given that the PAV ' x ' appears as an argument of ' BIGGER-THAN ' in E_{1b}, the system searches for what can be made to correspond with this predicate in E_{2b}. Only BIGGER-THAN(MOBY-DICK, KIKI) can be made to match with BIGGER-THAN(MOBY-DICK, x). So the aim now is to wipe out the structural differences between these two elements. In E_{2b}, ' x ' is instantiated by ' JONAS '. As we assume that individuals with different names are distinct (JONAS and KIKI are two distinct individuals), it is necessary to introduce another PAV, to be instantiated by ' x ' in E_1 and by ' KIKI ' in E_2.

E_{1c}: *(CETACEAN u_2 u_1)(x) & MAMMAL(MOBY-DICK) & BIGGER-THAN(MOBY-DICK, y)*
  [(x = FLIPPER) (u_1 = DOLPHIN) (u_2 = DENTICETE) (y = x) (y = FLIPPER)]
E_{2c}: *(CETACEAN u_2 u_1)(x) & WHALE(MOBY-DICK) & BIGGER-THAN(MOBY-DICK, y)*
  [(x = JONAS) (u_1 = WHALE) (u_2 = MYSTICETE) (y = KIKI)]

The algorithm then introduces a PAV instantiated by ' MOBY-DICK ', to bring the last elements of the two expressions into structural correspondence. This goes against our intuition, since the two elements are equal. In section 2.3 it will be seen that inappropriately introduced variables are to be eliminated.

E_{1d}: (CETACEAN u_2 u_1)(x) & MAMMAL(z) & BIGGER-THAN(z, y)
[(x = FLIPPER) (u_1 = DOLPHIN) (u_2 = DENTICETE) (y = x)
(y = FLIPPER) (z = MOBY-DICK)]
E_{2d}: (CETACEAN u_2 u_1)(x) & WHALE(z) & BIGGER-THAN(z, y)
[(x = JONAS) (u_1 = WHALE) (u_2 = MYSTICETE) (y = KIKI) (z = MOBY-DICK)]

The structural differences between the BIGGER-THAN predicates of E_{1d} and E_{2d} have been eliminated. Since MAMMAL(z) does not appear in E_{2d}, elements which can be matched with this predicate are to be sought in this expression. We find WHALE(z). So finally these atoms are replaced by their common ancestor, which is ' MAMMAL ' .

E_{1e}: (CETACEAN u_2 u_1)(x) & MAMMAL(u_5 u_4 u_3)(z) & BIGGER-THAN(z, y)
[(x = FLIPPER) (u_1 = DOLPHIN) (u_2 = DENTICETE) (y = x)
(y = FLIPPER) (z = MOBY-DICK)]
E_{2e}: (CETACEAN u_2 u_1)(x) & MAMMAL(u_5 u_4 u_3)(z) & BIGGER-THAN(z, y)
[(x = JONAS) (u_1 = WHALE) (u_2 = MYSTICETE) (y = KIKI) (z = MOBY-DICK)
(u_3 = u_1) (u_3 = WHALE) (u_4 = u_2)
(u_4 = MYSTICETE) (u_5 = CETACEAN)]

2.2 Introduction of links

All the links contained in the examples have been deduced on the basis of the examples. Nevertheless, as Michalski has shown [Michalski 1983], there can also be hidden links.

Numerical relations between variables, valid in all examples, can be detected by examining their variation taking them two by two.

Thus, we neglected attempt to detect that the length of the tails of 'MOBY-DICK', ' FLIPPER ' and ' OUM ' varies according to their overall size.

In accordance with these relations, there can be an attempt to introduce new relations between variables.

When two variables vary in the same way in all the examples, we should try to show up a constancy in their relationship. For example, it might perhaps be detected that the ratio of the length of the tail to the body is constant in the cetaceans.

Here, to avoid becoming too lengthy, we shall only add a single type of link, indicating that the instances of two Tentative Generalization Variables are different. In other words, in a given expression, we have (x ≠ y) when no example exists in which ' x ' and ' y ' have the same value.

For example, ' x ' and ' y ' take the value ' FLIPPER ' in E_1; consequently we have (x = y) in the formula expressing E_1.

In E_2, we have x = JONAS and y = KIKI; hence the (x ≠ y) in this formula.

After introducing these these equalities and inequalities the expressions become:

E_{1f}: *(CETACEAN u_2 u_1)(x) & MAMMAL(u_5 u_4 u_3)(z) & BIGGER-THAN(z, y)*
   [(x = FLIPPER) (u_1 = DOLPHIN) (u_2 = DENTICETE) (y = x) (y = FLIPPER)
   (z = MOBY-DICK) (x ≠ z) (y ≠ z)]
E_{2f}: *(CETACEAN u_2 u_1)(x) & MAMMAL(u_5 u_4 u_3)(z) & BIGGER-THAN(z, y)*
   [(x = JONAS) (u_1 = WHALE) (u_2 = MYSTICETE) (y = KIKI) (z = MOBY-DICK)
   (u_3 = u_1) (u_4 = u_2) (u_5 = CETACEAN)
   (x ≠ y) (x ≠ z) (y ≠ z)]

As we have assumed that two constants with different names represent different individuals or predicates, the claim that the Tentative Generalization Variables ' x ' and ' y ' are different is not really inductive, since x = FLIPPER and y = KIKI.

The only links that will be represented explicitly are links (equalities and inequalities) between two Tentative Generalization Variables and links indicating that a Tentative Generalization Variable is instantiated by a constant (equalities between a variable and a constant).

We leave "May-be-the-same" links implicit to respect the traditional convention that for any expression ' f ', f(x, y) is more general than f(x, x).

The equality link is important when VSPs are introduced, because it enables the climbing of the generalization tree to be refined.

Suppose we want to generalize the two examples:

E_{11}: *WHALE(TOTO) & WHALE(TITI)*
E_{12}: *DOLPHIN(NONO) & DOLPHIN(NINI).*

The traditional generalization, which says "there are two cetaceans" , forgets the information that the two cetaceans in each pair are of the same kind. By preserving the links between the variables, we generalize correctly to:
   (CETACEAN u) (x) & (CETACEAN v) (y) [x ≠ y) & (u = v)]

Exercise 22
****

Find another pair of examples of the same type, where the equality u = v is not valid. Establish that they do contain indeed a piece of information similar to the one of the two examples above.

****

2.3 Elimination of the differences

The removal of links and of predicates which are not common to all the examples constitutes the only inductive step in our generalization algorithm. We shall thus obtain the most restrictive generalization possible, in which there will be no disjunction.

The examples
> E_{13}: *DOLPHIN(FLIPPER)*
> E_{14}: *DOLPHIN(OUM)*

will thus be generalized to DOLPHIN(x), whereas the nearest generalization $E_{13} \lor E_{14}$ *is DOLPHIN(x)[(x = FLIPPER) $\lor$ (x = OUM)].*

So this stage is inductive; there is no guarantee that we have not over-generalized. *Similarly, when we generalize DOLPHIN(A) and WHALE(B), we obtain CETACEAN(x), whereas another valid and less strong generalization is: CETACEAN(x) & $\neg$ CACHALOT(x), for example.*

At this stage, the generalization of example 3 becomes
> *G: (CETACEAN u_2 u_1)(x) & MAMMAL(u_5 u_4 u_3)(z) & BIGGER-THAN(z, y)*
> *[(z = MOBY-DICK) (x ≠ z) (y ≠ z)]*

The links concerning u_1, ..., u_5 are eliminated. For instance, in E_{1f} we had (u_3 "May be the same" WHALE) whereas in E_{2f} we had (u_3 = WHALE). These two links are different from each other and consequently dropped.

Only at this moment do the Tentative Generalization Variables x, y, u_1, u_2, u_3, u_4, u_5 become true variables, resulting from generalization.

2.4 Simplification

The equalities present in the links are propagated and the uninstantiated PSVs are eliminated.

We finally obtain the generalization:
> *G': (CETACEAN u_2 u_1)(x) & MAMMAL(MOBY-DICK) & BIGGER-THAN(MOBY-DICK, y)*
> *[(x ≠ MOBY-DICK) (y ≠ MOBY-DICK)]*

Intuitively, we would have been more inclined to prevent MOBY-DICK from being variablized.

Note that this algorithm replaces MOBY-DICK by a PAV in the initial stage, but then, at the end of the process, realizes that the variablization was unnecessary. So this PAV is not a generalization variable.

There will be no illustration here of other simplifications, which go farther than the one described in the above example, which was given only to show how the process functions.

3   USING AXIOMS AND IDEMPOTENCE

Structural matching gives this algorithm its originality.

In contrast with other programs for learning by similarity detection which use the dropping condition rule [Michalski 83], we have tried to "fill in the gaps" (when they exist) between the expressions to be generalized.

Example 4.
E_1: *DOLPHIN(FLIPPER) & GREY(FLIPPER)*
 and
E_2: *DOLPHIN(KIKI) & DOLPHIN(OUM)*

We establish that E_1 has a "gap" in relation to E_2 (' DOLPHIN ' or any other element of E_1 appears in it no more than once) and that E_2 also has a "gap" in relation to E_1 (there is no trace to be found in it of GREY or of any other element of E_1).

By using the dropping condition rule, the system would produce the generalization DOLPHIN(x). The algorithm must seek to reveal a predicate which can correspond to DOLPHIN(KIKI) in E_1, and then a predicate which can correspond to GREY(FLIPPER) in E_1, using the idempotence of & and the axioms. In this case, the idempotence of & enables us to transform E_1 into

E_1': *DOLPHIN(FLIPPER) & DOLPHIN(FLIPPER) & GREY(FLIPPER)*

and the application of axiom Ax_2 of section 1.3 will transform E_2 into

E_2': *DOLPHIN(KIKI) & DOLPHIN(OUM) & COLORED(KIKI)*

Thus the two expressions will correspond with respect to their structures, and they will finally be generalized to DOLPHIN(x) & DOLPHIN(y) & COLORED(x).
Here, ' x ' and ' y ' are two variables which can be instantiated in the same way.

Note that the idempotence of the logical & and the axioms are used only to "fill in the gaps". This makes it possible to carry out the re-writing needed by Structural

Matching. In this way we avoid getting into an infinite loop, and this justifies the convention for equivalences adopted in section 1.3.

When neither idempotence nor the axioms enable us to "fill in a gap" (failure of Structural Matching), the system resorts to using the dropping condition rule during the third stage of the elimination of differences.

4 A DEFINITION OF GENERALIZATION

This section is to be skipped by "theory-haters".

The above algorithm presupposes a new definition of the notion of the generalization of several expressions.

This definition contrasts with the standard definition as given by Vere [Vere 80] in the sense that it does not in an unqualified way admit the dropping condition rule as a valid rule of generalization.

The implicit definition of generalization following from the algorithm we have just described will be called **restricted generalization**.

As we shall see, this definition is compatible with the traditional definition given in logic.

Definition

G is the **restricted generalization** of $E_1, E_2, ..., E_n$ iff $\exists\ \sigma_1, \sigma_2, ..., \sigma_n$ such that
$\forall\ i \in [1, n]$, $E_i =_T \sigma_i\ G$, where $=_T$ designates equality modulo the equational theory which defines the semantics of the domain in which the generalization is carried out.

However, there are cases where this definition is inadequate, even though it enables generalization to be done in the framework of a theory of first- order logic. In particular, it does not enable us to eliminate useless terms, and hence to restrict ourselves to the significant terms. To confront this difficulty, learning theorists such as Vere [Vere 80], Michalski [Michalski 84], Hayes-Roth [Hayes-Roth 78] etc ... have introduced a restricted definition of generalization which confines it to a subset of propositional logic, consisting of conjunctions of atomic propositions.

We are now going to show that it is the role of negative examples to determine whether or not to use the dropping condition rule or the adding conjuncts rule explained in chapter 6.

5   USE OF NEGATIVE EXAMPLES

The generalizations of E can be numerous and there is no knowing which to choose. The quest is for generalizations which allow the positive examples as instances and reject the negative examples.

5.1   Use of the negative examples to "over-generalize" a description

Generalizing examples gives us a description which the examples are instances of. But often this description is very complex, and one would like to be able to simplify it while keeping only the right descriptors.

The negative examples are there to direct this "over-generalization" and test the description.

For example, the generalization algorithm discussed earlier clearly gives a generalization with a simple formula, but there can be many links between its variables. It would be a good idea to simplify them.

The principle adopted is: the useful links in the generalization of the examples are those which enable the negative examples to be refuted. In other words, the negative example is applied to the generalization.
 If it is not in structural correspondence with the generalization, nothing can be deduced except that it is indeed a negative example.
 If it is in structural correspondence with the generalization, we look at the links which are responsible for the negative example 's "failure", and these are the links we keep.

A detailed description of this process will be found in [Kodratoff et al. 1985].

5.2   Disjunctive generalization by the use of negative examples

We have defined a generalization algorithm which enables conjunctive generalized formulae to be obtained. Obviously, however, disjunctions have to appear in some formulae. We claim that one task of the negative examples is to guide us to the disjunctions, as will now be shown.

Assume we have a set E of positive examples and a set NE of negative examples.
 We are seeking a characterization of the positive examples in disjunctive form. By "characterization", we understand a feature which is true for the positive examples and false for the negative examples.

Let P be a feature confirmed for all the negative examples.

Apply P to the positive examples. This then yields a partition of E, $\{P_E, \neg\, P_E\}$, where P_E is the set of positive examples which confirm P and $\neg\, P_E$ is the set of positive examples which do not confirm P.

The positive examples in $\neg\, P_E$ are characterized by the feature $\neg$ P; $\neg$ P is true for $\neg\, P_E$ and false for the negative examples.

It is sufficient to find a feature Q which is true for the the positive examples of P_E and false for the negative examples.

The description of the positive examples which we are looking for is
$$\neg\, P \vee Q$$

The mechanism will be illustrated by the following example, inspired by Michalski's [Michalski 1984] example of the "Eastbound and Westbound Trains".

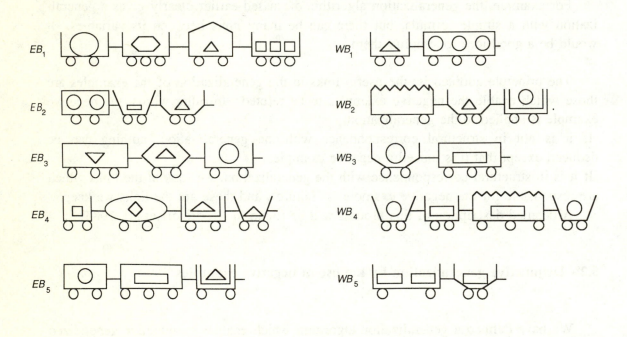

Figure 2

We are trying to generalize the goods transported by each train.

The negative examples here are labelled EB_i and the positive examples are labelled WB_i. Each good is represented by a variable which takes the value 1 if it is in the train, otherwise 0. Thus, x_1 represents the delta Δ, x_2 the circle, x_3 the empty car, x_4 the long rectangle, x_5 the short rectangle, x_6 the square, x_7 the hexagon, x_8 the nabla

∇, and finally x_9 the rhombus.

The table obtained is the following:

	x_1	x_2	x_3	x_4	x_5	x_6	x_7	x_8	x_9
EB_1	1	1	0	0	0	1	1	0	0
EB_2	1	1	0	0	1	0	0	0	0
EB_3	1	1	0	0	0	0	0	1	0
EB_4	1	0	0	0	0	1	0	0	1
EB_5	1	1	0	1	0	0	0	0	0
WB_1	1	1	0	0	0	0	0	0	0
WB_2	1	1	1	0	0	0	0	0	0
WB_3	0	1	0	1	0	0	0	0	0
WB_4	0	1	0	1	1	0	0	0	0
WB_5	0	0	0	0	1	0	0	0	0

The negative examples confirm the features: $x_1 = 1$ & $x_3 = 0$. Looking at the partition of the positive examples generated by

$$P: \quad x_1 = 1$$

It induces a partition of the WBs since WB_1 and WB_2 confirm $x_1 = 1$; WB_3, WB_4 and WB_5 do not confirm it.
It follows that

$$P_E = \{WB_1, WB_2\} \quad and \quad \neg P_E = \{WB_3, WB_4, WB_5\}$$

We are looking for a feature Q confirmed for WB_1 and WB_2 and false for the negative examples.

$$Q: (x_1 = 1) \ \& \ (x_2 = 1) \ \& \ (x_4 = 0) \ \& \ ... \ \& \ (x_9 = 0) \text{ is suitable.}$$

So the characterization of the positive examples is:

$$(x_1) \vee ((x_1 =)1 \ \& \ (x_2 = 1) \ \& \ (x_4 = 0) \ \& \ ... \ \& \ (x_9 = 0))$$

which means that a positive example either contains no delta or contains nothing but a circle and a delta. So a characterization of "Westbound" is
either contains no delta or contains nothing but a circle and a delta.

We could have studied the partition generated by the feature

$$P': x_3 = 0.$$

In this case, no feature Q characterizing the positive examples which confirmed P' would be found.

The roles of the positive and negative examples could be reversed: the result would be a characterization of the negative examples in disjunctive form.

It is a case of learning by clustering: the examples are partitioned into p classes E_1,

$E_2, ..., E_p$, a generalization G_i of the examples of E_i is found and a generalization of the whole set of examples is:

$$G_1 \lor G_2 \lor ... \lor G_p.$$

5.3   Systematic use of the negative examples

Before beginning this slightly difficult section, I wish to tell the reader the origin of these results.

The article in "Machine Learning 2" of which Ganascia and I are the co-authors received Ryszard Michalski as referee. In the first version of this article, we said that if the recognition function is

SPHERE(x) & BLACK(x)

and if the negative example

SPHERE(A) & BLACK(A)

were applied to this function, then "obviously" the modification to be made to the function would be to transform it into

SPHERE(x) & BLACK(y) & (x ≠ y).

Obviously, indeed, this new recognition function is similar to the previous one and now rejects the negative example.

In his comments, Ryszard did not find this obvious and asked why we should not arrive at

SPHERE(x) & BLACK(y) & (x ≠ A) or
SPHERE(x) & BLACK(y) & (y ≠ A)

I found that Ryszard's suggestion diminished the whole point of using the negative examples, and so I undertook to show him that his suggestion was absurd. The result is the theory presented below.

My reason for wanting to tell you this anecdote is that if you read this section, you will see that the conclusion of all this theory is that I was completely wrong, and that the generalization proposed by Ryszard is exactly right!

The examples are given in the form of a logical formula (generally purely conjunctive) which is (again in general) completely instantiated, i.e. it contains no variables. Let us call one of the formulae F(A).

Starting from these examples, we generate a set of existential theorems (in purely conjunctive form) in which some of the constants are replaced by existentially-quantified variables. Let us call such theorems ∃x [F(x)], where ' x ' is of course a vector of variables. If it turns out that one of the theorems implies the others, we shall say we have obtained the best theorem of the set.

If we can prove, within a given universe, that no other theorem can be added to the set (of course a change of universe can invalidate the completeness proof), then we shall say that the set of deducible theorems is complete, and that the best theorem of the set can be deduced from the examples.

The suppression of the existential quantifiers transforms this theorem into a recognition function $F(x)$ which can be TRUE or FALSE, depending on the instantiation of its variables. Using a less formal vocabulary, we talk of values of variables, rather than of instantiations of variables. This is done because the "value" we use is not always a constant; it can also be a function which calculates the required value, and in that case "instantiation" is the right word.

The description by a predicate $P(x)$ of the domain in which this $F(x)$ takes the value TRUE enables us to invent a theorem: $\forall x \ [P(x) \Rightarrow F(x)]$, which may become a rule.

Let us return to the negative examples.

Suppose that, starting from a given set of positive examples, we have obtained the recognition function:
$$F(x, y): BLACK(x) \ \& \ SPHERE(y)$$
Furthermore, suppose that a negative example is given by:
$$NE_1: BLACK(A) \ \& \ SPHERE(A)$$

On the basis of a set of negative examples (which may be reduced to a single element), we can thus deduce existential theorems concerning these negative examples. Let us call this kind of theorem $\exists x \ [NF(x)]$ (recall that we used $\exists x \ [F(x)]$ for the existential theorems deduced from these examples).

As before, our judgment here is that these theorems must be stated in conjunctive form. Otherwise we would have the possibility of finding the disjunction of all the negative examples as a theorem. As in the case of the positive examples, this must be avoided if we want the learning to be able to take place.

From NE_1 we can deduce, for example:

$T_1: BLACK(A) \ \& \ \exists y \ [SPHERE(y)]$
$T_2: \exists x \ [BLACK(x)] \ \& \ \exists y \ [SPHERE(y)]$
$T_3: \exists x \ [BLACK(x) \ \& \ SPHERE(x)]$
$T_4: BLACK(A)$

Paying proper attention to the implications of existential theorems, which are not very familiar, we see that NE_1 implies each T_i, that T_1 implies T_2 and T_4, that T_3 implies T_2, and that no other implications hold between them.
In this case, NE_1 also belongs (trivially) to the set of theorems which can be deduced from NE_1 because just one (negative) example is used.

As in the case of the positive examples, we want to obtain the formula which is "nearest" to the examples. So we try here to obtain the best theorem from the set of those which can be deduced from the ((here) negative) examples.

In this special case, the only (negative) example also belongs to the set of theorems, so that NE_1 is the best.

The positive examples express the fact that such-and-such a feature, common to the positive examples, exists. On the other hand, the negative examples express the fact that none of the examples contains such-and-such a feature. Hence the positive examples must confirm the theorem obtained by negating the one which best expresses the features of the negative examples.

If we choose a more general theorem, calling it T'', which does not imply all the other theorems deducible from the negative examples, then there could be some positive examples (call them x_0) for which:

$$\neg F(x_0) \Rightarrow \neg T''(x_0)$$

even if the correct $NF(x_0)$ is such that

$$[F(x_0) \Rightarrow \neg[NF(x_0)]]$$

From this we conclude that the positive examples enable us to find the recognition functions and that the negative examples enable us to find the theorems which must be negated by all TRUE instances of the recognition function.

If $\exists x \, [NF(x)]$ is the best theorem deduced from the negative examples, then the instances of ' x ' which belong to the positive examples must confirm $\neg \exists x \, [NF(x)]$. In other words, **we have to prove**

$$\forall x \, [F(x) \Rightarrow \neg NF(x)]$$

in order to confirm that the domain of the positive examples does not overlap with the domain of the negative examples.

However, it may happen that they overlap, and we are going to study the consequences of this.

Since the best theorem is NE_1 itself, the theorem which must be confirmed by the examples is $\neg NE_1$, i.e.

$$\neg [BLACK(A) \, \& \, SPHERE(A)]$$

We must try to prove

$$\forall x, y \, [[BLACK(x) \, \& \, SPHERE(y)] \Rightarrow \neg [BLACK(A) \, \& \, SPHERE(A)]]$$

and, of course, we shall fail.

If the proof of $\forall x \, [F(x) \Rightarrow \neg NF(x)]$ succeeds, we shall be able to use this negative example to over-generalize or to find new disjunctive generalizations, like those in sections 5.1 and 5.2 above.

If the proof of $\forall x \ [F(x) \Rightarrow \neg NF(x)]$ fails, this means that the positive examples intersect the negative ones; we must then try to construct a new generalization which implies $\neg \ NF(x)$. We now suggest a method for doing this. It uses an attempt to prove a particular theorem, called Th. The reason for which Th is chosen cannot be understood immediately, and the reader is asked to wait a little before being able to see the interesting results of proving it.

$$\text{Th} : \exists x \ [F(x) \Rightarrow NF(x)]$$

Let us try to prove that
$$\exists x, y \ [[BLACK(x) \ \& \ SPHERE(y)] \Rightarrow [BLACK(A) \ \& \ SPHERE(A)]].$$

5.3.1 First case: Th is false

There can be two reasons for this failure.

- The first is where it can actually be proved that $\forall x \ [F(x) \Rightarrow \neg NF(x)]$

In this situation, the features of the new negative example are indeed different from those of the positive examples; nothing needs to be changed.

- The second is where there is no way of proving either Th or $\forall x \ [F(x) \Rightarrow \neg \ NF(x)]$.

Here we are faced with a total failure from which nothing can be learned. We know nothing except that an important feature of the domain is missing, the one which would make one of the two proofs succeed.

5.3.2 Second case: Th is proved and reduces to the empty clause

We prove it by refutation, by trying to prove that the empty clause can be deduced from $\neg$ Th. As Th is provable, a way will be found, and each success gives us a substitution σ which is an instance of the substitutions to be carried out on x to confirm Th. By doing all the possible proofs in the case where their number is finite, or, in the case where it is infinite, by inventing a function which covers all the cases (this part is not developed here; see Appendix 2) we define the set of x_i such that $F(x_i) \Rightarrow NF(x_i)$. Let us call this set E_i:

$$E_i = \{ \ x_i \ / \ [F(x_i) \Rightarrow NF(x_i)] \}.$$

You can see now that the only purpose of Th is to serve to define the domain E_i.

****

A property of Th. One has:
$$\forall x \ [[F(x) \ \& \ \neg[x \in E_i]] \Rightarrow \neg \ NF(x)].$$
In other words, we have found the modification of F(x) we were looking for: No negative example confirms $[F(x) \ \& \ \neg[x \in E_i]]$.

Proof:

Since x belongs to the set for which the implication $F(x_i) \Rightarrow NF(x_i)$ is FALSE, we can conclude that NF(x) is FALSE in all the cases where F(x) is TRUE.

****

To prove
$$\exists x \; \exists y \; [[BLACK(x) \& SPHERE(y)] \Rightarrow [BLACK(A) \& SPHERE(A)]]$$
We try to derive the empty clause from its negation ¬Th. As usual, [Kowalski 1979] the theorem is transformed into clauses as follows (see section 1.2 of Chapter 2).

$$\neg \; \exists x \; \exists y \; [[BLACK(x) \& SPHERE(y)] \Rightarrow [BLACK(A) \& SPHERE(A)]] =$$
$$\neg \; \exists x \; \exists y \; [\neg \; [BLACK(x) \& SPHERE(y)] \lor [BLACK(A) \& SPHERE(A)]] =$$
$$\forall x \; \forall y \; [[BLACK(x) \& SPHERE(y)] \& \neg[BLACK(A) \& SPHERE(A)]]$$

So it is equivalent to the set of clauses

BLACK(x)	:-	
SPHERE(y)	:-	
	:-	BLACK(A), SPHERE(A)

This set generates the empty clause just once, with the substitution
$$\sigma = \{ \; x \leftarrow A, y \leftarrow A \; \}.$$
So the set $\{x = A, y = A\} = E_i$ is the set for which Th is valid. As was proved above, the conjunction of $\neg \; [(x = A) \& (y = A)]$ with BLACK(x) & SPHERE(y) will yield the generalization we are looking for:
$$[BLACK(x) \& SPHERE(y)] \& [(x \neq A) \lor (y \neq A)]$$
which is the result of our method.

It is the generalization which retains as much as possible of what has been deduced from the positive examples and which excludes the negative examples.

It is clear from this that the information deducible from a single negative example cannot be too subtle.

Bear in mind that this is the best specialization that can be drawn from negative examples. Trying to deduce a more general rule could result in over-generalization and the loss of essential information.

For another example, consider the case where several negative examples are available.

In the case where the following negative example is added
$$NE_2: BLACK(A) \& SPHERE(D)$$
then the generalization based on f(x, y), NE_1 and NE_2, in accordance with our method, must be
$$[BLACK(x) \& SPHERE(y) \& (x \neq A)]$$

Consider now the case where one provides NE_1 and, instead of NE_2, the additional

negative example:
$$NE_3 = BLACK(B) \ \& \ SPHERE(B)$$

The theorem to be deduced on the basis of NE_1 and NE_3 is
$$\exists x \ [BLACK(x) \ \& \ SPHERE(x)].$$
In this case, Th is
$$\exists x, y \ [[BLACK(x) \ \& \ SPHERE(y)] \Rightarrow [BLACK(x) \ \& \ SPHERE(x)]]$$
which is TRUE just for the substitution $\{y \leftarrow x\}$; thus E_i is characterized by $x = y$ and we have $\neg \ [x \in E_i]$ if $x \neq y$. It follows that the right generalization in this case is
$$[BLACK(x) \ \& \ SPHERE(y) \ \& \ (x \neq y)]$$

5.3.3 Third case: Th is proved but does not reduce to the empty clause

Since we assume that we are using resolution to deduce the empty clause from ¬Th, it follows that a subset of clauses remains which do not reduce to the empty clause. Let us call this set R(x) (remainder).

We assume here that R(x) is unique. The case where it is not is still a matter for research.

Let us consider the expression F(x) & ¬ R(x) and let us try to prove
$$Th' : \exists x \ [[F(x) \ \& \ \neg R(x)] \Rightarrow NF(x)]$$
Its negation is
$$\forall x \ [F(x) \ \& \ \neg R(x) \ \& \ \neg NF(x)]$$
which can be converted into three clauses:

    F(x) :-
    :- R(x)
    :- NF(x)

and, as R(x) is nothing but the remainder from the resolution of $\forall x \ [F(x) \ \& \ \neg NF(x)]$, i.e. from the clauses   F(x) :- and   :- NF(x).

Now let the set of values which confirm Th' be called E_i.

To draw a conclusion from the foregoing reasoning, R must be looked at more closely. In view of the conjunctive form of the theorem
$$\forall x \ [F(x) \ \& \ \neg R(x) \ \& \ \neg NF(x)],$$
we can always suppose that each clause either contains atoms which originate exclusively from F(x) (say, R'(x)) or atoms which originate exclusively from NF(x) (say, NR'(x)). It follows that R(x) has the form :
$$R'(x) \ \& \ \neg NR'(x).$$
Finally, one obtains
$$F(x) = F'(x) \ \& \ R'(x) \text{ and } NF(x) = NF'(x) \ \& \ R''(x).$$

During the proof of Th', R' resolves some predicates of ¬ NF and ¬ NR' resolves some predicates of F.

It follows that, on the basis of the proofs of

$$\exists x \, [[F(x) \, \& \, \neg R(x)] \Rightarrow NF(x)],$$
we can construct a domain E_i in the way shown above and prove that
$$\forall x \, [[F'(x) \, \& \, \neg[x \in E_i]] \Rightarrow \neg NF'(x)]$$
by the same reasoning as was given above.

Let us now use the two following tautologies

from $A \Rightarrow C$, it can be deduced that $A \, \& \, B \Rightarrow C$

from $A \Rightarrow C$, it can be deduced that $A \, \& \, D \Rightarrow C \vee D$

to find that
$$\forall x \, [[F(x) \, \& \, \neg[x \in E_i] \, \& \, \neg R''(x)] \Rightarrow \neg NF(x)]$$
which is the interesting form we wanted to construct.

5.3.4 The general form

The final definition which we can now give of the best formula that can be deduced from the formula $F(x)$ together with the negative examples generalizing to $NF(x)$ is:

$$[F(x) \, \& \, \neg R''(x) \, \& \, \neg[x \in E_i]]$$

This is the right recognition function.

Two simple examples will now be described, showing that our definitions correspond to the well-known behavior of intuitive learning when the negative and positive examples do not match over one predicate.

First case:

The generalization based on the positive examples contains more predicates than the negative example.

Let $F(x) = BLACK(x) \, \& \, SPHERE(y)$ and let $BLACK(A)$ be the negative example.
The attempt to prove
$$\exists x \, \exists y \, [[BLACK(x) \, \& \, SPHERE(y)] \Rightarrow BLACK(A)] \; \text{succeeds with } R =$$
SPHERE(y).
We replace $F(x)$ by $F(x) \, \& \, \neg R'$, and attempt to find a non-trivial proof to
$$\exists x \, \exists y \, [[BLACK(x) \, \& \, SPHERE(y) \, \& \, \neg SPHERE(y)] \Rightarrow BLACK(A)]$$
The trivial proof would be that FALSE implies anything, therefore one must attempt to prove $\neg \exists x, y \, [BLACK(x) \Rightarrow BLACK(A)]$. Substitution $\{x \leftarrow A\}$ describes the domain where this expression is not valid. One therefore has to add it to the initial generalization.
We find that the best generalization is
$$[BLACK(x) \, \& \, SPHERE(y) \, \& \, (x \neq A)]$$

Second case:

The generalization based on the positive examples contains fewer predicates than the negative example.

Let BLACK(x) be the generalization based on the positive examples and SPHERE(A) & BLACK(A) the negative example.

The remainder is ¬ SPHERE(A) = ¬ NR', whose conjunction with BLACK(x) enables us to find the empty clause with {x ← A}.

Consequently, the best recognition function is

[BLACK(x) & SPHERE(A) & (x ≠ A)]

CONCLUSION

Chapters 8 and 9 describe what has been called "Similarity-Based Learning" in which one learns the similarities among a set of positive examples, but also the dissimilarities between them from a set a negative examples.

We have stressed the difference between the "empirical" and the "rational" approaches. The empirical one is based on Michalski's work and the rational one is based on our work at Orsay. The aim of our presentation is to teach ML simply and not to describe how we worked on it, so notice that the difference between the approaches has been over-emphasized.

Nevertheless, other people are pushing the rational approach farther, and increasing the element of theorem-proving in it. This attempt at making generalization (an essentially inductive process) more deductive is due to young new-comers in the field of ML in Australia and in France.

Techniques known as Statistics must not be confused with those that are here being called "numeric". The methods of statistical analysis will not be touched on here, except to say that they spring from Applied Mathematics and that they are still completely independent of ML.

On the other hand numeric methods, which in fact are what is called "Clustering Analysis", can be and are used in ML. But with a specific view to ML applications and independently of Clustering Analysis, Quinlan has introduced a numeric approach involving a measure of the amount of information contained in each descriptor.

In this chapter, both these approaches will be described.

1 A MEASURE OF THE AMOUNT OF INFORMATION ASSOCIATED WITH EACH DESCRIPTOR

This is Quinlan's method.

The example to be used now is drawn from an article by Quinlan in the first volume of the book *Machine Learning*. It was chosen by Quinlan to illustrate his numeric method for creating efficient classification procedures, and we shall show how this same example can be used to illustrate the symbolic method.

1.1 Description of the example

The examples available illustrate two different concepts called concept A and concept B, and presented as follows.

CONCEPT A			CONCEPT B		
size	nationality	family	size	nationality	family
small	German	single	small	Italian	single
large	French	single	large	German	married
large	German	single	large	Italian	single
			large	Italian	married
			small	German	married

Table 1.

So there are 3 examples of concept A and 5 examples of concept B, and the problem is to find a method enabling concept A to be efficiently differentiated from concept B.

One possible method consists in first of all asking the question: What is the value of nationality? In this way we obtain the clustering below.

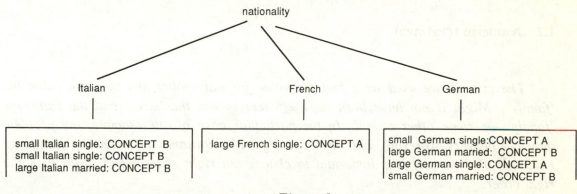

Figure 1.

It will be seen that the nationality criterion selects only concept B for Italian nationality and only concept A for French nationality, but that concepts remain mixed with respect to German nationality. So in order to discriminate these two concepts completely we are obliged to use a further criterion. Trying that of the value for 'family', we obtain the clustering below.

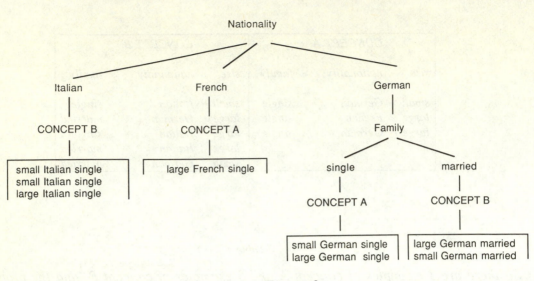

Figure 2.

This shows that if we choose to test firstly the value for 'nationality' and secondly the value for 'family', then the two-level discrimination tree presented above enables us to distinguish concepts A and B with certainty.

1.2 Numeric treatment

The criteria we used were first the value for nationality and then the value for 'family'. Might it not have been more efficient to use the 'size' and the value for 'family', or some other order? In the particular case of our example, the problem may not be very worrying, but when dealing with thousands of examples describing hundreds of concepts, it is important to choose the right criteria and to do it in the right order.

At the beginning the examples are mixed and 3 out of a total of 8 describe concept A while 5 out of 8 describe concept B. We shall estimate the initial disorder by the pair (3/8, 5/8). In reality, researchers use a more complicated measure which is connected with information theory and which will not be described here because it would make no difference to the nature of the reasoning.

Our goal is to arrive at perfectly sorted clusters as in Figure 2. In this figure, the terminal clusters are perfectly sorted, which is marked by the fact that their disorder is (0, 1) (for clusters that contain only samples of concept B) or (1, 0) (for clusters that contain only samples of concepts A). For example, in the first cluster on the left there are three examples of concept B out of three members of the cluster and no examples of concept A, therefore the disorder is (0, 3/3) which reduces to (0, 1).

We are going to estimate the efficiency of a criterion by the distance between the values of the initial pairs and the values of those obtained after applying the criterion.

Taking the criterion of nationality, section 1.1 shows that we obtain three clusters whose value pairs are: (0, 1), (1, 0) (1/2, 1/2).

If we applied the 'size' criterion first, we would separate the examples into two *clusters. One of them, containing the examples whose 'size' is small, has 1 example of concept A and two examples of concept B, so its value pair is (1/3, 2/3). The other, containing the examples whose 'size' is 'large' has two examples of concept A and two examples of concept B, so its value pair is (2/5, 3/5). Note that the gain in comparison with the initial values (3/8, 5/8) is very slight in each cluster, in any case less significant than when the nationality is the first criterion chosen.*

If we applied the criterion of the value for 'family' first, we would separate the examples into two clusters. One of them, containing the examples whose value for 'family' is 'single', has three examples of concept A and two examples of concept B, so its value pair is (3/5, 2/5). The other, for which the value for 'family' is 'married', has zero examples of concept A and three examples of concept B, so it gives (0, 1). So it does matter much whether the first criterion to be applied is the value for 'family' or the value for nationality; the precise calculation shows an advantage of about 10 per cent for putting the test for nationality first.

The numeric method consists in iterating this process on the clusters and choosing the set of criteria which lead to the best value.

Quinlan applies this method in the article mentioned to chess end-games with white king and rook against black king and knight.

The criteria to be chosen describe the respective positions of the pieces on the chess-board, for example: white rook is more than two spaces from the black king.

Of course, the problem of discovering these criteria remains untouched; but it can be seen, nevertheless, that this enables the most useful criteria to be chosen.

At a subsequent stage, Quinlan used higher-level descriptors, which recognize "situations" as being an attribute, for more details, one must see Quinlan's paper in Machine learning, volume 1, but also his paper in the first issue of the new journal "Machine Learning".

The principle we have just described has been applied to other cases and constitutes the heart of a commercial learning system. Measures of the statistical value of a classification have been added to this system, making it less sensitive to noise.

1.3 Symbolic treatment

The question being asked is no longer which is the most efficient but which is the most significant. Do some attributes have more significance than others?

The measure used is no longer the relative number of examples sorted by a criterion, but the similarity between formulae describing the examples.

Looking at concept B, we notice that none of the attributes, neither that of 'nationality', nor that of 'family', nor that of 'size' take a constant value for all the examples. Either the attributes describing concept B are badly chosen or "concept B" in actual fact covers several different concepts.

Looking at concept A, it is clear that the examples all have their value for the attribute 'family' in common, viz. 'single'. It can be concluded that this attribute is significant and describes concept A. Now it would be a good idea to also distinguish the 'single' examples of A from those of B which are also 'single'. To do this, B will be divided into two clusters: those which are 'single' and those which are not, as shown below:

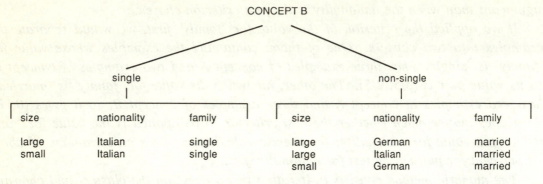

Figure 3.

The 'single' criterion can already serve to recognize all the members of concept A and reject all those of concept B whose value for 'family' is 'married'. So we shall try to see if the members of concept B display some common characteristic enabling them to be distinguished from those of concept A. The above clustering makes it immediately clear that their 'nationality' is Italian and that by contrast none of the members of concept A (refer to Table 1.) have Italian 'nationality'. It follows from this that the criterion 'single' and 'non-Italian' enables concept A to be recognized uniquely and is not true for any of the members of concept B.

Note that we have "invented" a concept - admittedly unspectacular in an example made to illustrate numeric learning - while relying only on explicit knowledge.

Now that this concept has been invented we accept that the descriptors used had a meaning, and so we begin setting ourselves the question of the efficiency of our criterion. Quinlan's analysis shows that it is worth using the 'nationality' attribute first, of course, but our analysis has shown that a significant notion corresponding to the descriptors used was indeed there, hidden in the definition of concepts A and B.

2 APPLICATION OF DATA ANALYSIS

2.1 Simplified description of the methods of Clustering Analysis

2.1.1 Items

By way of support for the imagination, suppose that we wish to use Data Analysis for Pattern Recognition. An "item" is then one of the patterns we wish to recognize.

There are two representations of a pattern, on the one hand a name, and on the other hand an internal representation which describes the values taken by certain parameters for the given item. This last is the representation we are going to look into.

Thus the item X_i is characterized by n values of these parameters: x_{i1}, x_{i2}, ..., x_{in}.

Let X be the domain of the x_{ij}. This is the item space.

We say that x_{ij} is the value of a variable Y_j associated with the jth parameter.

We say each x_{ij} corresponds to an observation carried out for each of the parameters describing the item X_i. So in this case, we have assumed that there were n observations.

When working on, say, m items at once, we thus obtain a list of n values for each of them, given that we have a list of n variables.

Thus, a table of dimensions n*m will reproduce the results of the n observations performed on m items.

	Y_1	Y_2		Y_j	...	Y_n
X_1	x_{11}	x_{12}	...	x_{1j}	...	x_{1n}
X_2	x_{21}	...				x_{2n}
...						
X_i	x_{i1}	...				x_{in}
...						
X_m	x_{m1}	...		x_{mj}	...	x_{mn}

2.1.2 Distances and measures of similarity

A **distance** between two items X_i and X_q is defined as a function ' d ' of X *cross* X in the positive reals having the properties of

(1) reflexivity: d(i, i) = 0

(2) symmetry: d(i, q) = d(q, i)

(3) triangular inequality: d(i, q) ≤ d(i, p) + d(p, q) where i, q, have been written for X_i, X_q respectively.

A **dissimilarity measure** satisfies (1) and (2) only.

A **similarity measure** 's' only satisfies (2) and (1'):

(1') : r(i, i) = r(q, q) > r(i, q).

An **ultrametric distance** satisfies (1) and (2) and, instead of (3):

(3') : δ(i, q) ≤ SUP (δ(i, p), δ(p, q)).

A large number of dissimilarity measures have been proposed; for example, that due to the Shebyshev metric:

$$d\ (X_i, X_q) = MAX_j\ \text{ABS}(x_{ij} - x_{qj}).$$

Here too is Kendall's measure which uses an intermediate function

$$\Delta_{jk}^i = 1 \text{ if } x_{ij} > x_{ik},$$
$$= -1 \text{ if } x_{ij} < x_{ik},$$
$$= 0 \text{ if } x_{ij} = x_{ik}.$$

This functions allows to define the distance : $d(X_i, X_q) = 1 - 2/(n(n-1)) * \Sigma_{j<k}\ \Delta_{jk}^q\ *\Delta_{jk}^i.$

Others will be found in the specialized literature [Diday & Al. 1982].

2.1.3 Clusterings

A **partition** of a set E is a set of disjoint subsets of E covering E.

A **clustering** is a partition P of a set E of m objects $\{X_i\}$, obtained by using a similarity measure.

Let P be a clustering and let P_r be one of its elements, which will from now on be called a cluster. P_r is called **homogeneous** when for each pair of items (X_i, X_j) of P_r and for each X_k not belonging to P_r, we have :

$$d(X_i, X_j) \leq d(X_i, X_k), \text{ and }\ d(X_i, X_j) \leq d(X_j, X_k).$$

When this property is exhibited by any cluster of a clustering, two items of the same cluster are closer to each other than to any other item not belonging to this cluster.

This property is desirable but rarely exhibited by the distances in general use. This problem is solved by defining, for each distance ' d ' an associated ultrametric δ such that δ exhibits the property of homogeneity.

The usefulness of all the notions defined above is that they enable us to give conditions for building "clean" hierarchies (whose links are free both of inversions and intersections): a homogeneous clustering can be visualized in the form of such a hierarchy.

To do this, it must also be remembered that a hierarchy is called an indexed hierarchy when the depth of each node in the hierarchy is measured by a function f which is monotonic at every level.

Thus, the following theorem can be set out: There exists a bijection between the set of ultrametrics and the set of indexed hierarchies.

2.1.4 Clustering algorithms

Many ways of carrying out the clustering exist, depending on the number of clusters required and on whether the preferred results are "strings" or "blotches".

Generally speaking, the problem is solved as follows: a distance ' d ' is defined between any two elements x and y, and a distance δ between any element x and any class of elements C.

Then the growth of strings will be promoted by defining
$$\delta(x, C) = MIN_{y \in C} \, d(x, y)$$
and that of blotches by defining
$$\delta(x, C) = MAX_{y \in C} \, d(x, y)$$

By way of example, here are two algorithms whose only claim is that they are simple to understand.

First algorithm : Clustering algorithm generating strings

Take a number of the closer neighbors, on the basis of which a maximum measure of membership of the cluster is to be defined.

Begin at a point (chosen at random, for example) and search for its 4 nearest neighbors.

Measure the six distances between the neighbors and define a maximum distance for membership by the average of these six distances. Let D be this value.

Return to the starting-point and apply the following algorithm recursively.

For the current point, calculate its distance ' d ' from its closest neighbor.

If d < D, then incorporate the closest neighbor into the cluster being calculated, and make it the current point.

If d > D, then the calculation of this cluster is terminated. Choose a new current point to calculate the next cluster.

Second Algorithm : Clustering algorithm generating blotches

It is similar to the previous one, except that one has to first choose a distance from a cluster of points to a point.

The new current point, chosen in step with the building of the cluster, is not the one which is nearest to its predecessor, but the one which is closest to the cluster already built.

Example.
Suppose that we wish to incorporate 4 points A, B, C and D, arranged as follows:

$$D$$

$$B \qquad C$$

$$A$$

and whose Euclidean distances are d(A, B) = 1; d(B, C) = 1.3; d(B, D) = 1.2; d(A, D) = 2.2; d(A, C) = 1.64.

Suppose that 'A' and 'B' are already incorporated and that the question is whether 'D' or 'C' should be the next point to be put in the cluster.

If we use an algorithm for strings then 'D', of course, is the one to be incorporated.

If we use a distance for blotches, for example the arithmetic mean of the distances between the points in the blotch the 'C' will be the point incorporated, since d(A, D) + d(B, D) = 3.4, but d(A, C) + d(B, C) = 2.94.

2.1.5 Hierarchies

Let E be a set of objects $\{X_1, ..., X_m\}$. Let P(E) be the set of subsets of E. $H \subset P(E)$ is said to be a **hierarchy** iff

(1) $E \in H$

(2) $X_i \in H$

(3) If h, h' $\in$ H then we have one of the following alternatives

(3.1) either h $\cap$ h' = $\varnothing$

(3.2) or, either h $\subset$ h' or h' $\subset$ h.

In other words, in a hierarchy the clusters are all disjoint.

In Artificial Intelligence, the noun "hierarchy" often (especially among English-speakers) stands for a less precise notion called tangled hierarchy, in which the clusters are not necessarily disjoint.

These two notions do satisfy (1), (2) and (3.1), but (3.2) becomes

(3.2') or, h $\cap$ h' $\in$ H.

This is all that is required of a tangled hierarchy where a child can have any number of parents.

A **pyramid**, for which each child is required to have at most two parents, additionally satisfies

(4) - There exists an order O on E compatible with H.

This means that if ' d ' is the distance on E associated with H, an order O exists on E such that if x_i, x_j and x_k are in this order with respect to O, then $d(x_i, x_k)$ = MAX$\{d(x_i, x_j), d(x_j, x_k)\}$.

An advantage of pyramids is that they always have a graphic representation without intersection of edges.

To build a hierarchy, we take a distance which is used iteratively to do clusterings. At each step we confine ourselves to the items in one cluster as possible candidates for subsequent clusterings.

2.2 Application to learning

Obviously this kind of technique constitutes a possible method for learning, since it enables clusterings of the data to be carried out.

Suppose, for example, that we wanted to recognize printed characters. Beginning with a set of characters, we can first transform it into a table like that of the n measurements on m items. In this case, we can have m = 26. The number of measurements n is given by the number of parameters describing the letters, such as:

number of horizontal segments, number of vertical segments, number of diagonal segments, number of points where there are curves, etc...

A clustering algorithm is then applied to these data. The clusters thus obtained reflect the letters which resemble each other the most and which must be distinguished in the last instance. Each cluster's common parameters which are not shared with other clusters will serve to distinguish the clusters from each other.

Exercise 23
****

Choose some letters and descriptors. Apply a clustering algorithm similar to those given above. Build the associated recognition tree. Analyze the "learning" achieved.

This exercise was the exam problem for the Orsay University Computer Science Department's "Learning" course in 1985-6. About ten different solutions were put forward by the students.

****

3 CONCEPTUAL CLUSTERING

Michalski gave a good introduction to this problem with the following example, shown as figure 1 in chapter 1. Looking at this figure, what ought we to recognize: two circles or two parts of a moon face to face?

The notion of a circle is such a strong one for humans that they have some difficulty in seeing anything other than two circles in this drawing.

To analyze this drawing, suppose we use a "curve follower" which begins, say, at the lowest point on the left-hand shape and starts moving toward the right. So when it comes to a junction, it has to ask itself whether to continue along the left-hand curve or the right-hand curve, as shown in the figure. This depends on how it chooses its way.

Suppose first that the algorithm for following curves says: if a choice has to be made, trace the tangent T to the curve already followed, then continue along the curve which is also at a tangent to T. Then this algorithm has to recognize two circles, as we do.

Suppose now that algorithm chooses instead to follow the curve which causes the greatest variations in the derivative, i.e. the most angular curve possible, then this other algorithm has to recognize two moons face to face.

This example clearly shows that symbolic recognition can depend on numeric factors, it being well understood that the choice between maximizing and minimizing variations in the derivative is a symbolic choice which can also be expressed as the choice between the detection of angular shapes and rounded shapes.

The way we have just followed in our analysis of this example clearly shows the power of numeric methods of Clustering Analysis, and their ability to take account, in a roundabout way, of symbolic factors.

This section must now turn to the problem of the direct use of symbolic knowledge to help with Clustering Analysis.

In the case of the example above, we might also use methods inspired by Gestalt theory. We would then start off by taking an ordered series of shapes to be recognized, if necessary by filling in some lines, and only after this would an algorithm for following outlines be used.

The corresponding algorithm would contain a series of definitions of, say, squares, circles, rectangles, ellipses, rhombuses, etc ..., then of angular shapes etc ... which the system would try to recognize first, before using an algorithm for following curves. By applying this algorithm to the drawing of the two circles, we would find that its content offers no possibility of recognizing squares (for example) because it does not have any angles; of course, the circles would be recognized.

More generally, numeric methods can indeed take account of a piece of semantic information by "concealing" it in a distance or a choice criterion. But in general, semantics is not one of the parameters that they use.

It is desirable to be able to use a Clustering Analysis algorithm which includes semantic information in the form of a parameter. This is one of the aims of the approach described in this section.

There is another aim too, which is harder to communicate.

Suppose that a classification algorithm clusters certain examples together. The algorithm has "reasons" for carrying out this clustering, of course, but these reasons depend on statistical concepts such as variance, which do not automatically belong to the knowledge of the domain expert who has to interpret the system's results. So it is important that the reasons for the clusterings should be explained to these experts in their own vocabulary. This requires the classification algorithm to be capable of carrying out meaningful clusterings in the expert's vocabulary.

There is something which makes the examples picked out by the expert describable in terms of his vocabulary. Finding this something is precisely the goal of conceptual generalization, as explained in chapters 6 and 7.

Thus our suggestion is to apply these conceptual generalization algorithms to the clusterings carried out by the classification algorithm in order to find the "explanation" for these clusterings.

This will enable us to talk better with the expert.

Finally (and this is the subject of the following sections) we also want to be able to favor the clustering of those examples whose generalized description is interesting to the expert. This requires us to include a kind of "forecast" in the generalization algorithm, or rather, to include a sort of estimation of the "value" of the conceptual generalization that will be obtained by doing one clustering rather than another. Of course, it is always difficult to estimate the result of a process like this before it has been executed. Let us now see how this is possible, without ever having the formal assurance that the result will be the best.

3.1 Similarity and good generalization of examples

In principle, when examples are clustered for good reasons, it ought to be possible to find a recognition function for this clustering, expressed by these very reasons.

One of the characteristics of numeric Clustering Analysis is that it does not respect this principle. In a sense, this is one of its strengths, enabling it to suggest descriptors to the expert which he had not suspected.

As we said, this is not our goal here; we want to describe the data in the actual language of the expert and not to suggest ways of increasing his vocabulary to him.

If we happen to discover a category he did not know, then we see our role as being to explain the significance of that category to him in his vocabulary.

Thus we wish to cluster together those examples which have a "good" common description, i.e. one which relies on features which, when conjoined, supply good explanations to the user.

In the absence of semantic knowledge showing which are the best descriptors to cluster in a recognition function, we can try to maximize the number of common descriptors.

The idea of using a generalization algorithm to do this job may spring immediately to mind. It would indeed be possible to try all the possible generalizations of all the examples, two by two, three by three, ..., n by n, and to see which are the clusterings which give the best generalization.

The problem with this method is that any generalization algorithm is extremely expensive for time. Even a much lesser combinatorial undertaking would be unmanageable.

Another argument is that often the generalization of a given set of examples is not unique. So in addition there would have to be a search for all possible generalizations of all possible clusterings. Clearly the problem needs to be simplified in order to make it manageable.

This is what we are now going to do by defining an assessment criterion for the value of future generalization of a clustering.

This criterion will enable us to perform a rapid assessment of the worthwhileness of incorporating an example into an already existing clustering.

Let $\{E_p\}$ be a clustering already found. Let E_i and E_j be two examples not belonging to $\{E_p\}$.

Now we shall say that the clustering of $\{E_p\}$ with E_i is **more promising** than the clustering of $\{E_p\}$ with E_j when the number of descriptors in common between $\{E_p\}$ and E_i is bigger than the number of descriptors in common between $\{E_p\}$ and E_j.

To evaluate this definition in practice, we are going to define a similarity vector between examples, then extend it into a similarity vector between a cluster and an example.

This will be done in three stages:
1 - digitalization of the examples
2 - similarity over the common parts
3 - similarity over the residual parts.
These stages are to be illustrated as we go through the following example.

Suppose we were starting with the following two examples.

E_1: FRENCHMAN(Claude) & ENGLISHMAN(Mike) & ALGERIAN(Fahrid) & ENGLISHMAN(Steve) & FRENCHMAN(Gilles)
E_2: SWISS(Pierre) & FRENCHMAN(Alain) & ENGLISHMAN(Bob) & ENGLISHMAN(Peter) & DANE(Pete) & DANE(Yan)

1 - digitalization of the examples

Instead of keeping all the information contained in the examples, we only keep the number of occurrences of each descriptor.
So in our example, the numeric vectors obtained are

$$E_1': \quad (natl{=}fren) \quad (natl{=}engl) \quad (natl{=}alg)$$
$$2 \qquad\qquad 2 \qquad\qquad 1$$

$$E_2': \quad (natl{=}fren) \quad (natl{=}engl) \quad (natl{=}swiss) \quad (natl{=}dan)$$
$$1 \qquad\qquad 2 \qquad\qquad 1 \qquad\qquad 2$$

2 - Similarity over the common parts.

The least number of occurrences of each descriptor constitutes the vector $SIM(E_1, E_2)$.

In our example, we obtain

$$SIM \quad (natl{=}fren) \quad (natl{=}engl)$$
$$1 \qquad\qquad 2$$

3 - Similarity over the residual parts

It depends on the links which could exist between the descriptors.

These links can be expressed either by theorems or by taxonomies, as we have already seen in chapters 6 and 7.

In our example, we shall use only the following taxonomy

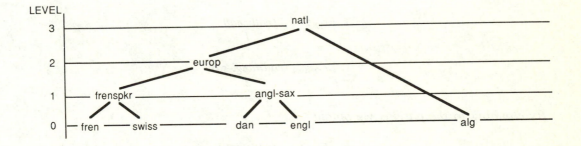

where natl, europ, frenspkr, angl-sax, fren, swiss, dan, engl and alg are abbreviations for 'nationality', European, French-speaking, Anglo-Saxon, Frenchman, Swiss, Dane, Englishman and Algerian respectively.

The taxonomy is ordered by levels of generality; natl is its level 3, europ is level 2, frenspkr and angl-sax are level 1, and fren, swiss, dan, engl and alg are level zero.

To compare the residual parts, we replace each descriptor by its parent.

We then compare the vectors obtained as at the stage of similarity over the common parts, and we add the common parts in the similarity vector.

We iterate the process until one of the two residual vectors is empty. The process of determining the similarity vector is then ended.

Let the residual parts of E_1' and E_2' be called Er_{11} and Er_{21}. They are given by

$$Er_{11}: \quad (natl=fren) \quad (natl=alg)$$
$$1 \qquad\qquad 1$$

$$Er_{21}: \quad (natl=swiss) \quad (natl=dan)$$
$$1 \qquad\qquad 2$$

By climbing to the parents of the descriptors of Er_{11} and Er_{21}, we obtain

$$Er_{11}': \quad (natl=frenspkr) \quad (natl=natl)$$
$$1 \qquad\qquad 1$$

$$Er_{21}': \quad (natl=frenspkr) \quad (natl=angl\text{-}sax)$$
$$1 \qquad\qquad 2$$

This step enables us to detect a French-speaker common to the two examples in addition to the 'Frenchman' already found.

The similarity vector then becomes

$$SIM \quad (natl=fren) \quad (natl=engl) \quad (natl=frenspkr)$$
$$1 \qquad\qquad 2 \qquad\qquad 1$$

The residual vectors Er_{12} and Er_{22} are then

$$Er_{12}: \quad (natl=natl)$$
$$1$$

$$Er_{22}: \quad (natl=angl\text{-}sax)$$
$$2$$

By climbing to the parents we obtain

$$Er_{12}': \quad (natl=natl)$$
$$1$$

$$Er_{22}': \quad (natl=europ)$$
$$2$$

which adds nothing to the similarity. In the end, after the last iteration, we shall have

$$SIM \quad (natl=fren) \quad (natl=engl) \quad (natl=frenspkr) \quad (natl=natl)$$
$$1 \qquad\qquad 2 \qquad\qquad 1 \qquad\qquad 1$$

At the end of this process, we have a vector which describes in a certain way the richness of the future generalization between E_1 and E_2.

It is then possible either to use this vector to define a numeric distance between examples, or to use it as it is to compare two examples.

In both cases, it is easy to see that we shall be able to define a similarity vector between more than two examples, and thus to compare the similarity between a cluster of examples and a new one which we are trying to incorporate into the cluster.

So we shall incorporate the one which modifies the cluster's similarity vector the least.

There are many different procedures for achieving this; the interested reader will find one in [Benamou & Al. 1986].

3.2 Dissimilarity and discriminant generalization

It is customary in Clustering Analysis to take the view that dissimilarity is another aspect of similarity. In other words, it is hypothesized that the more similar two examples are, the less dissimilar they are (which seems to go without saying).

The introduction of the notion of symbolic similarity justifies the rejection of this hypothesis. Indeed, there can very easily be some respects in which two examples are very similar and others in which they are very different.

For example, imagine descriptions of particular people. It is perfectly possible to have complete similarity between the personalities of two people and complete dissimilarity between their professions.

Since our ambition is to recognize symbolic characteristics like these, we must prohibit ourselves from "averaging" over similarity and dissimilarity.

Now the goal is no longer to evaluate our generalization's usefulness for recognizing concepts, but to evaluate its usefulness for discriminating concepts.

It is customary to require recognition functions to be characteristic (i.e. to recognize all the positive examples) and at the same time discriminant (i.e. to reject all the negative examples).

This condition is no longer so obligatory in a framework of symbolic learning.

In order to recognize concepts without accepting any counter-example, we need consistent functions. In order to recognize al the examples of the concepts, we need characteristic functions.

Requiring a function to fulfill both roles at the same time means taking the risk of missing another consistent function which would recognize more efficiently, and it also means taking the risk of missing a characteristic function which would describe much better.

So we propose that there should be distinct criteria of similarity and dissimilarity.

A similarity criterion will serve to recognize a clustering whose recognition function is rich. The dissimilarity criterion will then serve just to decide between the clusters displaying the same similarity.

The dissimilarity criteria will serve to cluster the examples in clusters which are well-distinguished. Then the similarity criterion will serve just to decide between the clusters displaying the same dissimilarity.

Two different sorts of information can be used to build two vectors of dissimilarity. Once again, it will be possible to combine them in many ways to arrive at a dissimilarity measure; there is an example in [Benamou & Al. 1986].

1 - First sort of information : Vector of omissions

This vector notes how many times the dropping condition rule will have to be used on the descriptors which do not occur in both examples at once (see chapter 6) in order to bring them both into structural matching.

Clearly E_1' lacks a Swiss and two Danes to "fill in the gaps" with respect to E_2'. Symmetrically, E_2' would need an Algerian to fill in its gaps with respect to E_1'. It follows that the vector of omissions, V_{drop}, is given by

$$V_{drop} \quad \begin{matrix} (natl=alg) \\ 1 \end{matrix} \quad \begin{matrix} (natl=swiss) \\ 1 \end{matrix} \quad \begin{matrix} (natl=dan) \\ 2 \end{matrix}$$

2 - Second form of information : Vector of repetitions

For each descriptor common to both examples, count the number of times it would have to be duplicated in order to be equally numerous in both examples. The vector of repetitions, V_{rep}, measures a more subtle difference than the vector of omissions, but in cases where the examples are very similar, this is just the vector which enables the examples to be differentiated.

Let us recall that on the basis of the examples

$$E_1': \quad \begin{matrix} (natl=fren) \\ 2 \end{matrix} \quad \begin{matrix} (natl=engl) \\ 2 \end{matrix} \quad \begin{matrix} (natl=alg) \\ 1 \end{matrix}$$

$$E_2': \quad \begin{matrix} (natl=fren) \\ 1 \end{matrix} \quad \begin{matrix} (natl=engl) \\ 2 \end{matrix} \quad \begin{matrix} (natl=swiss) \\ 1 \end{matrix} \quad \begin{matrix} (natl=dan) \\ 2 \end{matrix}$$

we found the following similarity vector

SIM	(natl=fren)	(natl=engl)	(natl=frenspkr)	(natl=natl)
	1	2	1	1

The vectors E_1' and E_2' are then re-written, adding the values for the descriptors of the children of the highest parent in the hierarchy used for the calculation of SIM.

So they become

E_1'':

(natl=fren)	(natl=engl)	(natl=alg)	(natl=frenspkr)
2	2	1	2

(natl=angl-sax)	(natl=europ)	(natl=natl)
2	4	5

E_2'':

(natl=fren)	(natl=engl)	(natl=swiss)	(natl=dan)
1	2	1	2

(natl=frenspkr)	(natl=angl-sax)	(natl=europ)	(natl=natl)
2	4	6	6

The values of the descriptors 'swiss', 'dan' and 'alg' are ignored, since they have already been taken into account in V_{drop}.

On the other hand, looking at the descriptors common to both examples, E_1'' lacks two Anglo-Saxons, two Europeans, and one person of whatever 'nationality' in order to become identical to E_2''.

Symmetrically, looking at the descriptors common to both, E_2'' lacks one Frenchman in order to become identical to E_1''.

Finally, one has

V_{rep}	(natl=fren)	(natl=angl-sax)	(natl=europ)	(natl=natl)
	1	2	2	1

3.3 Conclusion

The farther use of the dissimilarity vectors and of the similarity vector depends on the numeric techniques that one may wish to apply to them.

This becomes too technical to be described here.

Nevertheless, the idea is clear. The calculation of these vectors is a kind of small approximate generalization which can be included in a Clustering Analysis algorithm.

The difficulty consists in correctly evaluating the approximation to the final generalization.

If we stay too far away from the final generalization, then we are almost in a standard Clustering Analysis algorithm.

If we refine the generalization too much, then the new algorithm will be too greedy for time.

The process of "deep" understanding of a text is certainly one of the most interesting challenges to Artificial Intelligence : it so happens that, on the one hand, the problems arising from the understanding of a text have not been solved at present and, on the other hand, that we are all more or less expert at interpreting texts, so that we can quite easily see what the problem is.

Not all of these problems are going to be tackled in this chapter, and in particular, we shall neglect the one which is standardly held to belong to the province of natural language understanding: the mechanisms for transforming written text into an internal representation usable by a machine.

The natural language understanding specialists have thought up a very large number of ways of representing the knowledge contained in a text.

Never forget that in general, transitions from a text to its internal representation are not always obvious except for those that severely restrict the "naturalness" of the language.

By way of parenthesis, let us point to the increasing number of systems that are turning up, written by non-linguists and non-AI specialists who, as far as they are concerned, have solved the problem of natural language understanding. The simple fact is that they are unaware of the problems of multiplicity of points of view, of belief, of non-monotonicity, of contradictory and uncertain data, of temporality, to mention only the main ones raised by AI. The linguists would have another mass of them to suggest, such as that of the recognition of meaningless but syntactically correct sentences: what to do about the sentence "The word dog does not bite"? (Example suggested by M. Gross on the radio station France-Culture).

For this reason we want to insist here on the fact that converting a text into PRO-LOG clause form, which we take for granted here, is in reality an extremely difficult problem.

In addition to the problems of syntax, which are not trivial, there exist all the problems we mention above and which are clustered under the name of truth maintenance [Doyle 1979], as they take into account all the variabilities of truth-values during the transcription of a text into its internal representation. The exercise about the fable of the fox and the crow given at the end of this chapter clearly shows that the understanding of the motives of the fox depends on an analysis of the contrary beliefs of the fox and the crow, even in a text which children understand immediately.

And so, with the aim of illustrating the problem of the control of micro-worlds, we are going to assume that all these problems have been solved.

The problem of the control of micro-worlds, for its part, is connected with ML in a typical manner. We talked about it already in section 9 of chapter 4, where it was clear that the state of the art in this field is hardly sophisticated.

However, we consider that this problem, although tackled relatively little in ML research, is one of the key ones and a logical outcome of ML.

The control of micro-worlds is one of the keys to ML

We hope that the whole of this book makes clear what progress has recently been made in ML; not all the problems are solved, far from it, but on the one hand they are now clearly defined, and on the other hand a certain number of simple and effective techniques have now been born.

One common characteristic of all these modern methods is that they require a precise description of the features of the universe in which the learning takes place.

So there are two restrictions on their capacity to apply in a realistic environment.

1 - the total amount of knowledge used to solve a problem becomes very large as soon as it ceases to be a toy problem.

For example, suppose we want to build a learning system for livestock rearing. Of course, all the information concerning the micro-world of veterinary problems will be needed, but also concerning the "common sense of country life" (animals can take this path but not that one, etc ...), that connected with the micro-world of conjectural models of the economy, that connected with the micro-world of national and European politics (the political decisions of Euro-countries are important data for a European farmer), that connected with the micro-world of international information (the Chernobyl accident had consequences for European agriculture), to name only the most obvious ones.

If all the rules concerning all the domains are dumped wholesale into the system, it will be engulfed.

Furthermore, the lack of modularity in this kind of system makes rule acquisition very difficult.

2 - It is very likely that some rules which are valid in one domain will become invalid in another. It is indispensable to control contradictory rules without getting

into dead-ends.

In particular, any matter of common-sense is a compromise between contradictory rules, but the same problem turns up even in the most technical areas.

In our example, a standard case is that where the farmer takes the decision to slaughter diseased livestock. It is obvious that the acquisition of all the rules that lead to such a decision cannot take place at the same time.

These two restrictions will be removed when we get a "taxonomy" of micro-worlds (we call it a "taxonomy" because there will always be a certain cross-checking between concepts) such that the rules that are valid for a parent are valid for its offspring. This entitles us to assign rules to two different concepts even where some of the rules may be contradictory.

Such a "taxonomy" could take an appearance similar to this one

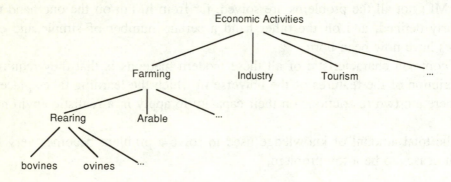

The choices connected with the slicing-up of the micro-worlds, with their relative positions, with the rules associated with them, are quite often unexpressed choices, but their importance is capital.

For example, it is necessary to know that in the universe of farms that run guesthouses for tourists as a sideline, the rules concerning agriculture and those concerning tourism have to be analyzed and compared.

In a phase of learning, it will be necessary to analyze all the contradictions (e.g. concerning the time for getting up) and to find a solution to the which could be dependent on a mass of other factors.

In a phase of utilization the rules of the new micro-worlds *of agriculture and tourism* which remain valid must be distinctly marked, and a mixed micro-world must be developed where new rules will be added.

In conclusion, the methods developed hitherto are valid in a single micro-world and will only be able to find realistic applications if they are incorporated into a system for the control of micro-worlds.

The control of micro-worlds is a logical outcome for ML

It is not, of course, the only logical outcome for ML, since even the development of techniques valid in a single micro-world is not yet a fully-solved problem.

The point is simply to emphasize that a complete system of learning, which must of course have information right from the start about the contents and interrelationships of the micro-worlds, must also be capable of the three following operations:
- adding or modifying a rule in a given micro-world
- modifying the rules that enable the current micro-world to be recognized
- modifying the interrelationships between the micro-worlds, i.e. modifying the "taxonomy" of the micro-worlds.

These capacities portray a system which is capable of adapting to changes in its universe while still using its old knowledge. This is just what is expected from a system endowed with the ability to learn.

The first operation has already been abundantly illustrated here.

We shall say little of the third operation, except to remark that it necessitates the same kind of techniques as the second, the one we shall now describe.

In fact, we shall now show how the detection of the cause of an error can enable the recognition function for a micro-world to be modified.

The technique we are going to use to find explanations is called "debugging"; a detailed account of it will be found in E. Shapiro's thesis [Shapiro 1983].

We shall see how these explanations can be used to improve the recognition functions for a micro-world. This process is quite complex, which is why the reader must not get impatient with the numerous technical details we shall meet on our way.

1 RECOGNITION OF MICRO-WORLDS

So we are going to assume that the sentences of natural language have been converted into clause form, in accordance with a process that we shall not talk about, but which might be, say, a logical syntactico-semantic analyzer.

1.1 Description of the example

The last International Workshop on Machine Learning took place near New York

City, in a high-quality but slightly stilted hotel.

Roger Shank, one of the leaders of natural language understanding who is very interested in problems of creativity in ML, gave a talk on learning in which he upheld the opinion that learning occurs essentially through a kind of resolution of contradictions.

To illustrate his topic, he used a self-description of Skytop Lodge, which strongly insisted on the fact that Skytop Lodge was a very "relaxed" area, where the greatest simplicity of dress prevailed.

It so happens that, at the same time, the participants in the seminar were very disturbed by the fact that they were required to wear a jacket and tie to dinner. Indeed, many jokes were made about this, and there were even photographs taken of people who will never again be seen in such distinguished attire.

We are now going to present what is almost a PROLOG version of Schank's argumentation.

Take a simple case where only one character exists: the "AI researcher". In the universe of the character, there are theorems which say

relaxed area $\Rightarrow$ simple clothes

simple clothes $\Rightarrow$ $\neg$ (vest and tie at supper)

This can be converted into clauses like

C_1:   SIMPLE-CLOTHES(x, y) :- RELAXED-PLACE(y)
C_2:   :- SIMPLE-CLOTHES(x, y), WEARS(JACKET&TIE, DINNER, x, y)

where x is a character and y is the place where he is.

It will be noticed that C_2 is not a PROLOG clause, but a "query".

We are assuming in this chapter that queries can be controlled in the same way as other clauses. (Start of a PROLOG parenthesis) In PROLOG, one would have to transform this query into a normal clause by using the 'NOT'.

For instance, one could write C_2 under the form NOT SIMPLE-CLOTHES(x, y) :- WEARS(JACKET&TIE, DINNER, x, y), or, as well, NOT WEARS(JACKET&TIE, DINNER, x, y) :- SIMPLE-CLOTHES(x, y). (End of PROLOG parenthesis).

The character must have worn a jacket and tie to dinner the day before, which is written

C_3: WEARS(JACKET&TIE, DINNER, AI-RESEARCHER, SKYTOP-LODGE) :-

On the other hand, reading the self-description above, the "AI researcher" must add to his knowledge the fact, declared in the text, that

C_4: RELAXED-PLACE(SKYTOP-LODGE) :-

This leads to a contradiction (note that we aren't going to use PROLOG resolution!).

****

Use PROLOG resolution and see what that would yield.

****

C_4 *and* C_1 *resolve to*

$\quad\quad C_5$:   SIMPLE-CLOTHES(x, SKYTOP-LODGE)   :-

C_5 *and* C_2 *resolve to*

$\quad\quad C_6$: :- WEARS(JACKET&TIE, DINNER, x, SKYTOP-LODGE)

And finally C_3 *and* C_6 *resolve to the empty clause with* {x <-- AI-RESEARCHER}.

This contradiction between clauses is a logical representation of the contradiction which is evoked in the mind of the AI-researcher when he reads the self-description of Skytop Lodge.

To find out where the contradiction comes from, write the resolution tree that led to the empty clause.

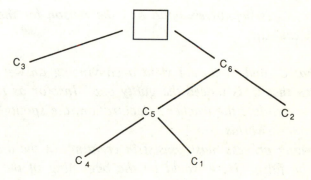

1.2 Debugging

Let us analyze the credibility of the clauses used.

C_3 *is a part of the personal experience of '* AI-RESEARCHER *', so he cannot contradict it.*
C_6 *is a deduction derived from* C_5 *and* C_2, *so the latter are what must be considered.*
C_2 *is a part of '* AI-RESEARCHER *' knowledge; it will have to be examined.*
C_5 *is a deduction derived from* C_4 *and* C_1.
C_4 *is a statement drawn from the text; it will have to be examined.*
C_1 *is a part of '* AI-RESEARCHER *' knowledge; it will have to be examined.*

All in all, three clauses are detected which could be responsible for the contradiction. So an explanation of this contradiction could be derived from these three clauses.

Exercise 25
****

Describe how C_4 and C_1 could be called into question.

****

At this point we shall only discuss C_2; other explanations would be found by discussing the others, as can be seen by doing the above exercise.

C_2:   :- SIMPLE-CLOTHES(x, y), WEARS(JACKET&TIE, DINNER(x, y)

is a piece of knowledge about SIMPLE-CLOTHES, and so we must check whether there is any other information about this predicate.

It must be assumed that a sort of dictionary exists (containing more details than an ordinary dictionary) which describes the predicates.

Two cases are possible.

1 - in this dictionary, there is no information concerning the possible existence of other micro-worlds different from those of ' AI-RESEARCHER '.

In this case, C_2 is definitively valid and the reason for the contradiction must be looked for in C_4 and C_1.

Suppose that C_4 and C_1 do not yield a convincing answer either, and/or that the teacher declares that C_2 is indeed the guilty one. Insofar as nothing can be found in the dictionary to validate the teacher's declaration, the spotlight must now shift to the "taxonomy" of micro-worlds.

So the learning process must consist in creating, in the dictionary, a micro-world where C_2 will be false. Here would be the beginning of the creation of the micro-world of people who wear evening dress to dinner.

2 - In this dictionary there exists a snobbishly-dressed micro-world, and instead of C_2, there would be a rule like

C_2':   :- SIMPLE-CLOTHES(x, y), WEARS(EVENING-DRESS, DINNER, x, y)

Furthermore, in this micro-world, wearing a jacket and tie is a way of wearing simple clothes (anything else is called, say, "slovenly"). Thus we have

C_2'':   SIMPLE-CLOTHES(x, y) :- WEARS(JACKET&TIE, u, x, y)

This rule cannot be present at the same time as C_2, which is why it is necessary to put the various pieces of knowledge about the various micro-worlds into different "boxes" which can only send each other information in very specific cases.

In this micro-world,

C_1:   *SIMPLE-CLOTHES(x, y) :- RELAXED-PLACE(y)*
C_2'':   *SIMPLE-CLOTHES(x, y) :- WEARS(JACKET&TIE, u, x, y)*
C_3: *WEARS(JACKET&TIE, DINNER, AI-RESEARCHER, SKYTOP-LODGE) :-*
C_4: *RELAXED-PLACE(SKYTOP-LODGE) :-*

C_4 *and* C_1 *lead to*

C_7:   *SIMPLE-CLOTHES(x, SKYTOP-LODGE) :-*

and C_3 *and* C_2'' *lead to*

C_7:   *SIMPLE-CLOTHES(AI-RESEARCHER, SKYTOP-LODGE) :-*

which is not contradictory.

The existence of two micro-worlds using different definitions for a concept, where one introduces a contradiction but the other does not, can be itemized as the following standard "explanation" of contradiction in general.

Letting U and U' be two micro-worlds, such as the above, the explanation is
The character from micro-world U has not noticed that he is in micro-world U'.
A catalog of such general explanations, associated with an explanation comparer, (for the case where the process is continued by assuming that C_2 is valid but that C_4 and then C_1 are to be analyzed successively) would make it possible to give an account of extremely subtle mental processes, the foundation stone of these processes being the logical debugging of programs.

So it is clear that the character used a recognition function for ' AI-RESEARCHER ' micro-world that was erroneous.
In our description we have not made this recognition function explicit, but it is of course a function containing many predicates, and we are not going to try to spell it out here.
Let us assume that the recognition function is a function F(x) which, among other things, contains an item referring to the price of hotels habitually frequented by AI researchers.
So let F(x) =   ... & HOTEL-CHARGE < 200 dollars per day & ...
The ' AI-RESEARCHER ' micro-world had been selected by applying a heuristic.

This heuristic can be expressed by
IF one of the clauses contains a character K THEN go to character K's micro-world
This heuristic is always justified so long as you can check that you really do have to go to this micro-world.

In our example, F(x) took the value TRUE because we had gone to the ' AI-RESEARCHER ' micro-world.

We saw that this led to a contradiction, so we shall now need to modify F(x).

We find out, then, that the daily charge at Skytop Lodge is 120 dollars per day and modify F(x) to

$$F'(x) = \quad ... \ \& \ HOTEL\text{-}CHARGE < 120 \ dollars \ per \ day \ \& \ ...$$

More generally, we are back with a standard case of example-based learning as studied in ML.

The erroneous recognition function recognized a situation which was in reality a negative example. So we considered the problem of modifying the recognition function to make it reject this new negative example.

Here, a complete description of Skytop Lodge was to become a negative example to the ' AI-RESEARCHER ' micro-world.

2 DETECTION OF LIES

This section describes another application of logical debugging, that in which the explanation is connected with the presence of a false piece of information in a character's data, and when this false piece of information has been introduced by a second character. We then say that he lied to the first.

In a world where several characters are present simultaneously, it is not rare for their knowledge to be in contradiction. This can be quite simply because they are not of the same opinion, which can constitute a possible explanation of the contradiction.

We are now going to illustrate the case of another possible cause, which arises when one of the characters lies to the other.

This section is presented as an exercise. The reader is invited to make a certain effort. To help him, partial solutions will be given for him to complete.

Exercise 26
****

Study the following text to convert it into clause form.
The fox and the crow

1 - The crow was perched on a tree with a piece of cheese in his beak.
2 - The fox came to the foot of the tree.
3 - The fox said to the crow:
4 - "Crow, what a beautiful voice you have; please sing to me."

5 - The crow was very flattered by this, and began to sing.
6 - As he did so, the cheese fell from his beak.
7 - The fox seized the cheese and ran off, laughing.
(From Aesop.)

The information contained in the above text is to be represented just with the help of the following clauses.

Perched (Crow, Tree)	:-
Holds (Crow, Cheese, Beak)	:-
Comes-to (Fox, Tree)	:-
Beautiful-voice (Crow)	:-
Flattered (Crow)	:-
Sings (Crow)	:-
Falls (Cheese, Beak)	:-
Seizes (Fox, Cheese)	:-
Runs-off (Fox)	:-
Laughs (Fox)	:-

In a case like this one, it is necessary to avoid mixing the clauses which represent the knowledge of the various characters, here that of the fox and the crow.

The knowledge of each character will be put in a "box" bearing the name of the character.

Furthermore, it is necessary to have another box available, which we shall call the "Master" box, in which the knowledge of the various characters can be compared.

Finally, if the only information used were that contained in the clauses of the text, then there could be no question of understanding it; information from outside is required, which is implicitly contained in certain key-words of the text.

Here, the title and the remark "from Aesop" tell us we have a fable about two animals. So information has to be available about the animals of fable, which are a mixture of animal and human.

Furthermore, this information from outside is not used blindly. Only at the time when it is needed is it added to the Master box with the purpose of showing up contradictions. The control mechanism for this information is certainly very complicated. The reader is asked to use his intuition to fetch the information from outside at the right moment, to add it to the Master box.

The information from outside, which must be used appropriately by the Master box, is the following:

The crow does not have a beautiful voice.
If you do not have a beautiful voice, then you should not sing.
If a bird sings, then it cannot hold a thing in its beak.
When a thing cannot be held in its beak, then this thing falls.

Part of the exercise is to show that the fourth sentence of the text is absurd.

1 - FIRST QUESTION

Convert the information from outside which was given above into First-Order Logic, using only the predicates in the clauses given. Convert these theorems into clause form, without using the PROLOG "NOT".

2 - SECOND QUESTION

Extract all the information you can from the four clauses thus obtained, using resolution.
Note the absurdity of a certain conclusion outside the context of the fable.

3 - THIRD QUESTION

Create three "boxes" containing the information known to the crow, the fox and the Master. Give the state of each after reading each sentence, up to and including sentence 4.

Temporality is to be controlled in a trivial way. A "time" is associated with each sentence. Clauses drawn from successive sentences belong to successive times; those deduced from the same sentence are contemporaneous.

(Rest of question 3:) Show how the formalism of the boxes enables account to be taken of such information as "the fox says to the crow" without needing to use a predicate of the type "Says (x, y)".
N.B. The words of the fox are added to the box or boxes like the rest of the information in the text.

4 - FOURTH QUESTION

Use the information contained in the theorems given above (i.e., the theorems themselves in clause form) to show that the fox knows that the cheese falls "at the same time as" he asks the crow to sing.

5 - FIFTH QUESTION

Show how the information from outside given above has to be modified to prevent the absurd conclusion found in question 2 from appearing.

****

Answer to question 1:

	:-	*Beautiful-voice (Crow)*
Beautiful-voice (x)	:-	*Sings (x)*
	:-	*Sings (x), Holds (x, y, Beak)*
Holds (x, y, Beak); Falls (y)	:-	

So the fourth clause not a Horn clause.

Answer to question 2:

	:-	*Sings (Crow)*
Falls (y)	:-	*Sings(x)*

So if anyone sings, "everything" (i.e. the trees, the characters etc ..) falls, which is of course absurd.

Answer to question 3

Sentence 1.

Fox	Crow	Master
	Perched(Crow,Tree) :-	
	Holds(Crow, Cheese, Beak) :-	

Sentence 2.

Fox	Crow	Master
	Perched(Crow,Tree) :-	
	Holds(Crow, Cheese, Beak) :-	
Comes-to(Fox,Tree) :-		

Sentence 3.

Fox	Crow	Master
		Perched(Crow,Tree) :-
		Holds(Crow, Cheese, Beak) :-
Comes-to(Fox,Tree) :-		

Sentence 4 (initial phase)

Fox	Crow	Master
		Perched(Crow,Tree) :- Holds(Crow, Cheese, Beak) :-
Comes-to(Fox,Tree) :-		
		:- Beautiful-voice(Crow) Sings(Crow) :-

Answer to question 4:

The knowledge is put in the fox's box, to which the common knowledge of the Master box is added.

Sentence 4 (intermediate phase)

Fox	Crow	Master
Perched(Crow,Tree) :- Holds(Crow, Cheese, Beak) :-		Perched(Crow,Tree) :- Holds(Crow, Cheese, Beak) :-
Comes-to(Fox,Tree) :-		
Beautiful-voice(Crow) :- Sings(Crow) :- :- Beautiful-voice (Crow) Beautiful-voice (x) :- Sings (x) :- Sings (x), Holds (x, y, Beak) Holds (x, y, Beak); Falls (y) :-		:- Beautiful-voice(Crow) Sings(Crow) :-

There is a contradiction between Beautiful-voice (Crow) :- and :- Beautiful-voice (Crow) which can be resolved by removing Beautiful-voice (Crow) :- from the fox's knowledge.

This yields:

Sentence 4 (final phase)

Fox	Crow	Master
Perched(Crow,Tree) :- Holds(Crow, Cheese, Beak) :-		Perched(Crow,Tree) :- Holds(Crow, Cheese, Beak) :-
Comes-to(Fox,Tree) :-		
Sings(Crow) :- :- Beautiful-voice (Crow) Falls (Cheese) :-	Beautiful-voice(Crow) :-	Sings(Crow) :-

Thus, by simulating the fox's knowledge and assuming that the fox knows that the crow does not have a beautiful voice, we do indeed find that he knows that the cheese is going to fall. To put it more precisely, it can be deduced that the information *concerning the falling of the cheese is accessible to the fox as soon as he speaks.*

Answer to question 5:

Add the information that if ' x ' sings and ' x ' holds ' y ' in its beak, then ' y ' falls.

It is now up to the reader to use this to detect the lie that the fox tells the crow.

We are tempted to believe that most learning should go by analogy since we are very much used to analogy when attending a lecture. In fact, this chapter will show how much difficult it is to implement an analogy mechanism.

1 A DEFINITION OF ANALOGY

1.1 Definitions

Let us suppose that we dispose of a piece of information that can be put into the form of a doublet (A, B) in which it is known that B depends causally on A, in some way that does not need to be very formal nor strict. In the following of this chapter, we shall call this relation β. Suppose now that we find an other piece of information (A', B') that can be put into the same form, and such that there exists some resemblance between A and A'. In the following of this chapter we shall call this relation α. Let us call β' the causal dependency between A' and B', and α' the similarity dependency between B and B', as shown in the figure below.

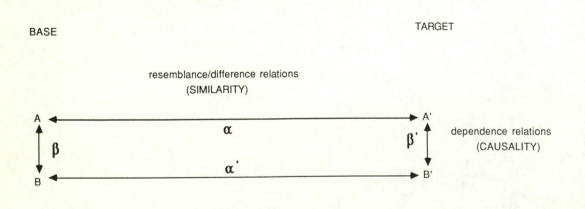

Figure 1.

We can then define **analogy** in many ways. We shall give here three of them. In all cases, it is supposed that we know more or less precisely A, B, A', α, and β, and that we try to invent B' or to justify its plausibility.

One compares B and B': they are analogous in the way A and A' are similar, taking into account the relation β between A and B. In other words, in this first kind of analogy, we try to find some similarity relationship between B and B', namely we try to infer α'. From α', we can of course deduce what B' is.

Another way compares A' and B': they are analogous in the way A and B are causally dependent, and taking into account the relation α between A and A'. In other words, in the second kind of analogy, we try to find some causality relationship between A' and B', namely we try to infer β'.

A third which will be illustrated in great detail in the next section (this is Winston's definition of analogy) is such that β = β', α = α'. The relation α is an approximate matching between A and A', α' is an exact matching between B and B'. A' is exactly known, and analogy tries to answer the question: Is B' TRUE? Therefore, B' is considered as exactly known, even if it is just an hypothesis. The analogy process consists in adjusting together α and A so that they fit with A'. Once A and α are thus chosen, it becomes possible to adjust B and β so that they fit with B'. In other words the analogy process consists in a search for causality relations that will explain why (A, B) is analogous to (A', B').

In many cases, the relation α is reduced to the belonging to a common ancestor.

For instance, consider 'A = John is an American human male ', and 'B = John is greedy'. Suppose that the relation of causality between A and B uses a property inherited from a common ancestor, for instance 'β = John is greedy because this is part of the human nature '. Then, considering the case of 'A' = Jane is an American human female ', and since 'α = human male and human female are both human', one will find, by analogy that 'β' = Jane is greedy'.

The difference with the straightforward syllogism is simply that β is not a real implication. This use of analogy reduces it to an ill-grounded syllogism. It can be interesting when one discusses where the property is inherited from.

In the above example, one can discuss if the "good" analogy stems from their humanity or their Americanness.

The analogy problem then reduces to the choice of the cluster to which both A and B belong. This is the problem of clustering analysis that has already been presented in chapter 10. In this chapter, we will instead present the case where the relation α is more complex than having a common ancestor, as shown by the following example.
As an other instance of a well-known way to use analogy, the reader will find interesting to read Carbonell's papers (see for instance, [Carbonell 1983]. His use of analogy is "analogous" to Winston's in that sense that he also looks for causality relationships.

The main difference is that the causality relationship, in Carbonell's view of analogy, is different in the base and in the target. The game is then to find out the target causality relationships from the ones in the base, and a supposedly correct description of both base and target. In other words, (A, B) and (A', B') are well-known, and analogy consists in finding some α, (*a', and β to be able to invent a β' that will fit with B and B'.

1.2   A complete example

Let us illustrate analogy by a case where the result of the analogy is wrong, but where the analogy itself is correct and non-trivial.

Let 'A = Earth has an atmosphere of 1013 MB containing oxygen', 'B = Earth is inhabited by humans', 'A' = Mars has an atmosphere of 5 MB containing oxygen', 'α = both Earth and Mars have an atmosphere containing oxygen, but the atmospheric pressure is 1013 on Earth, and 5 on Mars', and 'β = the presence of oxygen allows life, 1013 MB is enough for humans'.

The analogy problem is to complete the following diagram when some of its parts are missing.

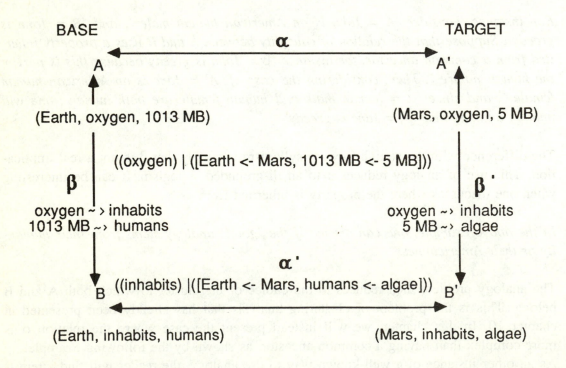

Figure 2.

1.2.1 Analogy between B and B'

Analogy will first look for what is common to A and A', and try to keep it in α'.

From β, one sees that the presence of oxygen allows life, therefore α' must say that some forms of life inhabit Mars. Because of β again, and since Mars' atmospheric pressure is 5 MB only, one looks for some beings such that '5 MB is enough for these beings'. Suppose that we know that, for instance, algae can live under an atmospheric pressure of 5 MB, and that they indeed need oxygen to live, then one can attempt to use
'α' = both Earth and Mars have an atmosphere containing oxygen, but Earth is inhabited by humans, while Mars is inhabited by algae
which, of course immediately gives B'.

1.2.2 Analogy between A' and B'

It will first look for what is common to A and B, and try to maintain it in β'.
From α, one sees that both Earth and Mars have oxygen, therefore the part of β that says 'the presence of oxygen allows life ' is kept in β'. Because of α again, one sees that the difference between Mars and Earth is in the difference of atmospheric pressure, from which one concludes that one has to transform the statement '1013 MB is enough for humans' into another statement relative to 5 MB. As before, let us suppose that we know that, for instance, algae can live under an atmospheric pressure of 5 MB, and that they need oxygen to live. We can therefore transform '1013 MB is enough for humans' into '5 MB is enough for algae. Then β' is: 'oxygen allows life for algae and a pressure of 5 MB is enough for them'. From that we can obviously find B'.

1.2.3 Finding the causality relation allowing an analogy to be drawn

This third case is a bit more complicated to illustrate because, to be realistic, we need a knowledge base from which A can be extracted.
Let us therefore suppose that we have access to a huge knowledge base KB about earth-life, in which the A above is contained together with a lot of information about life conditions on Earth.
Suppose that we know for sure that A' = 'The atmosphere of Mars contains oxygen and its atmospheric pressure is 5MB'. Suppose also that we are asking the question: Is there any reason for us to believe that some algae live on Mars? Therefore, B' is assumed to be 'algae live on Mars'.
Now, the process of analogy will be finding some information within KB that is relevant to A'. In this simple example, we can easily find that A = 'Earth atmosphere contains oxygen and its pressure is 1013MB'. In a more realistic example in the next section, you will see that finding A within KB is a tedious process.
Now that A has been found, we try to determine B by finding in KB "something" that

lives on Earth **and** *has a causality relationship with oxygen and atmospheric pressure. As a counter-example, algae also live on Earth but a 1013MB pressure has no causality relationship with it. Suppose, as an example, that there is a causality relationship between oxygen, atmospheric pressure, and the presence of humans on Earth. The β is discovered as 'humans need oxygen and a 1013MB atmospheric pressure to live ', and B is discovered as 'humans live on Earth'.*

Now, since we are **assuming** *that β = β', we can answer that algae live on Mars because they need oxygen (as humans do on Earth), and they need a 5MB atmospheric pressure (unlike the humans that need a 1013MB pressure).*

2 WINSTON's USE OF ANALOGY

In this section we shall describe a realistic example of learning from analogy which is found in [Winston 1982]. As already said, it belongs to the third kind of process described above. It can be summarized as follows.

   - GIVEN

1 - a knowledge base (that will here a precis of the story of Macbeth). In what follows, this will be called the "base-story".

2 - an exercise about the knowledge base. This exercise contains

2.1 - another precis of a similar story, called here the "target-story".

2.2 - a question about the validity of an hypothesis about the target-story.

   - FIND

a general rule illustrated in both stories.

2.1 Description of the example

Consider the following precis of Macbeth (called MA in the following), given by a teacher as precedent. This precis is an instance of what we shall call the base-story in what follows. It will contain the base of the analogy to come. In this section, the most difficult step of the analogy will be finding which sub-set of the base is relevant.

In MA there is Macbeth, Lady-Macbeth, Duncan and Macduff. Macbeth is an evil noble. Lady-Macbeth is a greedy ambitious woman. Ducan is a king. Macduff is a loyal noble. Macbeth is evil because Macbeth is weak and because Macbeth married Lady-Macbeth and because Lady-Macbeth is greedy. Lady-Macbeth persuades Macbeth to want to be king. Lady-Macbeth influenced Macbeth because Lady-Macbeth is greedy and because Macbeth married Lady-Macbeth. Macbeth murders Duncan with Lady-Macbeth using a knife because Macbeth wants to be king and because Macbeth is evil. Lady-Macbeth kills Lady-Macbeth. Macduff is angry. Macduff kills Macbeth because Macbeth murdered Ducan and because Macduff is loyal.

Consider the following exercise which is an instance of the target of the analogy. In the particular case of analogy developed by Winston the causal relations are the same in the base and in the target.

> *In EX1 there is a particular man (man-1) and a particular woman (woman-1). The man married the woman. The man is weak and the woman is greedy.*
> *Question: Show that the man in EX1 may be evil.*

The teacher tells the student that the base-story is to be considered as a precedent, and the student has to find why the question is answered by YES (*why the man in EX1 may be evil*). Furthermore, he should find a rule the antecedent of which is the least general common representation of the base and target stories, and the conclusion of which is the answer to the question of the exercise.

In this example, one should learn, from MA and EX1, the following rule.

> IF   *any man who is weak is married to any woman who is greedy*
> THEN   *the man may be evil.*

Winston's proposal amounts to giving a representation of MA and EX1 as semantic nets and retrieving common links between the two nets. If the man common to MA and EX1 is evil in MA, one can conclude that he may also be evil in EX1. Typically, this supposes that MA contains far more details than EX1 (in other words, that it is an instance of EX1) and that some details of MA can be transferred to EX1. Let us first look at the semantic net which is equivalent to MA. It can be represented by

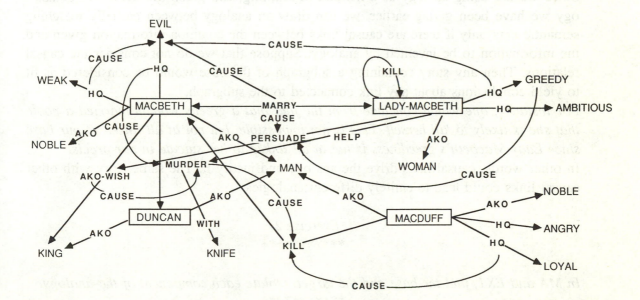

Figure 3. The semantic net representing the story told in MA.

In this figure, AKO = A-KIND-OF, HQ = HAS-QUALITY, AKO-WISH = WISH-TO-BECOME-A-KIND-OF. Notice that MA never says that Macbeth is a man, while the semantic net does. We introduced this information in order to avoid having to deduce it from theorems of the kind ∀x, y [MARRY(x, y) & WOMAN(y) ⇒ MAN(x)].

The semantic net associated with EX1 can be represented as follows.

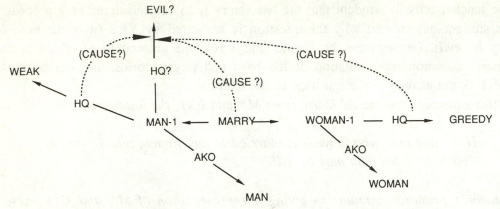

Figure 4. The semantic net representing the story told in EX1.
The causal links in dotted lines are implicit in EX1 once it has been said that MA is the precedent for EX1.

Let us comment on the causal links we put in figure 4.
Since we are using analogy as a method of learning, and given the definition of analogy we have been giving earlier, we can draw an analogy between partially matching semantic nets only if there are causal links between the common information given and the information to be invented by analogy. Suppose that we do not consider the causal relations. Then any story containing a subgraph of the base would be considered as fit to yield conclusions about any link connected to the subgraph.
For instance, one would conclude from the fact that a greedy woman married a noble that she is likely to kill herself. This is not impossible, but not at all linked to our base since Lady-Macbeth's greediness is not at all linked to her suicide in our precis.
In other words, causal links drive the analogy and justify it. The same story with other causal links could lead to entirely different analogies.

Exercise 27
****

In MA and EX1, find the base and the target. Isolate each component of the analogy.
****

2.2 An implementation of this problem

We shall now discuss of PROLOG implementation of Winston's learning by analogy method. We shall make our problem more simple by making the hypothesis that EX1 is always more general than MA. This cannot be always the case since the base-story could well contain some general statements, and the target-story some peculiarities. For instance, the target could contain the fact that the man is a prince (instead of a noble), and the analogy should work exactly in the same way, which is not the case with our hypothesis. The noble of the base could not be recognized as an instance of the prince of the target, and the analogy would fail. In order to overcome this drawback, we would have to use a unifier instead of a simple pattern-matcher. The latter will be enough for our simple present purposes, we raised this question just to show that we are not implementing the full method of Winston, but a simpler sub-case of it.

2.2.1 The knowledge base

This gives the representation of MA as a set of clauses.

Facts

AKO(Macbeth, man)
AKO(Lady-Macbeth, woman)
AKO(Duncan, man)
AKO(Macduff, man)
SOC-POS(Macbeth, noble)
SOC-POS(Duncan, king)
SOC-POS(Macduff, noble)
SOC-REL(Macbeth, Lady-Macbeth, MARRY)
PSY-FEATURE(Macbeth, evil)
PSY-FEATURE(Macbeth, weak)
PSY-FEATURE(Lady-Macbeth, ambitious)
PSY-FEATURE(Lady-Macbeth, greedy)
PSY-FEATURE(Macduff, loyal)
PERSUADE(Lady-Macbeth, Macbeth, king)
MURDER(Macbeth, Ducan, knife)
MURDER(Lady-Macbeth, Lady-Macbeth, WEAPON))
PSY-STATE(Macduff, angry)
KILL(Macduff, Macbeth, WEAPON)))

Causal links in MA

CAUSE(PERSUADE(Lady-Macbeth, Macbeth, king)) :- SOC-REL(Macbeth, Lady-Macbeth, MARRY), PSY-FEATURE(Lady-Macbeth, greedy)

CAUSE(PSY-FEATURE(Macbeth, evil)) :- PSY-FEATURE(Macbeth, weak), SOC-REL(Macbeth, Lady-Macbeth, MARRY), PSY-FEATURE(Lady-Macbeth, greedy))

CAUSE(MURDER(Macbeth, Ducan, knife)) :- PERSUADE(Lady-Macbeth, Macbeth, king), PSY-FEATURE(Macbeth, evil)

CAUSE(KILL(Macduff, Macbeth, WEAPON)) :- MURDER(Macbeth, Ducan, knife), PSY-FEATURE(Macduff, loyal))

Theorems

MURDER(x, y, z) :- KILL(x, y, z), PSY-FEATURE(x, evil)
MARRIED(x, y) :- SOC-REL(x, y, MARRY)
DEAD(x) :- KILL(x, y, WEAPON))
SOC-POS(x, noble) :- SOC-POS(x, prince)
WEAPON :- KNIFE

EX1

AKO(man1, man)
AKO(woman1, woman)
SOC-REL(man1, woman1, MARRY)
PSY-FEATURE(man1, weak)
PSY-FEATURE(woman1, greedy)
?   :- PSY-FEATURE(man1, evil)

2.2.2 Partial matching algorithm

KB denotes a large knowledge base of which MA is an instance, and EX any exercise about KB, of which EX1 is an instance.

Analogies can be drawn about different types of characters. We suppose that characters of the same kind are put together into clusters. This information in implicit in the precis we have been using.
In our example, let us suppose that the clusters are the following. {Macbeth, Lady-Macbeth, Duncan, Macduff, man1, woman1}, {man, woman}, {noble, king, prince}, {evil, weak, ambitious, loyal, greedy, angry}, {knife}, {weapon}. We choose to attempt to draw analogies about the first cluster. This will be implemented in step 1 by choosing to generalize within this cluster.
  STEP 1.
Generalize EX by variablizing those of its constants which belong to the chosen cluster. This generalization will be called GEX. The corresponding substitutions will be called {T}.

Here we chose to generalize in the first cluster, therefore man1 and woman1 are replaced by variables. This gives
                    Generalization of EX1 = GEX1

AKO(x, man)
AKO(y, woman)
SOC-REL(x, y, MARRY)
PSY-FEATURE(x, weak)
PSY-FEATURE(y, greedy)
?   :- PSY-FEATURE(x, evil)

STEP 2.

Present the question of GEX to KB.

If this question is answered by YES, with the substitutions {σ} then

2.1 - delete the question from GEX, this gives GEX'

2.2 - apply {σ} to GEX'

2.3 - choose one of the clauses of GEX', and transform it into a question, and go back to the beginning of step 2 with this new question, where GEX' takes the place of GEX.

Each clause of EX will become, after an appropriate transformation, a question for KB. If all the questions are answered by YES, with a set of substitutions {Σ}, then continue to step 3, otherwise the analogy fails.

The question '? :- PSY-FEATURE(x, evil)' elicits the answer YES from MA, with the substitution [x ← Macbeth]. The question is deleted from GEX1 and the substitution is applied to GEX1 which becomes

GEX1'

AKO(Macbeth, man)
AKO(y, woman)
SOC-REL(Macbeth, y, MARRY)
PSY-FEATURE(Macbeth, weak)
PSY-FEATURE(y, greedy)

Now each statement of GEX1' becomes a question, presented to MA. Querying MA on
?   :-AKO(Macbeth, man) yields the empty clause. Querying MA on
?   :-SOC-REL(Macbeth, y, MARRY) yields the empty clause with the substitution [y ←Lady-Macbeth] which is also applied to GEX1'. This gives GEX1".

GEX1"

AKO(Lady-Macbeth, woman)
PSY-FEATURE(Macbeth, weak)
PSY-FEATURE(Lady-Macbeth, greedy)

By querying MA on each clause of GEX1" successively one finally obtains the empty clause. This shows that all the relations of evil between Macbeth and Lady-Macbeth may apply as well to man1 and woman1.

2.2.3 Looking for causality links

This is not enough to draw a valid analogy, we still have to check that the YES we obtained for the first question finds its causes in the information contained in EX. This is done during

STEP 3

3.1 - Look for the cause of the success the first question.

If there is no such cause, the analogy fails.

If there is such a cause, it is expressed in a clause the head of which starts with a 'CAUSE', called a causal clause in the following.

3.2 -

- Isolate the conditions of the causal clause selected at step 3.1.

- Apply the replacement $\Sigma^{-1} * T$ to these conditions. This amounts to replacing in KB the characters of the clausal cause by the corresponding characters of EX.

- Query EX on the conditions thus partially instantiated

If all are answered by YES, then the analogy is justified, otherwise it fails.

The reason why the first question has been answered YES is given by the causal clause instantiated by the substitutions that lead to a success.

This is not enough to draw a valid analogy, we still have to check that this evil finds also its causes in EX1. This is done by finding the cause of evil in Macbeth which is CAUSE(PSY-FEATURE(Macbeth, evil)) :-

> *PSY-FEATURE(Macbeth, weak),*
> *SOC-REL(Macbeth, Lady-Macbeth, MARRY),*
> *PSY-FEATURE(Lady-Macbeth, greedy))*

by replacing Macbeth and Lady-Macbeth by man1 and woman1, we obtain the three questions

? PSY-FEATURE(man1, weak)

? SOC-REL(Man1, woman1, MARRY)

? PSY-FEATURE(woman1, greedy)

that ask in EX1 if the conditions for man1 being evil are fulfilled.

All these questions are answered YES by EX1, which allows us to conclude that the analogy between the couples (Macbeth, Lady-Macbeth) and (man1, woman1) is justified for evil.

2.2.4 Finding a general rule

STEP 4

The causal clause is found to be applicable to two sets of instances. It is generalized to the common parents of these instances, thus generating a general rule.

We can generalize the causality to the common parents of the elements of the above couple. Since one has

AKO(man1, man)

226

AKO(woman1, woman)
AKO(Macbeth, man)
AKO(Lady-Macbeth, woman)
one can generalize to any kind of men and women, obtaining the new rule

CAUSE((PSY-FEATURE(man, evil)) :- PSY-FEATURE(man, weak), SOC- REL(man, woman, MARRY), PSY-FEATURE(woman, greedy))

Exercise 28
****

Apply the same method to the following EX2. Point out the place where it fails.

AKO(man2, man)
AKO(woman2, woman)
AKO(man4, man)
AKO(man3, man)
SOC-POS(man2, noble)
SOC-POS(man4, king)
SOC-POS(man3, prince)
SOC-REL(man2, woman2, MARRY)
PSY-FEATURE(man2, evil)
PSY-FEATURE(woman2, greedy)
PSY-FEATURE(man3, loyal)
? KILL(man3, man2)

****

In conclusion let me point out that the above algorithm has received about 10 implementations from my graduate students, as one of their graduation chores. None of the groups performed exactly the same implementation but all succeeded in making running programs on this problem and also on some complications of it. For instance, they had to introduce causality clauses expressing the fact that Macbeth and his wife wish to raise their social status, and use this causality for drawing better analogies.

Appendix 1
Equivalence Between Theorems and Clauses

This appendix gives the notions of logic needed to understand the equivalence between a proof that a theorem is satisfiable and a proof that a set of clauses is satisfiable. For more details, the reader will refer to [Chang & Lee 1973].

1 INTERPRETATION

Definition 1.

An **interpretation** of the formula F in a first-order logic consists in a non-empty domain D and an assignment defined as follows:

(i)   An element of D is associated with each constant in F.

(ii)   An application of D^n toward D is associated with each n-ary function symbol.

(iii)   An application of D^n toward {TRUE, FALSE} is associated with each n-ary predicate symbol.

For each interpretation of the formula on a domain D, the formula can be evaluated to TRUE or FALSE in accordance with the following rules:

(i)   If the truth-values of the formulae G and H are evaluated, then the truth-values of the formulae $\neg G$, G & H, G $\vee$ H, G $\Rightarrow$ H and G $\Leftrightarrow$ H are evaluated using the following table.

G	H	$\neg G$	G&H	G$\vee$H	G$\Rightarrow$H	G$\Leftrightarrow$H
TRUE	TRUE	FALSE	TRUE	TRUE	TRUE	TRUE
TRUE	FALSE	FALSE	FALSE	TRUE	FALSE	FALSE
FALSE	TRUE	TRUE	FALSE	TRUE	TRUE	FALSE
FALSE	FALSE	TRUE	FALSE	FALSE	TRUE	TRUE

(ii) $\forall x$ G is evaluated to TRUE if the truth-value of is evaluated to TRUE for each d of D, otherwise, it is evaluated to FALSE.

(iii) $\exists x$ G is evaluated to TRUE if the truth-value of is evaluated to TRUE for at least one d of D, otherwise, it is evaluated to FALSE.

No formula containing free variables can be evaluated.

Example 1.

Consider the formula $\forall x \, [P(x) \Rightarrow \exists y \, Q(x, y)]$ and the following interpretation of this formula

Domain: $D = $ NATURAL INTEGERS

Assignments for P:

P(0)	P(1)	P(2)	P(3)	...	P(n)	...
FALSE	FALSE	TRUE	TRUE	...	TRUE	...

Assignments for Q:

$Q(0, 0) \rightarrow$ TRUE

$Q(1, 1) \rightarrow$ TRUE

$Q(x, y) \rightarrow$ TRUE if $x = y + 2$ for $x > 1$.

We can check that the given formula is TRUE in this interpretation.

Of course, since P(0) and P(1) are evaluated to TRUE, the values of $Q(0,y)$ and $Q(1, y)$ are indifferent (even though a value must be chosen), i.e. whether they take the value TRUE or the value FALSE makes no difference to the validity of the interpretation.

Notation.

In the rest of this appendix, an atom or formula ' P ' whose truth-value is indifferent will be written *P. Of course, P and ¬P cannot both be present in the interpretation, one of the two has to be chosen, but this choice is unimportant.

*So in the example above, we have *Q(0, y) and *Q(1, y).*

Example 2.

The formula $\forall z \, B(z) \Rightarrow (A(f(z)) \, \& \, \neg R(f(z), z))$ involves a unary function f, two unary predicates, A and B, and a 2-ary predicate R.

Let us define a particular interpretation as follows:

Domain: $D = \{a, b, c, d\}$.

Assignments for f:

f(a)	f(b)	f(c)	f(d)
c	d	c	d

Assignments for A:

a	b	c	d
FALSE	FALSE	TRUE	TRUE

229

Of course, since A has only f(z) as argument, the values of A(a) and A(b) can be indifferent, i.e. we have: *A(a) and *A(b).

Assignments for B:

a	b	c	d
TRUE	TRUE	FALSE	FALSE

The assignments for R(y, x) are deduced from the following table:

y＼x	c	d
a	FALSE	TRUE
b	TRUE	FALSE

where y can take the values c, d (because of the fact that y is always instantiated by f(z)) and where x can take the values a and b because B(c) and B(d) are FALSE and hence imply everything.

The given formula is clearly TRUE under the given interpretation.

Definition 2.

A formula G is **satisfiable** if and only if there exists an interpretation I such that G evaluates to TRUE in I. If the formula G is TRUE in an interpretation I, we can say that I is a **model** of G and that I **satisfies** G.

Definition 3.

A formula G is **unsatisfiable** if and only if no interpretation exists which satisfies G.

Definition 4.

A formula G is **valid** if and only if each interpretation of G satisfies G.

Definition 5.

A formula G is a logical consequence of the formulae $F_1, F_2, ..., F_n$ if and only if for each interpretation I such that $F_1, F_2, ..., F_n$ is true in I, G is also TRUE in I.

The following two theorems express the relationship between validity or unsatisfiability and logical consequence.

Theorem 1.

Given the formulae $F_1, F_2, ..., F_n$ and a formula G, G is a logical consequence of $F_1, F_2, ..., F_n$ if and only if the formula: $F_1 \& F_2 \& ... \& F_n \Rightarrow G$ is valid.

Proof: systematic use of definitions 1 - 5.

Theorem 2.

G is a logical consequence of F_1, F_2, ..., F_n if and only if the formula : F_1 & F_2 & ...& F_n & ¬G is unsatisfiable.

These theorems are very important. They show that proving that a particular formula is a logical consequence of a finite set of formulae is equivalent to proving that certain related formulae are valid or unsatisfiable.

If G is the logical consequence of F_1, F_2, ..., F_n, the formula F_1, F_2, ..., F_n ⇒ G is called a **theorem**, and G is also called the **conclusion** of the theorem.

Example 3.

Let us consider the formulae

F_1: ∀z B(z) ⇒ (A(f(z)) & ¬R(f(z), z))

F_2: ∀y A(y) ⇒ ¬B(y)

F_3: B(a).

We are going to prove that the formula ¬B(f(a)) is a logical consequence of F_1, F_2 and F_3.

Let us use theorem 2. ¬B(f(a)) is a logical consequence of F_1, F_2 and F_3 if the formula G: F_1 & F_2 & F_3 & B(f(a)) is unsatisfiable.

By definition 3, this is true if there is no interpretation which satisfies G. Let us assume that I is an interpretation in which G evaluates to TRUE.

Thus, by definition 1, we know that F_1, F_2, F_3 and B(f(a)) all evaluate to TRUE in I. Since 'a' occurs in F_3, since 'f(a)' occurs in ¬B(f(a)), and since 'f' is the only function occurring in the formulae F_1, F_2, and F_3, the elements 'a' and 'f(a)' must certainly be considered in I.

Therefore, for a and f(a) we have

$F_1[z \leftarrow a]$

(1)   B(a) ⇒ A(f(a)) & ¬R(f(a), a) evaluates to TRUE

$F_1[z \leftarrow f(a)]$

(2)   B(f(a)) ⇒ A(f(f(a))) & ¬R(f(f(a)), f(a)) evaluates to TRUE

$F_2[z \leftarrow a]$

(3)   A(a) ⇒ ¬B(a) evaluates to TRUE

$F_2[z \leftarrow f(a)]$

(4)   A(f(a)) ⇒ ¬B(f(a)) evaluates to TRUE

F_3

(5)   B(a) evaluates to TRUE

F_4

(6)   *B(f(a)) evaluates to TRUE*

In each interpretation, B(a) (i.e. F_3) is evaluated to TRUE.

Because of this, through (1), we infer that A(f(a)) & ¬R(f(a), a) must be TRUE in I.

This is so if and only if A(f(a)) & ¬R(f(a), a) both evaluate to TRUE. We then have

(7)   *A(f(a)) evaluates to TRUE.*

(8)   *¬R(f(a), a) evaluates to TRUE.*

Then, in view of (7), we infer, starting from (4), that ¬B(f(a)) must evaluate to TRUE in I. But this is in contradiction with (6).

Exercise 29
****

Find the smallest interpretation that satisfies the following set of 6 clauses.

(S_1) ∃z [B(z)]

(S_2) ∀x ∀y [A(x) & A(y) ⟹ ∃z [B(z) & R(x, z) & R(y, z)]]

(S_3) ∀x ∀y [A(x) & A(y) & x ≠ y ⟹ ∃z [B(z) & R(x, z) & R(y, z) & (∀q [B(q) & R(x, q) & R(y, q) ⟹ (z=q)])]]

(S_4) ∀z [B(z) ⟹ ∃x ∃y [x ≠ y & A(x) & A(y) & R(x, z) & R(y, z)]]

(S_5) ∀z [B(z) ⟹ ∃x [A(x) & ¬ R(x, z)]]

(S_6) ∀y [A(y) ⟹ ¬B(y)]

****

2 THE HERBRAND UNIVERSE OF A SET OF CLAUSES

In first-order logic, if there is an infinite number of domains, then there is an infinite number of interpretations of a formula. Thus it is not possible to verify that a formula is valid or that a formula is unsatisfiable by evaluating the formula for all its possible interpretations.

Exercise 30

****

Is it possible to do it in propositional logic ?

****

But there is another way of checking the validity of formulae which gives a restriction on a suitable domain.

This very important approach to automatic theorem-proving was set out by Herbrand in 1930. In 1965 Robinson established the resolution principle, which improved efficiency far more than all other method issued from Herbrand's ideas.

But Herbrand's results are really a "pre-formulation" of the resolution principle.

2.1 Conversion of formulae into Skolem form

The definition of a Skolem form has been given in section 1.1 of chapter 2.

Definition 6.

A **clause** is a finite disjunction of literals. When a clause contains no literal, we call it an **empty clause**.

A set of clauses S is considered as a conjunction of all its clauses, where each variable is considered as being universally quantified.

According to this convention, a standard form can be represented simply by a set of clauses.

Example 4.

The standard form of the formula: $\forall z\ B(z) \Rightarrow \exists x\ (A(x)\ \&\ \neg R(x, z))$ can be represented by the set $\{\ \neg B(z) \vee A(f(z)),\ \neg B(z) \vee \neg R(f(z), z)\ \}$.

The following theorem shows that we can eliminate the existential quantifiers without modifying the property of unsatisfiability.

Theorem 3.

Let S be a set of clauses representing a standard form of the formula F. F is unsatisfiable if and only if S is unsatisfiable.

Proof

Let us write the formula to be proved as $F = Q_1 x_1, ..., Q_n x_n \ M(x_1, ..., x_1)$ where each Q_i is either $\forall$ or $\exists$ and where M is the body of the formula.

Case 1 - Elimination of an $\exists$.

Suppose that Q_r is the the first $\exists$, i.e. that the formula is of the form
$F = \forall x_1 \ \cdots \ \forall x_{r-1} \exists x_r \, Q_{r+1} x_{r+1} \ \cdots \ Q_n x_n \ M(x_1, ..., x_n)$.

Letting f be the Skolem function corresponding to x_r, the Skolemized form of F is
$F_1 = \forall x_1 \ \cdots \ \forall x_{r-1} \, Q_{r+1} x_{r+1} \ \cdots \ Q_n x_n \ M(x_1, ..., f(x_1, ..., x_{r-1}), x_{r+1}, ..., x_n)$.

Case 1.1

Suppose that F_1 is satisfiable, then an interpretation I exists such that F_1 is TRUE in I. Therefore, F is also TRUE in I since the instance, necessary to satisfy the existential, is exactly $f(x_1, ..., x_{r-1})$.
Therefore, F is also satisfiable.

Case 1.2

Supposing that F is satisfiable, then an interpretation I exists on a domain D such that F is TRUE in I. So for all $x_1, \ ..., \ x_{r-1}$, an x_r exists such that $Q_{r+1} x_{r+1} \ \cdots \ Q_n x_n \ M(x_1, ..., x_{r-1}, x_r, x_{r+1}, ..., x_n)$ is true in I.
Let us extend I by adding to it a function f defined by
$$f(x_1, ..., x_{r-1}) = x_r.$$

Let I' be this extension. Then for all $x_1, \ ..., \ x_{r-1}$, we have $Q_{r+1} x_{r+1} \ \cdots \ Q_n x_n \ M(x_1, ..., x_{r-1}, f(x_1, ..., x_{r-1}), ..., x_{r+1}, ..., x_n)$ is TRUE in I' and so F_1 is satisfiable.

Case 2 - Elimination of several $\exists$.

The proof above is iterated to obtain a proof by induction on the number of $\exists$.

Let S be a standard form of the formula F. If F is unsatisfiable, then theorem 3 shows that F and S are identical in relation to their context. But if F is not unsatisfiable, we note that, in general, F is not equivalent to S, as the following example shows.

Example 5.
Let F = ∃x P(x) and S = P(a). Let I be the interpretation defined below:
Domain: D = {1, 2}.
Assignment for a: a ← 1
Assignment for P:

P(1)	P(2)
FALSE	TRUE

F is TRUE in I, but S is FALSE in I. Hence F ≠ S.

Remark: THE STANDARD FORM OF A FORMULA IS NOT ALWAYS UNIQUE, as is shown by example 6 below.

For greater simplicity, when we transform a formula F into a standard form S, we have to replace the existential quantifier by Skolem functions which must be as simple as possible (the ones used have the fewest arguments).

Example 6.
The reader will verify that from the formula ∀x ∀y [A(x) & B(y) ⟹ ∃z R(x, z)] two different Skolem forms can be obtained

$$\forall x\, \forall y\, \exists z\, [\neg A(x) \lor \neg B(y) \lor R(x, z)] \text{ and}$$
$$\forall x\, \exists z\, \forall y\, [\neg A(x) \lor \neg B(y) \lor R(x, z)]$$

The first form will require a Skolem function dependent on the variables x and y, whereas the second form requires a Skolem function dependent only on x.
So the second will be chosen, the additional variables being merely a superficial complication of the satisfiability proofs.

2.2 Skolemization and unsatisfiability

If we have $F = F_1 \& ... \& F_n$, we can separately obtain a set S_i of clauses, where each S_i represents a standard form of F_i, i = 1, 2, ..., n. Let $S = S_1 \cup ... \cup S_n$.
F is unsatisfiable if and only if S is unsatisfiable.

Example 7.
Consider the formulae
F_1: *∀z B(z) ⟹ (A(f(z)) & ¬R(f(z), z))*

F_2: $\forall y\ A(y) \Rightarrow \neg B(y)$

F_3: $B(a)$.

The formula $\neg B(f(a))$ is a logical consequence of F_1, F_2 and F_3. By theorem 2, this is true if and only if F_1 & F_2 & F_3 & $B(f(a))$ is unsatisfiable.

Theorem 3 indicates that this is true if and only if the set of clauses representing this last formula is unsatisfiable.

Given the previous remark, a set S can be represented as a union of S_1, S_2, S_3 and S_4:

$S_1 = \{\neg B(z) \vee \neg A(f(z)), \neg B(z) \vee R(f(z), z)\}$

$S_2 = \{ \neg A(y) \vee \neg B(y) \}$

$S_3 = \{ B(a) \}$

$S_4 = \{ B(f(a)) \}$.

Example 8.

Let us find the smallest interpretation in which F_1, F_2, F_3 and F_4 are satisfied.

F_3 and F_4 give $a, f(a) \in D$.

In the required interpretation we must have

(1) $B(a)$

(2) $\neg B(f(a))$

From F_1 we infer that $A(f(a))$ evaluates to TRUE.

(3) $B(a) \Rightarrow A(f(a))$ & $\neg R(f(a), a)$ must be evaluated to TRUE because of (1). This is so if

(4) $A(f(a))$ and (5) $\neg R(f(a), a)$ are both evaluated to TRUE.

For $f(a)$ we have

(6) $B(f(a)) \Rightarrow A(f(f(a)))$ & $\neg R(f(f(a)), f(a))$ must be evaluated to TRUE. In view of (2), this is TRUE if *$[A(f(f(a)))$ & $\neg R(f(f(a)), f(a))]$.

Furthermore, we obtain that $f(f(a)) \in D$. Formulas (1) and (2) give $a \neq f(a)$. So we can write $f(a) = b$. We have 3 possibilities:

(i) $f(f(a)) = a$

(ii) $f(f(a)) = b$

(iii) $b \neq f(f(a)) \neq a$. Consider the evaluation of F_2 for a. We obtain that

(7) $A(a) \Rightarrow \neg B(a)$ must be evaluated to TRUE. From (1) we infer that

(8) $\neg A(a)$ must be evaluated to TRUE. Suppose now that $f(f(a)) = a$. From (6) we have obtained that *$[A(f(f(a)))$ & $\neg R(f(f(a)), f(a))]$.

Looking at (8), it can be seen that evaluation to TRUE is not possible. Hence we finally choose to evaluate $A(f(f(a)))$ & $\neg R(f(f(a)), f(a))$ to FALSE.

Thereafter, we have *$[\neg R(f(f(a)), f(a))]$, i.e. *$\neg R(a, f(a))$.

As there are no restrictions on our choice, let us evaluate $\neg R(a, f(a))$ to FALSE.

We can then begin to build the required interpretation I:

Domain D = {a, b}

 Assignments for A:

a	b
FALSE	TRUE

 Assignments for B:

a	b
TRUE	FALSE

 Assignments for R:

	a	b
a	*x	TRUE
b	FALSE	*x

*where *x means that the corresponding value may be TRUE as well as FALSE.*

2.3 Herbrand Universe, H-interpretations

Definition 7.

Let H_0 be the set of constants appearing in S. If no constant appears in S, then H_0 constitutes a single constant, say $H_0 = \{a\}$.

For i = 0, 1, 2 ..., let $H_i + 1$ be the union of H_i and the set of all terms of the form $f(t_1, ..., t_n)$ for all the n-ary functions f occurring in S where t_j, j = 1, ..., n are members of the set H_i.

Each H_i is called a set of constants of the ith rank of S, and the limit of H_i when i tends to infinity is called the **Herbrand Universe** of S.

Example 9.

 The Herbrand Universe for the set of clauses given in example 4 is H = $\{a, f(a), f(f(a)), ... \}$

Example 10.

 Let S = $\{P(f(x), a, g(y), b), Q(h(a, z))\}$. Then

$H_0 = \{a, b\}$

$H_1 = \{a, b, f(a), f(b), g(a), g(b), h(a, a), h(a, b), h(b, a), h(b, b)\}$

$H_2 = \{a, b, f(a), f(b), g(a), g(b), h(a, a), h(a, b), ..., f(f(a)), f(f(b)), f(g(a)), f(g(b)), f(h(a, a)), f(h(a, b)), ..., g(f(a)), g(f(b)), g(g(a)), g(g(b)), g(h(a, a)), g(h(a, b)), ..., h(a, f(a)), h(a, f(b)), h(a, g(a)), h(a, g(b)), h(a, h(a, a)), h(a, h(a, b)), ...\}$.

Definition 8.

Let S be a set of clauses. The set of ground atoms of the form $P(t_1, ..., t_n)$ for all the n-ary predicates occurring in S, where $t_1, ..., t_n$ are elements of the Herbrand Universe of S, is called the **Herbrand Base** of S.

Definition 9.

A **ground instance** of a clause C of a set S of clauses is a clause obtained by replacing all variables in C by elements of the Herbrand Universe of S.

Definition 10.

Let S be a set of clauses, let H be the Herbrand Universe of S and let I be an interpretation of S on H.

I is called an **H-interpretation** of S if it satisfies the following conditions:

1. I maps each constant in S with itself.
2. Let f be an n-ary function symbol and let $t_1, ..., t_n$ be elements of H. In I, one attributes to f a function which maps $(t_1, ..., t_n)$ (an element in H^n) on $f(t_1, ..., t_n)$ (an element in H).

There is no restriction on the assignment to each symbol of an n-ary predicate in S. Let $A = \{A_1, ..., A_n, ...\}$ be the atom set of S.

An H-interpretation I can conveniently be represented by the set $I = \{m_1, m_2, ..., m_n, ...\}$, in which m_j is either A_j or $\neg A_j$ for $j = 1, 2, ...$ The meaning of this set is that if m_j is A_j then A_j is assigned the value TRUE; otherwise A_j is assigned the value FALSE.

Example 11.

For the formula of example 4, we have the Herbrand base $A = \{ B(a), A(f(a)), R(f(a), a), B(f(a)), A(f(f(a))), R(f(f(a)), f(a)), ...\}$ and some of the H-interpretations are
$I_1 = \{ \neg B(a), A(f(a)), R(f(a), a), \neg B(f(a)), A(f(f(a))), \neg R(f(f(a)), f(a)), ...\}$,
$I_2 = \{ B(a), A(f(a)), R(f(a), a), \neg B(f(a)), A(f(f(a))), R(f(f(a)), f(a)), ...\}$.

Definition 11.

Given an interpretation I on a domain D, an **H-interpretation** HI corresponding to I is an interpretation which satisfies the following condition.

Let $t_1, ..., t_n$ be elements of H (the Herbrand Universe of S). Each t_i is associated with a d_i in D. If $P(d_1, ..., d_n)$ is associated with TRUE, FALSE, then $P(t_1, ..., t_n)$ is associated with TRUE, FALSE, respectively in HI.

Example 12.

In example 8, we have built an interpretation $I = \{ \neg A(a), A(b), B(a), \neg B(b), *R(a, a), *R(a, b), \neg R(b, a), *R(b, b)\}$

$H = \{ a, f(a), f(f(a)), ... \}$.

Let $fn(a) = a$ for n odd, and $fn(a) = f(a)$ for n even. We have $HI = \{\neg A(a), A(f(a)),$

238

¬A(f(a)), A(f(f(a))), ..., B(a), ¬B(f(a)), B(f(a)), ¬B(f(f(a))), ..., *R(a, a), *R(f(a), f(a)), *R(f(f(a)), f(f(a))), ..., *R(a, f(a)), *R(f(f(a)), f(f(f(a)))), ..., ¬R(f(a), a), ¬R(f(f(f(a))), f(f(a))), ... }.

Lemma:

If an interpretation I on a domain D satisfies a set S of clauses, then each of the H-interpretations corresponding to I also satisfies S.

Exercise 31
****

Prove the lemma.

****

Theorem 4.

A set of clauses S is unsatisfiable if and only if S is false under all the H-interpretations of S.

Exercise 32
****

Prove Theorem 4.

****

3 SEMANTIC TREES

The above lemma and theorem 4 enable us to check the unsatisfiability of a set of clauses in the H-interpretations. However, it quickly becomes clear that the number of these interpretations is very great.

Semantic trees serve to systematize the treatment of H-interpretations.

There will be a discussion below of the way in which finding a proof for a set of clauses is equivalent to generating a certain semantic tree.

Definition 12

If A is an atom, then the two literals A and ¬A are said to be **complements of each otherr**, and the set {A, ¬A} is called a **complementary pair**.

If a clause C contains a complementary pair, C is a tautology.

Definition 13.

Let us give ourselves a set of clauses, and let A be a set of atoms of S. A **semantic tree** for S is a tree T where each branch is associated with a finite set of atoms of A or of formulae built from atoms of A, in such a way that:

(i) For each node N, there is only a finite number of branches L_1,

Let Q_i be a conjunction of all the literals in the set associated to L_i, $i = 1, ..., n$. Then $Q_1 \vee Q_2 \vee ... \vee Q_n$ is a valid propositional formula.

(ii) for each node N, let I(N) be the union of all the sets associated with the branches of the descending branch T which includes N. Then I(N) contains no complementary pair.

Example 13.

Let $S = S_1 \cup S_2 \cup S_3$ where S_1, S_2 and S_3 are given in example 7.

We then have

$S = \{B(z) \vee \neg A(f(z)), B(z) \vee R(f(z), z), \neg A(y) \vee \neg B(y), B(a)\}$
$H = \{a, f(a), f(f(a)), f(f(f(a))), ...\}$

The set of atoms is $A = \{A(a), A(f(a)), A(f(f(a))), ...,B(a), B(f(a)), B(f(f(a))), ...,R(a, a), R(f(a), f(a)), R(f(f(a)), f(f(a))), ...,R(f(a), a), R(f(f(a)), f(a)), R(f(f(f(a))), f(f(a))), ..., R(f(f(a)), a), R(f(f(f(a))), f(a)), R(f(f(f(f(a)))), f(f(a))), ...\}$

Two corresponding semantic trees are given by T_1 and T_2.

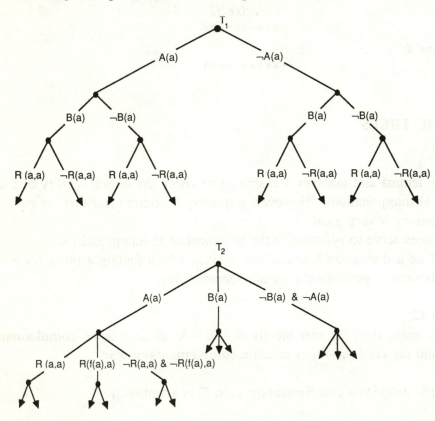

Definition 14.

Let $A = \{A_1, A_2, ... A_k, ...\}$ be the atom set of a set S of clauses. A semantic tree for S is called complete if and only if for each leaf N of the semantic tree, I(N) contains either A_i or $\neg A_i$ for each i.

240

Example 14.

Let $A = \{P, Q, R\}$ be a set of S of clauses. Then each of the trees T_3 and T_4 is a complete tree for S.

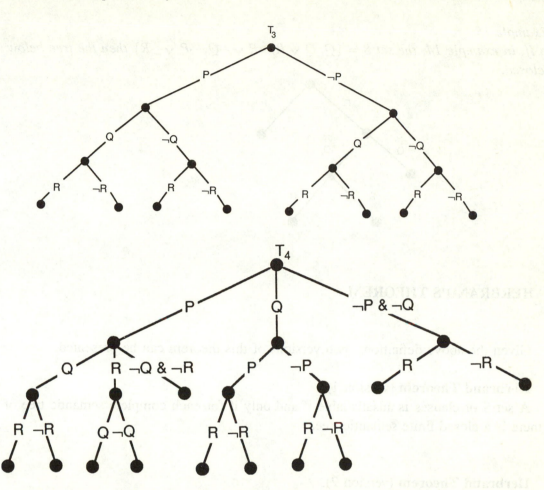

A complete semantic tree for S corresponds to an exhaustive search for all possible interpretations for S.

If S is unsatisfiable, then S is not TRUE in each of these interpretations.

Thus, we can stop the growth of the nodes beginning with a node N if I(N) falsifies S.

Definition 15.

A node N is a **failure node** if I(N) falsifies some ground instances of a clause in S, but it is not the case that for each node N', parent of N, I(N') falsifies an ground instance of a clause in S.

Definition 16.

A semantic tree T is called **closed** if and only if each branch terminates in a failure node.

Definition 17.

A node N of a closed semantic tree is called an **inference node** if all the nodes which are immediate descendants of N are failure nodes.

Example 15.

If, in example 14, the set S = {Q, Q ∨ R, ¬P ∨ ¬Q, ¬P ∨ ¬R} then the tree below is closed.

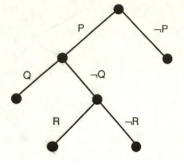

4 HERBRAND'S THEOREM

Given the above definitions, two versions of this theorem can be presented.

Herbrand Theorem (version 1).

A set S of clauses is unsatisfiable if and only if for each complete semantic tree of S there is a closed finite semantic tree.

Herbrand Theorem (version 2).

A set S of clauses is unsatisfiable if there is an unsatisfiable finite set S' of ground instances of clauses of S.

Clearly version 1 is connected with resolution and version 2 is connected with refutation, but this is not the subject here.

Appendix 2
Synthesis of Predicates

Let $\{E_i\}$ be a finite series of examples. On the basis of this series alone, it is not in general possible to predict the behavior of the elements of the series when it becomes infinite. It is important not to confuse this problem with that of finding the limit of $\{E_i\}$ when i tends to infinity. The aim here is to know the actual value of each of the E_i, whatever i may be.

Here are some examples taken from [Sloane 1973].

The standard problem is to find the "next" in a series whose first elements are given.
Find the law which generates the series:

$$1, 2, 3, 4, ..., 39, 42, 43, ...$$

One answer could be: it is the series of numbers n such that n**2 + n + 41 is a prime number.

Find the law which generates the series containing p occurrences of ' 1 ' at the beginning.

$$1, 1, 1, ..., 1, ... (p \; times)$$

One answer could be: the polynomial
$$(n - 1) (n - 2) (n - 3) ... (n - p) + 1.$$

The next example does not come from Sloane's book.

It is a mathematical game in which you ask your opponent to guess what is the law for which you propose examples, these examples not being necessarily successive. So this game is more difficult than the problem we are tackling.

The opponent can suggest an unlimited number of possible solutions which you have to reject if they do not fit the solution you are thinking of. At each of your opponent's mistakes, you have to give him a new example of the series you have in mind.

If the opponent gives in, then you have to give him a convincing solution, which eliminates the temptation to cheat.

A good way of winning at this game is to only give your opponent a meaningful subseries of the series you have in mind.

For example, supposing the law you are thinking of is "n is even", then you suggest to your opponent, as the first examples:

These examples make it clear that the number of possible solutions to such puzzles is infinite, and nothing indicates definitively which to choose.

However, in addition to the examples, you can impose conditions on the desired solution, thereby reducing the number of solutions and, in some cases, being able to find them. But do note that even if you are certain of the existence of a single solution spelling it out can still be an undecidable problem!

Clearly there is an infinite number of ways of continuing the series
$$\{0, 2, 4, 6, 8, ...\}.$$
However, if in addition we require the solution to make the difference between two successive terms equal to 2, completing it with the series of even numbers becomes trivial.

Definition.

The area of knowledge which deals with the conditions in which the values of infinite series can be calculated from their finite sub-series is referred to as **inductive inference**.

These conditions are in general very technical, and have only very little to do with ML.

A sub-domain of inductive inference, Program Synthesis, (now called Automatic Programming) is closer to our concerns. At the present time, the standard work on the subject is [Biermann et al. 1984]. In it a simple description will be found of the many methods developed to synthesize functions on the basis of of various kinds of data - from their properties, input/output, specifications, or informal descriptions.

Surprisingly enough, these authors have all tackled the problem of synthesizing functions and none of them has attempted to work on synthesizing predicates.

In fact, in ML we only very rarely need to build one element from others (which is the job of a function); but we do often need to recognize a feature of an element (which is the job of a predicate).

There are many programs capable of building a function that doubles the number of elements in a list, thus ensuring that this number is even.

On the other hand, the automatic construction of a predicate to recognize whether the number of elements in a list is even is a research problem unless you want to give an ad hoc solution. This problem is what exercise 33 is about.

This chapter is first going to give an example showing what makes synthesizing predicates on the basis of input/output a fundamental mechanism in ML. Following that we shall illustrate the problems raised by this form of synthesis.

1 MOTIVATION: AN EXAMPLE OF USEFUL SYNTHESIS IN ML

Let us consider an example of the learning of a recognition function from a set of positive examples E_i and of negative examples NE_i given by the following figures

E_1: ∇ Δ *, E_2: ∇ Δ, E_3:   *, E_4: ∇ []

NE_1: ∇ Δ * [], NE_2: ∇ *, NE_3: Δ →, NE_4: ∇ *

*Where ∇ is a NABLA, Δ is a DELTA, * is a STAR, [] is a RECTANGLE, → is an ARROW.*

In these examples, it must be understood that symbols are important only by their presence; their order does not matter. The fact that NE_2 and NE_4 are identical will not be used here, but it could be of use in numerical techniques.

*In order to study this problem, let us introduce variables to mark the presence or absence of a symbol in an example. Let x_1 be the variable associated with the symbol ∇, let x_2 be the variable associated with the symbol Δ , let x_3 be the variable associated with the symbol *, let x_4 be the variable associated with the symbol [], let x_5 be the variable associated with the symbol →.*

If the symbol associated with x_i is present in E_i, then $x_i = 1$; if it is absent, then $x_i = 0$.

So the problem is represented by the following table

	x_1	x_2	x_3	x_4	x_5
E_1	1	1	1	0	0
E_2	1	1	0	0	0
E_3	0	0	1	0	0
E_4	1	0	0	1	0
NE_1	1	1	1	1	0
NE_2	1	0	1	0	0
NE_3	0	1	0	0	1
NE_4	1	0	1	0	0

The reader can now attempt to find a predicate taking the value TRUE for the positive examples the value FALSE for the negative examples.

He will find an infinity of them, admittedly, but all will be of comparable complexity to the trivial expression:

$$(E_1 \lor E_2 \lor E_3 \lor E_4) \,\&\, \neg(NE_1 \lor NE_2 \lor NE_3 \lor NE_4)$$

Thus, by our definition of Artificial Intelligence, this solutions will be unsatisfactory because no explanation can be drawn from them.

The conclusion is that we have chosen an unsatisfactory way of representing the examples.

Now let us use our knowledge of geometric shapes. One possible taxonomy of shapes is

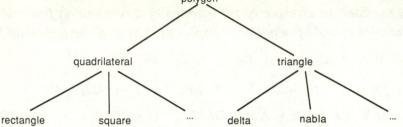

A nabla and a delta are triangles. Let us replace the variables x_1 and x_2 by the variable $x_{triangle}$, which counts the number of triangles in each example: $x_{triangle} = x_1 + x_2$.

We thus obtain a new representation of the examples.

	$x_{triangle}$	x_3	x_4	x_5
E_1	2	1	0	0
E_2	2	0	0	0
E_3	0	1	0	0
E_4	1	0	1	0
NE_1	2	1	1	0
NE_2	1	1	0	0
NE_3	1	0	0	1
NE_4	1	1	0	0

It might turn out that we still do not arrive at a good generalization. Let us reuse the taxonomy of shapes.

If we let $x_{polygon}$ be the variable associated with the polygon, it will count the number of polygons present in each example, so that we have $x_{polygon} = x_{triangle} + x_4$.

We thus obtain the new table:

	$x_{polygon}$	x_3	x_5
E_1	2	1	0
E_2	2	0	0
E_3	0	1	0
E_4	2	0	0
NE_1	3	1	0
NE_2	1	1	0
NE_3	1	0	1
NE_4	1	1	0

In the examples, $x_{polygon}$ takes the value 0 or 2, whereas in the negative examples, $x_{polygon}$ takes the value 1 or 3.

So a possible characterization of the examples is:
the number of polygons is even.

This example shows that a generalization algorithm must use the knowledge and, most importantly, must be able to modify the description used if it is meant to be applied to learning.

This example calls for two farther comments.

The first can be given in the form of a personal story.

In the innumerable discussions which gave birth to the ideas described in this book, one of our favorite themes was whether there are cases where learning ought not to take place. The data can be so confused that a learning system must indicate to its user that nothing can be gotten from them. The above example was created precisely in order to illustrate this thesis. It was only about a year after seeing it for the first time that I had the idea of applying the climbing the generalization tree technique to it, and saw, to my great astonishment, that the generalization given above appeared. Now that this kind of technique has become popular, this solution is coming to be found quite easily.

The second comment is about the difference between

> R_1:   *There is an even number of polygons, and*

> R_2: $(E_1 \lor E_2 \lor E_3 \lor E_4)$ & $\neg(NE_1 \lor NE_2 \lor NE_3 \lor NE_4)$.

It is intuitively clear that R_1 is a genuine explanation whereas R_2 is not. As far as we know, no formal definition of what makes an explanation "good" exists at present, and we are not going to solve this problem here.

Even so, let us give some indications about how to tackle it.

The closer a generalization is to the examples, the better it is. This is why, in a sense, R_2 is the best generalization that can be extracted from the examples. It is even the only one whose validity is certain. On the other hand, obviously, nothing has been learnt. To avoid falling into this kind of trap, we can impose conditions on the form of the generalization. For example, we can reject generalizations containing disjunctions. In R_2, the "$\neg$ &s" are going to generate $\lor$s, and according to this criterion, R_2 is not an authorized generalization.

On the other hand, R_1 is the most specific of the purely conjunctive generalizations that we have been able to find. So it is the best of those that satisfy this criterion. This is not what makes it an explanation.

The notion of the validity of an explanation depends on the prevailing environment. In our computer science environment, the notion of parity is extremely important, and belongs to an arsenal of concepts that we take to be explanatory. Suppose that the drawings we started with were about the world of medicine, where the notion of parity only turns up exceptionally. Then R_1 is still a valid generalization, but becomes a bad explanation.

Thus an explanation is valid when it uses the concepts known to the domain expert in the way he would use them, in the

In chapter 9, we indicated all the importance we attach to the notion of a micro-world. Here is a farther example of this importance.

To paraphrase the proverbs, "When in Rome explain as the Romans explain" (which does not mean "An explanation is often best left unsaid").

2 SYNTHESIS OF PREDICATES FROM INPUT/OUTPUTS

So we are given a finite series of values for which the predicate is TRUE, a series for which it is FALSE, and we wish to induce a recursive definition of the predicate, valid for an infinite number of values.

2.1 Getting computation traces

First of all it must be understood that there is no way of synthesizing a predicate (any more than a function or a program, incidentally) on the basis of raw input/output. The first operation in the synthesis consists in transforming the input/output into computation traces.

Definitions.

The representation of an input/output expressed as a function of a finite set of constructors and selectors belonging to the data type of the input/output is referred to as its **computation trace**.

When describing a data type, it is customary to define the operations which enable a representative of these data to be built, which are called the **constructors** of the type. Conversely, the operations which enable to extract elements from a representative of the type are called **selector**.

For the type LIST, the constructors are NIL and CONS, from which any list can be built. The selectors are CAR and CDR, which enable elements to be extracted from a list.

Constructors and selectors enable an order to be defined on the data, since, for any datum x, we have

$$\text{Constructor}(x) \geq x \text{ as well as}$$
$$\text{Selector}(x) \leq x.$$

These constructors and these selectors constitute the basic functions which serve as inputs to the synthesis.

Given these basic functions, it is also possible to define intermediate functions which can be used during the synthesis.

Example 1.
In the natural integers, the basic constructors are Successor (SUCC) which associates each integer with its successor, and 0, which is the smallest of the natural integers.
Hence, SUCC(SUCC(0)) is a computation trace of the integer 2.

Example 2.
The Predecessor (PRED) is a basic selector of natural integers.
Using SUCC and PRED gives each integer an infinite number of computation traces. For example, the integer 2 can be written
SUCC(PRED(SUCC(PRED(SUCC(SUCC(0)))))), etc...
In this case, the computation trace is not unique.

Example 3.
In lists, LISP provides
- *the constructor of the empty list: NIL*
- *the list constructor: CONS*
- *the selector for the head of the list: CAR*
- *the selector for the body of the list: CDR.*
In tree representation, it is clear that CAR selects the left-hand child of a list and

CDR the right-hand child.

For example, let the list be ((1) 2 3), whose tree representation is

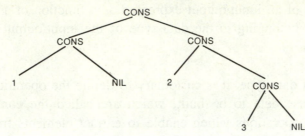

The CAR of this list, (1), does turn out to be the left-hand child of the highest CONS, and the CAR of this list, (2 3)), does turn out to be its right- hand child.

Thus, a computation trace of this list is

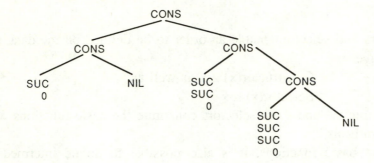

Example 4.

We might wish to only study the structures of lists, independently of their contents. The name of each atom then become insignificant. It is replaced by the position of the atom in the list.

Suppose, then, that the list ((1) 2 3) has to be considered in this way, i.e. that the integer nature of ' 1 ', ' 2 ' and ' 3 ' has no significance for us.

Let us refer to these lists, such as ((a) b c) or ((THIS) ISOKAY LIKETHIS?), as
'x'.

Then their computation trace (with respect to their structure) will be

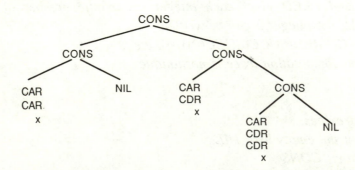

So we are going to need to use an algorithm associating computation traces with the data. It must exhibit the following property:

the algorithm associates a UNIQUE computation trace with each datum.

This condition of the uniqueness of the computation trace is in general difficult to fulfill. Let us take it that we wish to synthesize a function of the natural integers using the functions multiplication and division as the constructor and selector of the type.
 The computation trace for integers using these constructors and selectors is not unique. This means that the algorithm for synthesis has to contain a way of generating a unique trace.

In other words, the algorithm will have to be changed each time the constructors and selectors are modified.

2.2   Acquisition of recurrence relations on the computation traces

The data domain generally possesses an order. This order is used to order the series of inputs to the synthesis. As we are dealing with predicates, the outputs are always TRUE or FALSE.

With the data arranged in ascending order, we transform them into computation traces, and we search for recurrence relations between successive data pairs.
We have developed a direct search algorithm for relations of recurrence, [Kodratoff 1979], [Kodratoff & Jouanaud 1984], whereas others have found an indirect algorithm [Jouannaud & Guiho 1979].

As an example, let us study the synthesis of the predicate EVEN(x).

So the series of examples is {EVEN(0) = TRUE, EVEN(2) = TRUE,
EVEN(4) = TRUE, EVEN(6) = TRUE, EVEN(8) = TRUE, ...}
Let us convert the series {0, 2, 4, 6, 8, ...} into a computation trace, using only the constructor SUCC.
We obtain: {0, SUCC(SUCC(0)), SUCC(SUCC(SUCC(SUCC(0)))),
SUCC(SUCC(SUCC(SUCC(SUCC(SUCC(0)))))),
SUCC(SUCC(SUCC(SUCC(SUCC(SUCC(SUCC(SUCC(0)))))))), ... }.

Let us search for recurrence relations between successive data.
To do this, we are going to try to match each datum with the next one.
When the matching succeeds, we find recurrence relations, when it fails, we introduce new variables into the examples (i.e. we generalize the examples) so that the generalizations match.

We attempt successively to match 0 with SUCC(SUCC(0)),
to match SUCC(SUCC(0)) with SUCC(SUCC(SUCC(SUCC(0)))),

to match SUCC(SUCC(SUCC(SUCC(0)))) with
$$SUCC(SUCC(SUCC(SUCC(SUCC(SUCC(0)))))),$$
to match SUCC(SUCC(SUCC(SUCC(SUCC(SUCC(0)))))) with
$$SUCC(SUCC(SUCC(SUCC(SUCC(SUCC(SUCC(SUCC(0)))))))),$$
etc ...

All these matchings fail, and all for the same reason, namely that the constant 0 cannot be replaced by the expression SUCC(SUCC(0)). In fact, only a variable can receive a substitution (refer to section 2 for a definition).

In each value, the constant 0 is replaced by a variable in order to make the corresponding pair match. In general, we do not know any link between two successive pairs, which is why we have to give a different name to each variable thus introduced.

The series of computation traces becomes:

$\{z_0 \ [z_0 \leftarrow 0],$

$SUCC(SUCC(z_1)) \ [z_1 \leftarrow 0],$

$SUCC(SUCC(SUCC(SUCC(z_2)))) \ [z_2 \leftarrow 0],$

$SUCC(SUCC(SUCC(SUCC(SUCC(SUCC(z_3)))))) \ [z_3 \leftarrow 0],$

$SUCC(SUCC(SUCC(SUCC(SUCC(SUCC(SUCC(SUCC(z_4)))))))) \ [z_4 \leftarrow 0], \ ... \ \}.$

Let us study the series of computation traces which results from the above series when the substitutions are omitted.

Recall that these substitutions are the ones which make it possible to go from the new trace to the old trace.

The new series is:

$\{z_0,$

$SUCC(SUCC(z_1)),$

$SUCC(SUCC(SUCC(SUCC(z_2)))),$

$SUCC(SUCC(SUCC(SUCC(SUCC(SUCC(z_3)))))),$

$SUCC(SUCC(SUCC(SUCC(SUCC(SUCC(SUCC(SUCC(z_4)))))))), \ ... \ \}.$

This simple example makes it very tempting to remark that all the z_i receive the same substitution and so they must all be renamed by the same variable. When several variables are introduced, the problem cannot be solved in this way. For example, variables having different recurrence relations could receive the same substitution.

Once again we try to match the members of the new series of traces two by two. We successively try to match z_0 with SUCC(SUCC(z_1)),

to match SUCC(SUCC(z_1)) with SUCC(SUCC(SUCC(SUC(z_2)))),

to match SUCC(SUCC(SUCC(SUCC(z_2)))) with
$$SUCC(SUCC(SUCC(SUCC(SUCC(SUCC(z_3)))))),$$
to match SUCC(SUCC(SUCC(SUCC(SUCC(SUCC(z_3)))))) with

$$SUCC(SUCC(SUCC(SUCC(SUCC(SUCC(SUCC(SUCC(z_4)))))))),$$

etc ...

These matchings now succeed:

z_0 *matches with* $SUCC(SUCC(z_1))$ *provided the substitution* $[[z_0 \leftarrow SUCC(SUCC(z_1))]]$,
$SUCC(SUCC(z_1))$ *matches with* $SUCC(SUCC(SUCC(SUCC(z_2))))$ *provided the substitution* $[[z_1 \leftarrow SUCC(SUCC(z_2))]]$,
$SUCC(SUCC(SUCC(SUCC(z_2))))$ *matches with* $SUCC(SUCC(SUCC(SUCC(SUCC(SUCC(z_3))))))$ *provided the substitution* $[[z_2 \leftarrow SUCC(SUCC(z_3))]]$,
$SUCC(SUCC(SUCC(SUCC(SUCC(SUCC(z_3))))))$ *matches with* $SUCC(SUCC(SUCC(SUCC(SUCC(SUCC(SUCC(SUCC(z_4))))))))$ *provided the substitution* $[[z_3 \leftarrow SUCC(SUCC(z_4))]]$, *etc ...*

We have written these substitutions using a [[ ]] to distinguish them clearly from the first substitution, written [ ]. In fact, they represent two quite different things.

The substitutions written [ ] describe how, starting from the generalized series, the initial series can be found again.

The substitutions written [[ ]] describe how, starting from an element of the series, the next can be found.

When these successive substitutions have been found, the links between the generalization variables still remain to be detected.

Since these links are to express relations of recurrence, it is necessary for each variable ' x ' to occur in the expression which is substituted for it. This last statement may not be obvious to you. It will become obvious when you see the form of the function obtained.

In our example, let us first examine $[[z_0 \leftarrow SUCC(SUCC(z_1))]]$.

It is necessary for the variable z_0 *on the left of the substitution also to be on the right. The only variable present on the right has been called* z_1. *So its name must be changed to* z_0; *this is the only way to make* z_0 *appear on the right.*

So the next substitution, $[[z_1 \leftarrow SUCC(SUCC(z_2))]]$, *becomes* $[[z_0 \leftarrow SUCC(SUCC(z_2))]]$, *since we have replaced* z_1 *by* z_0. *The same reasoning then shows that* z_2 *must also be replaced by* z_0.

Thus we shall go from neighbor to neighbor showing that all the variables have to be replaced by z_0.

We get a new expression from the series of computation traces:

$\{t_0 = z_0 \ [z_0 \leftarrow 0],$
$t_1 = SUCC(SUCC(z_0)) \ [z_0 \leftarrow 0],$
$t_2 = SUCC(SUCC(SUCC(SUCC(z_0)))) \ [z_0 \leftarrow 0],$

$$t_3 = SUCC(SUCC(SUCC(SUCC(SUCC(SUCC(z_0)))))) \ [z_0 \leftarrow 0],$$
$$t_4 = SUCC(SUCC(SUCC(SUCC(SUCC(SUCC(SUCC(SUCC(z_0)))))))) \ [z_0 \leftarrow 0], \dots \ \}.$$

where each trace is named by a t_i.

This new series is such that each t_{i+1} can be calculated from t_i through the recurrence relation

$$t_{i+1}(z_0) = t_i \ (SUCC(SUCC(z_0)))$$

which derives directly from the constant substitution $[z_0 \leftarrow SUCC(SUCC(z_0))]$ which we discovered with the help of our matchings.

Of course, the fact that we have discovered a property of recurrence between five examples does not make it necessary that this property is valid for the infinite series of possible data to which the predicate applies.

The synthesized function is the one which extends infinitely the properties detected.

It can happen that the "right" properties are not detected, and the method is then at fault. However, for certain classes of simple functions which lack multiple properties, the method enables the right result to be obtained without fail.

2.3 Acquisition of recursive predicates from recurrence relations

What remains is to transform these recurrence relations into a recursive function, applying the methods set out in [Summers 1977] and [Kodratoff 1983, Kodratoff & Jouannaud 1984].

These methods will not be given in detail here, but their principle is extremely simple.

We define a recursive predicate by taking the initial values as the basic case. We then calculate its value by following the recurrence relations.

It is this latter calculation which can be a little complicated when working in a Functional Language and when the constructor used in the recurrence relations has no inverse.

If working in PROLOG, then we directly use the recurrence relations found previously.

If working in a Functional Language with a constructor that has an inverse, then we content ourselves with expressing t_i as a function of t_{i+1}, and this directly defines a standard recursive call.

So we are going to define the predicate EVEN(x) as follows. The basic case is given by the value the recurrence relations begin from, which here is 0.

So the basic case is:

(in PROLOG)   EVEN(0) :-

(in a Functional Language)   IF x = 0 THEN TRUE

The recursive case is then calculated by means of the recurrence relations.
If working in PROLOG, we use the recurrence relation directly, thus getting
$$EVEN(SUCC(SUCC(x))) :- EVEN(x)$$

In a Functional Language, the constructor SUCC has an inverse, namely, the selector PRED.
Thus, from
$$t_{i+1}(z_0) = t_i(SUCC(SUCC(z_0)))$$
it can be inferred that
$$t_i(z_0) = t_{i+1}(PRED(PRED(z_0)))$$

We can then write the recursive relation:
$$ELSE\ EVEN(PRED(PRED(x)))$$

In the end we have :

(in PROLOG)   EVEN(0) :-
                             EVEN(SUCC(SUCC(x))) :- EVEN(x)

(in a Functional Language) EVEN(x) $\Leftarrow$ IF x = 0 THEN TRUE ELSE EVEN(PRED(PRED(x))).

2.4 Synthesis of a predicate which gives the parity of the length of a list

Exercise 33
****

On the basis of input/outputs, synthesize a predicate which takes linear lists as its argument (i.e. lists containing no sublists) and which takes the value TRUE when the length of the list is even and FALSE when it is odd.

The examples

NIL $\rightarrow$ TRUE,   (A) $\rightarrow$ FALSE,   (A A) $\rightarrow$ TRUE , (A A A) $\rightarrow$ FALSE,
(A A A A) $\rightarrow$ TRUE, ...
must be converted into a computation trace like that of example 4 in section 2.1.

****

3 APPROACHES TO AUTOMATIC PROGRAMMING

3.1 Automatic Programming and ML

This section describes how programs can be synthesized from their specifications. This amounts to the invention of an algorithm that computes values fulfilling a given condition. This "**given condition**" is a set of relationships that link inputs and outputs. We shall assume here that these relationships are given in the form of a **formal specification**, in first order logics.

The **algorithm** is described by a program written in a target language.

Before giving any more details, let us explain why this is so, and give an example of how this problem may naturally occur while a learning system is running.

The main reason is that we do usually work with formal specifications in Machine Learning, but we usually prefer call them "**concept definitions**", or "**recognition functions**", or "**action conditions**". All three are things of the same kind, viz. sets of predicates (maybe containing variables whose values can make them) being either TRUE or FALSE.

As long as these three things are used to define concepts, or to recognize patterns, or to check whether a rule is to be fired, they play their usual role.

It may nevertheless happen that we want to use this knowledge not only as described above, but also in a generative way, with the purpose to generate either new instances of the concept, or new patterns recognizable by the concerned recognition function, or new instances of the actions to be done.

We are used to handling sets of predicates that recognize if a given individual is eating a cheese sandwich or listening to Bach's music. The problem of program synthesis is : given these predicates, generate cheese sandwiches and Bach's music.

Both problems are extremely difficult. Synthesizing a sorting function from the knowledge of what a sort is, or a unification algorithm from the definition of a unification are feasible but also very difficult tasks, as we shall see below.

In the context of an Apprentice System, we saw in chapter 1, the system, after noticing some relations among the variables, will have to produce new examples, satisfying some interesting contraints, and also the new relations it has learned. Each of these times, and each time it goes into a generation mode, the Apprentice will have to synthesize a function from its specifications.

Another typical case where generative abilities are needed is found in areas of intuitive knowledge where no formalized corpus of knowledge exists. Here, the only way to check the validity of the recognition functions that have been just learned is to use them to synthesize the patterns they recognize, and to use these patterns to assess them. This is what is done in the field of texture recognition, for example.

Suppose that we have a predicate EVEN(x) that decides whether a given integer ' x ' is even or not. We take this predicate as a datum, and do not concern ourselves on the way it is described internally.

This predicate can be used in order to recognize, in a set of integers, those that are even. This is fine as long as one wants only to recognize but, as soon as the system becomes active (for instance, when it needs to find itself new solutions), the predicate is not enough.

Then, supposing that we also need to generate an even integer, say greater than 11 and less than 45, we have to generate a function. This function is obviously linked to the predicate but the nature of the links may be very complicated to discover.

In our example, we can find at once the recursive definition of a function which generates an even integer between 11 and 45, if we suppose that we have a function RANDOM that returns a number between 1 and 100 after each call :

> *EVEN-GENER(x) ⇐ IF 11 ≤ x ≤ 45 THEN*
> *IF EVEN(x) THEN x*
> *ELSE EVEN-GENER(x-1)*
> *ELSE IF x < 11 THEN EVEN-GENER(x+2)*
> *ELSE EVEN-GENER(x-2)*

One must call this function under the form: EVEN-GENER(RANDOM).
This function is not totally trivial to invent because the domain has to be played with.

Exercise 34
****

Synthesize for yourself other functions that can generate even numbers between 11 and 45.

****

3.2 Different Types of Synthesis

3.2.1 Program synthesis from formal specification

In the set of predicates one starts from, the variables are quantified.

Those that must be considered as input variables are universally quantified. Those that must be considered as output variables are existentially quantified.

Therefore, one starts from a specification given as a theorem stating the relations between inputs and outputs. There exists a program that can compute the output ' z ' for each input ' x '. This is described by the following **Specification Theorem** (S_T)

$$S_T : \forall x \ [P(x) \Rightarrow \exists z \ [R(x, z)]]]$$

where P(x) specifies the domain of the input variable and R(x, z) is the relationship that links the inputs and the outputs.

The aim of the synthesis is to generate a function ' f ' such that

$$z = f(x) \text{ and } R(x, f(x)) \text{ holds.}$$

This approach is called the **deductive approach** to Program Synthesis because the synthesis is performed during a proof of S_T.

More details on this approach can be found in [Bierman & Al. 1984] and, for more recent results in [Franova 1987].

3.2.2 Program synthesis from computation traces or input-output examples

This topic has already been studied in greater detail in Section 2.

Recall that in Program Synthesis from specification, one starts from a description of the relationships between input and output variables.

Recall also that, when starting from examples, one must first introduce the relevant variables in order to transform the examples into computation traces.

Synthesis from computation traces uses examples of the function behaviour in order to induce those of its computational properties that repeat themselves ad infinitum.

One may well attempt to induce properties from the examples also. This is exactly what happens when one is learning concepts or recognition functions from examples, as seen in chapters 6 and 7. Once properties have been induced from the examples, they can be in turn treated as specifications, and program synthesis from specifications can be attempted on them.

A complete Apprentice should attempt both ways and check that coherent results are obtain. This is still a matter for long-term research.

3.2.3 Program Transformation

One starts from a program given in a runnable language.

Generally, it is considered that the computation time is not good or that it uses too much memory. The well-known Burstall and Darlington's method transforms recursive definitions into iterative ones [Burstall & Darlington 1977].

Let us give a standard example of it (see [Arsac & Al. 1982] for more examples).

Let us define a recursive function by considering the sequence $\{c_i\}$ of closed curves such that :
- the first, c_1, is arbitrary
- any c_i, $i \geq 2$, must intersect each other c_1, ..., c_{i-1} at exactly two distinct points
- three curves cannot intersect at the same point.

Then the number of plane regions thus defined is given by [Knuth 1973] :

$f(n) \Leftarrow IF\ n=1$
    $THEN\ 2$
    $ELSE\ f(n-1) + (2 * (n-1))$.

In the following the term f(n) will be called the "left-hand side" of f, and the conditional expression, its "right-hand side".

This formula is quite easily obtained by recursive reasoning on the number of curves.
When computing its value for a given n, we need a stack of size n in order to store intermediate results.
For example, f(3) must be computed as follows.

$f(3) = f(2) + (2 * 2)$ [level 1 of the stack]
Now we need to remember that f(3) is computed by adding 4 to the value of f(2). We compute f(2) :
$f(2) = f(1) + (2 * 1)$ [level 2 of the stack]
Again, we need to remember that f(2) is computed by adding 2 to f(1).
Finally,
$f(1) = 2$ [level 3 of the stack].
Now we can unstack and compute the value for the level 2 of the stack :
$f(2) = 2 + (2 * 1)$,
and then the value for level 1 :
$f(3) = 2 + (2 * 1) + (2 * 2) = 8$.

Let us now try to find a new way of computing this function, such that no stack is needed.

First step : invent a generalization g of f that matches the expression in the right-hand side of f.
Since this expression is

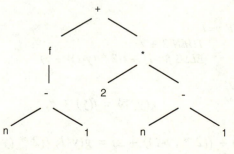

the function g must be something like

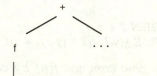

259

We can therefore choose

g(y, z) =

```
        +
       / \
      f   z
      |
      y
```

or, alternatively,

g(y, z) =

```
        +
       / \
      f   *
      |  / \
      y 2   z
```

Nothing can tell us in advance which is the efficient form, and we shall have to apply the following second step to each of them.

Let us now study :

$$g(y, z) = f(y) + z$$

Second step : Transformation into an iterative form.

Starting from the definition we are presently checking, we can write :

    g(y, z) = f(y) + z
            = (IF y=1
                THEN 2
                ELSE f(y-1) + (2 * (y-1))) + z

Using standard properties of conditionals [Manna & Al. 1972], we obtain

    g(y, z) = f(y) + z
            = IF y=1
                THEN 2 + z
                ELSE f(y-1) + ((2 * (y-1)) + z)

Now, using the fact that

$$g(y, z) = f(y) + z,$$

we see that

$$f(y-1) + ((2 * (y-1)) + z) = g(y-1, ((2 * (y-1)) + z)),$$

therefore, we can finally write

    g(y, z) = f(y) + z
            = IF y=1
                THEN 2 + z
                ELSE g(y-1, ((2 * (y-1)) + z)).

Since f(n) = g(n, 0), we can now compute f(n) by computing g(n, 0), that is, without using a stack.

For instance, f(3) = g(3, 0). We shall have to compute
$$g(3, 0) = g(2, 4) = g(1, 6) = 8$$
without need for remembering intermediate values. These are stored directly into the variable ' z ', called an **"accumulator"** *for this reason.*

As said above, program transformation methods have been mainly used in order to transform a recursive form into an iterative one, because they are more easily computed.

It must known that ease of computation is not the only criterion. For instance, J S. Moore [Moore 1973] shows that, in the context of proving properties about programs, recursive forms generally lead to tractable proofs, while it is generally very difficult to prove any property of an iterative form. Hence, transformation from iterative to recursive form would be also interesting.

The problem of program transformation can be described as that of analysing computation traces, and of discovering equivalent but different ways to perform the computation.

From the given form, we can always generate symbolic computation traces and apply to them the methods of synthesis from computation traces. This approach has been described with great detail in [Arsac & Al. 1982]. The method has been implemented by E. Papon in our research group under the name of "BMWk algorithm".

3.2.4   Program Translation

This case is seemingly similar to that of program transformation since we also start from a program given in a language, and translate it into another language. The difference is that now we make no attempt to alter the computation; on the contrary, the computations must be done in exactly the same way in both languages.
An example will make this clear.

Suppose that we are still concerned with the function given above as example, and that we want to translate its LISP expression into a FORTRAN expression.
In parenthesis, let us point to the fact that this kind of translation is rarely attempted since it is thought to be too difficult : we usually translate either a high level language into an assembler language, or a dialect into an other dialect.
At any rate, there would be no point in translating the recursive expression into FOR-TRAN, because this language does not allow recursive programs. We shall therefore assume that we want to translate a LISP iterative expression of the function into a FORTRAN iterative expression.
The two versions could be :

LISP version :

```
(DEFINE TAILRECUR (y z)
  (COND
    ((EQUAL y 1) (ADD z 2))
    (TRUE (TAILRECUR(SUB y 1)(ADD(MULT 2 (SUB y 1)) z)))))
```

FORTRAN version : ITER (y, z)

```
    IF (y.EQ.1) GO TO 2
    N = y - 1
        DO I = 1, N
        z = z + (2 * (y - 1))
        y = y - 1
        END
    GO TO 3
2   z = z + 2
3   CONTINUE
```

In spite of all the simplifications brought about by the fact that computations are invariant, the problem of program translation is still very difficult.

We shall not give much details here of how this problem has been handled, since it belongs to Software Technology rather than to AI.

Appendix 3
Machine Learning in Context

1 EPISTEMOLOGICAL REFLECTIONS ON THE PLACE OF AI IN SCIENCE

After having dealt with the purely technical problems, it will do no harm to put Machine Learning (ML) into the context of contemporary scientific thinking. In this, ML is strictly a sub-domain of Artificial Intelligence (AI), so we shall essentially be talking about AI in this chapter. Let us say right away that we do not claim to be giving the "low-down" on scientific thought, but only to recall some of its problems in a deliberately simplified form.

Here is an anecdote to show that the problem of the place of AI in science is far from being trivial, and that it still produces violent rejection reactions.

Recently, on March 11 1986, a Franco-American meeting on AI was being held. Among the guests was a very respected member of the French Computer Science community who made a noted speech in which he described AI as a "pre-science", just as Alchemy was a pre-science for the future science of Chemistry. Dreyfus had already said this long before [Dreyfus 1972].

Of course, the author of this book, like any member of the international AI community, can only be somewhat shocked by such declarations. But, rather than arguing - there is no shortage of arguments and they constitute a corpus which will soon be counted as banal - it seems to us much more interesting to show how, even from our own point of view, a rigorously orthodox scientist can be justified in protesting at AI.

However, even if it is right, in our opinion, that AI is fundamentally different from Science as it has found its culmination in modern physics, we are going to try to show that it is a "post" rather than a "pre" science.

Our argumentation is going to turn on the problem of the scientist's identification with his/her research topic or of his/her "alienation" (the word is taken from Brecht's theatrical technique of putting a distance between the actor and his/her role) from his/her research topic.

Science is born of an incessant effort by the scientists to detach themselves from the subject of their study. The concept of **scientific objectivity**, the keystone of the scientific edifice, implies: "I do not involve myself personally in all that", of: "all that I do is ascertain, you know", and also of: "I judge calmly because I have no personal interest in the matter." We do not wish to argue any more here about the importance of the concept of objectivity in the birth of scientific thought. The reader who may not know this is called on to read any history of science.

On the other hand, it is worth recalling several recent currents of thought which strongly question the reality of the objectivity of Science.

Criticisms of scientific objectivity

During the Seventies a dissident current was born, more or less tied to ecological preoccupations, whose main theme was: it is a shameless lie to say that Science is objective.

In France, it expressed itself mainly through three channels.

The confidential and very violent review, *Survivre et Vivre*, anarchistically inspired and profoundly anti-scientific.

The review *Impascience*, where the pun on "impasse", "science" and "impatience" was followed up by analyses, generally from scientists, reporting incidents they had experienced concerning sexism, racism and Science 's commitment to the Establishment.

Finally, the book *(Auto)-critique de la Science* [Lévy-Leblond & Jaubert 1975] is a collection of criticisms of science by recognized scientists.

The basic idea of all these criticisms is that Science is never objective, but always the expression of the will to power of a particular social group.

In quite an amusing way, it seems that, 15 years later, these arguments have neither been refuted nor assimilated. They were perceived in their time as a cat among the pigeons, and they remain so: life continues and the cat is still there.

One of the possible social consequences of AI, which we shall talk of in section 2, is precisely the assimilation of this cat.

Science and oriental philosophy

At the same time, a convergence was taking place between certain scientists and oriental thought.

Two books illustrated this movement well. Firstly, the *Tao of Physics* [Capra 1979] describes links between particle physics and Taoism in a rather mystical way.

Secondly, in a more popular and convincing manner, the book humorously entitled *Zen and the Art of Motor-cycle Maintenance* [Pirsig 1974] develops the argument that an understanding of a descriptive technical text (in this case, motor-cycle repair manuals) cannot be obtained without

- on the one hand a global understanding of the description, its functions and its general organization.

- on the other hand an identification of the reader with the object described, here an identification between the repairer and the motor-cycle.

You are referred to this book for a detailed argumentation, which is not the aim here. Simply remember that the most banal technical description can be held to require for its usefulness not an effort at distanciation (which would be the orthodox scientific attitude), but an effort to identify with the object described.

Right here is the essential difference between the western approach to Nature and the oriental approach.

In the western approach, the criterion of efficiency in action is one of maximum distanciation, whereas in the oriental approach, the criterion of efficiency in action is one of maximum identification with Nature.

In parentheses, let us pay homage to the small book by Eugen Herrigel, *Zen in the art of archery* [Herrigel 1985]. Herrigel manages to perform the feat of verbally describing an activity and sensations which might be thought to be incommunicable otherwise than by experiencing them oneself. This is the book where the unorthodox concept of efficiency through identification is described without using the usual panoply of Zen riddles.

Objectivity in Computer Science

Our analysis of the two "anti-science" movements given above is perhaps going to seem excessively cautious.

We believe that scientists delude the absolute objectivity, but it is also unrealistic to hold that scientific theories only represent the will to power of certain social groups. It is absurd to debate whether the measurement of the speed of light serves or does not serve certain financial interests. But let us take it for granted that the choice of investing in carrying out these measurements depends very much on those same financial interests.

Similarly, the myth of absolute objectivity is absurd because a human or a program created by a human is always needed to interpret the results of the measurements. On the other hand, it is completely reasonable, as the orthodox scientific attitude holds, to try to tend toward the greatest possible objectivity.

Where we depart from this cautious attitude is by claiming that the objective attitude limits the development of Science today.

A certain identification between the scientist and his/her topic of study is not only tolerable but desirable.

AI is the first Science to illustrate this position, and hence its odor of heresy.

The hackers' testimony

In our jargon, we call a person who spends all his/her time in front of a computer terminal a "hacker". These people indisputably experience a new kind of paranoia, that of identification with the computer system they are using. Certain hackers are malignant and turn out millions of lines of boring code. On the other hand, almost every computer scientist can testify that he/she has had his/her period of hacking, when he/she identified him/herself with the system he/she was writing, following which his/her program finally began to "work".

The non-objectivity of computer science

This is the sense in which we freely admit that AI, like the other areas of Computer Science, is not "objective", since the "objects" it studies are created by the (? pre-) scientist him/herself.

Computer programs express an objective reality (the topic they apply to) and a subjective reality (the mind of their designer) at the same time.

By way of example, let us recall the famous joke in which a user asks a programmer to build him/her a swing attached to the branch of a tree. In the outcome, the swing turns out to be suspended from a complex structure emerging from the tree which was the starting-point. The objective part of the program is the actions it carries out, here the swing itself. The subjective part of the program is the manner in which it carries them out, which reflects the mind of its programmer. The joke expresses the fact that simple problems can always be solved with methods reflecting a complicated mind.

All computer scientists interested in programs are conscious of this problem, and they can be divided into two categories according to their positions.

The heretics and the orthodox

The orthodox computer scientists (who tend to cluster as specialists in Software Engineering or Theoretical Computer Science) are those who seek to struggle against this situation in order to plunge their discipline back into traditional Science.

The heretics (more or less assembled under the banner of AI) are those who seek to take advantage of this situation to found a new scientific approach.

In our opinion, objectivity is not an end in itself, but the best means for ensuring communication between researchers, so that they can reproduce each others' results.

Now, as a result of the computer revolution, enactments of reality known as programs are available to us. Even without understanding anything about the style of a program, its informal specifications can be understood and used "objectively".

Standard Computer Science attempts to itemize, to solidify programming styles in order to make them uniform.

On the other hand, the AI approach consists in an attempt to liberate programming style. Not only does it simplify the programmer's task, but AI even claims that a day will come when it will increase the efficiency of the programs obtained.

Efficiency against Explicability

In our opinion, the essential manifestation of this new spirit is the prime importance which AI attaches to the concept of **explicability**, in contrast to that of **efficiency**.

Standardly, systems like those of Automata Theory, for instance, are built to model a natural phenomenon, and to do this in the most efficient way possible. A model is rejected just when it is not efficient enough.

What characterizes AI in relation to all the other approaches is that the system is also required to be able to furnish **explanations of its behavior**. It is necessary, admittedly, that the system's choices should not cause performance to deteriorate too much, but it is necessary above all for it to be able to keep in touch with the human experts about these choices.

Positive example
We have described the LEX system which is capable of carrying out formal integrations [Mitchell, Utgoff & Banerji 1983]. Suppose the system is asked to integrate 3cos x dx and that it chooses to integrate by parts with: u = 3x and dv = cos x dx.

LEX is capable of explanations in the sense that, at least in principle, it is capable, when asked the question: "Why have you chosen this way of integrating?", of giving the answer: "Because I had the option of choosing a ' u ' which is a polynomial and a ' dv ' whose functional part is a trigonometric function."
This explanation is what can intuitively be called a conceptual explanation.
In this case, furthermore, the choice is efficient.

Negative example
Let us consider commercial systems which play chess. At each move they make, they have to have analyzed the situation and to have a "reason" for making it. Nevertheless, the choice methods are tied to numerous coefficients, few of which have a conceptual equivalent.
Thus, these systems are not capable of explicability and, even if they reached world championship level, they would not belong to AI.
Such systems will become AI on the day when they will be able to explain a move by saying, for example: "I made this move because it is the best in a strategy of isolating the opposing queen with an attack from the left."

Our personal opinion is that the time when they become capable of such explanations will be precisely when they will reach world championship level.

Thus, the question whether or not a system is AI is not so much whether or not it models human intelligence as whether a human intelligence can understand its behavior in terms of clearly defined concepts.

To the extent that it models a human, this requirement becomes quite natural.

We think that the "AI approach" is characterized by the pre-eminence of explicability over efficiency.

It will be objected that there are famous AI systems, such as Samuel's CHECK-ERS [Samuel 1959, 1963] or Buchanan's META-DENDRAL [Buchanan & Mitchell 1978] whose cababilities for explaining are not very great. We freely admit it. Our argument is that the criticisms levelled against these systems by AI are concerned precisely with their lack of explicability rather than with their lack of efficiency.

Admittedly, the definitive criterion for judging AI requires efficiency, but it also requires the system to be able to explain itself.
To analyse on the explanations themselves, as the object of study, instead of trying to find explanations, is a completely new topic of Science.

Without developing any farther, let us emphasize in passing that explicability is precisely the means by which the expert or student can identify him/herself with the system he/she is studying.

Objectivity and communicability

As the reader will certainly have understood, we would be happy to abandon orthodox scientific objectivity, but only to immediately define a new form of objectivity, adapted to the computer revolution.

However, it is indisputable that orthodox objectivity has been useful for facilitating communication between scientists and hence for giving each scientist the means of verifying and reproducing his/her colleague 's results.

In the final analysis, whether our results express an eternal truth or a social truth ought not to concern us. The notion of eternal truth is deeply stained with religion anyhow and any scientist should distrust it.

Thus the reproducibility of scientific results seems to us far more important than their objectivity.

It can well be understood that a physicist measuring variations in the speed of light by floating an interferometer in a mercury cup should take enormous precautions about the objectivity of his/her experiment since it is difficult to reproduce. This kind of problem does not arise in AI, where (almost) anyone can reproduce other people 's programs on his/her own machine.

Objectivity no longer has to be monolithic; its expression must depend on the difficulty of reproducing the results.

Inventing a new means of expression

Science has therefore coded a method for transmitting information (lemmas, theorems, etc ...), based on the need for objectivity, and enabling results to be communicated fairly well.

To the extent that the researcher identifies with his/her research, this code becomes inoperative, since it is incapable of transmitting information about a personal experience.

On the other hand, there is a code, that of Literature, designed for the transmission of personal information.

In our opinion, one of the social problems of AI is to create a new code of expression, enabling its results to be transmitted. Until now, our approach has amounted to little more than: "Here are my programs, come and test them." It is in the process of being born and must not reproduce either the code of traditional Science or that of Literature.

A brilliant precursor in this field is Tom Mitchell (some of his scientific results are given in chapter 5). In his articles, and even more in his oral presentations, Tom Mitchell is capable of conveying this new information, a mixture of "objective" results and personal experiences; but only at the cost, he admits, of working frenziedly.

Pre-science or post-science?

One can of course hold that this identification with one 's research topic is perfectly retrograde.

Indeed, it is correct to say that the pre-sciences, Alchemy in particular, demand identification with the research topic rather than distanciation.

Thus we ourselves justify the position touched on at the beginning, at least in a certain sense.

On the other hand, our arguments do of course go in the direction of justifying identification with one 's research topic, taking into account the new situation created by computers. We even claim that it is a step forward for Science.

Strictly from the point of view of argumentation, we do not think that the clash between the two opinions can now be settled.

It is our special work as AI specialists to create this new code of communication, to bring to life models whose efficiency and explicability will demonstrate that our approach is justified by its results.

For the moment, only a few still debatable results in the field of games, Automatic Theorem-Proving and Diagnosis (Expert Systems) allow us to sense that we are on the right track.

The construction of scientific theories

The orthodox scientific method of development proceeds by a double alternation in the understanding of Nature.

First alternation: geniuses/toilers

In a first phase, some scientist of genius (a Leibnitz, a Herbrand, an Einstein, ...) expresses a new idea. Usually, this scientist spends a certain part of his/her life being vilified by the rest of the scientific community.

At this point I cannot resist the urge to let you know about two personal experiences.

*The first one concerns the above "his/**her**".*
*US readers may not be aware that **to-day** Mrs Curie is still accused of mixing her personal life and her job life, by some French scientists. I can testify that I heard the last such story in 1984, from a descendant of one of her students. Even if you believe these stories (they are actually highly dubious !), interest in them can be motivated by nothing other than hostility toward a female genius.*
The second one concerns my personal encounter with a representative of the vilifying scientific community.
In 1965, when I was preparing my doctoral dissertation on Paramagnetic Electronic Resonance, an old professor of Lyon University came to visit me in my laboratory.
When I explained to him that my work consisted in making electrons turn in a magnetic field, he interrupted me to declare that "all this business about Quantum Mechanics and Relativity is quite overdone. The wave theory of electromagnetism is sufficient to explain everything, as I've held all my life".
So I have seen, seen with my own eyes one of those fabled scientists who our schoolteachers told us were blind, because they struggled with all their might, in the name (of course) of scientific objectivity, against what we call "Modern Science".
In my everyday life, I am used to seeing these people: They fight with all their might against AI. But they are not yet acknowledged as ridiculous (in France), as this old professor from Lyons.

In a second phase an army of scientists comes, considered as being decent but not brilliant, who digest and formalize the ideas of the first ones. In this they accomplish a task which is far from being easy and which demands high intelligence and great modesty at the same time.

Second alternation: theoretician/experimentalist

There is also a traditional division of scientists into two races who will correct the defects of the geniuses in two ways.

The geniuses' lack of clarity or rigor is corrected by the theoreticians who reformulate, formalize and simplify the original ideas, often a bit luxuriant.

The experimentalists, however, trim away those parts of the geniuses' fantasies which are too wild, to fit them to concrete reality.

All this is well-known, and the reader can find more details in all the histories of Science.

This construction mechanism has shown itself to be perfectly efficient up to now.

It seems to us to be tied by deep ties to the era of industrial development which we have just known.

The construction of post-scientific theories

We are entering a post-industrial period (which continues and incorporates the industrial period without repudiating it, just as our post-science is not an anti-science), so it is not astonishing that Science too has to modify itself.

We have already described certain features of this new science: the questioning of scientific objectivity, the rejection of the absolute rule of distanciation between the scientist and the object of his/her study, the search for new means of communication between scientists.

Another consequence of this new scientific state of mind, of which AI is the first organized manifestation, is the suppression of the double alternation we have just pointed out.

First modification: continuous creativity

Orthodox science is creative in fits and starts, when a genius kindly appears - and bears the insults of his/her colleagues.

We think that creativity should no longer be confined to a few exceptional individuals, but that it is going to become a normal constituent of scientific activity.

Without confusing Art with Science, the continually creative aspect of artistic behavior must enter into every scientist.

The reason for this change seems to us to be twofold.

On the one hand, the extraordinary improvement in the quality of transmission of information enables ideas to be analyzed and understood much more rapidly.

On the other hand, the scientist's identification with his/her research topic forces him/her to express it as a personal deliverance, and no longer as an act in which he/she is not involved.

Second modification: simultaneous experimentation and theorizing

In the same way, it seems to us nonsensical to have a ditch separating theory from experiment.

A good theory is one that formalizes well, admittedly, but also one which yields results which can be used in practice.

A good experiment cannot spring from a parcel of confused ideas and hence must be based on valid theoretical foundations.

We are not claiming that traditional Science revelled in woolly theories and dubious experiments; on the contrary, its effort and its effect were to suppress both of these. Teams which contain theoreticians and experimentalists at the same time are becoming the rule today.

But we claim that, in the future, the very same individual will perform the experiments and establish the theories. We see two reasons for this.

The first comes from post-industrial demands which require the continually accelerated transfer of theoretical results into marketable products.

The second is due to the possibility for computers to model enactments of the Universe where fictitious experiments can be conducted.

An additional claim of this book

This book is of course designed to show the objective results of ML taken as a (contested) scientific discipline.

Thus the reader has been able to initiate him/herself into the concepts and methods which are becoming standard in ML.

But we also claim to have been trying to illustrate our ideas about this fabled new code of communication. So this text was written in a style which appeals both to rigorous thinking (like orthodox science) and to the reader's imagination (the post-scientific aspect).

Examples, commentaries and exercises, i.e. anything which should excite the imagination, were to be found in italics. Normal type was reserved for general descriptions, algorithms and even some theorems, i.e. anything which appeals to rigorous thinking.

The new code of communication discussed here is still being elaborated.

The reader is asked to kindly pardon our awkwardnesses in using it.

As we said in Section 1, for some years a strong pressure has been coming from scientists themselves in favor of recognizing that Science is not such an impartial tool as one would like to believe. It is embodied in our society, and reflects its good points and bad points.

In this appendix we are not going to discuss the well-foundedness of this assertion, which has now become quite banal, even if there are still a large number of scientists who believe themselves "pure".

We prefer to sincerely admit our state of original impurity once and for all, not to have a crisis of conscience about it, and to work.

As in the previous section, we shall take account of the fact that ML is a subdomain of AI, and we shall only talk of ML when we want to underline its particularities.

How Society influences Science, or, more specifically, ML, is a topic which may be exciting but which we scientists only view through the small end of the telescope: funds, posts, contracts; such are our worries.

In the United States, I found that non-computer scientists are a little bit disgusted to see the manna of official subsidies raining down on computer scientists while passing the other scientists by.

In Europe people talk a lot about Computer Science and even more about AI, but yet funds and jobs continue to go to other disciplines, often even in the name of computerizing these disciplines.

This example well shows that an analysis of the role played by Society in the development of ML must be fundamentally different in the USA from what it is in Europe.

The socialist countries are also a very distinct case from the others.

We admit to knowing little about the details of the situation in the USA. On the other hand to describe the situation in France would mean giving a lamentable list of promises never or belatedly kept, and of disappointed hopes.

All this is not very exciting.

On the other hand, the future role that ML will play in the establishment of new social relations seems to us to be much more universal. This is why, as far as interactions between Society and AI are concerned, we shall describe the future action of AI on Society rather than the present action of Society on AI.

2.1 ML, AI and SF

2.1.1 SF and AI: their place in society

Even if we have to be blamed for it ("What a casual approach!") we want to begin with a section on Science Fiction (SF), which has already described a thousand and one possibilities for our future society.

It is clear that SF occupies an important place in popular contemporary literature and that it is at the same time the reflection both of our present society and of our fears of what it could become.

The place of SF in literature seems to us to be perfectly comparable with that of AI in science. Like AI, SF attracts slightly crazy imaginations which reject the yoke of established ideas. The orthodox treat them both with the same somewhat scornful attention. They are not for really proper people, unless they become one of the mob.

Once again, strictly from the point of view of argumentation, there is no way of settling the issue. Will SF and AI meet the fate of romance literature, of which *Don Quixote* is a parody, or will they be among the principal gains of the twentieth century, along with atomic energy and feminism?

From all the possible arguments we shall just give one untraditional one, that of ridicule.

Medieval romances always attracted irony rather than anger. Atomic energy has certainly not made anybody laugh, feminism was ridiculed only at its beginnings, SF and AI attract more anger than irony.* This is admittedly a humoristic indication of their future success, but a sound one.

2.1.2 The validity of the problems taken up by SF

In a way that we find quite surprising, anticipations dealing with AI raise plenty of possible problems, but always in terms which seem to us to be improbable. We are going to analyze this with the aid of three examples: the amorous computer, the power-drunk computer and the robots subjected to the contradictions of Asimov's three laws of robotics.

One of the obvious roles of AI is to give more and more "personal" initiative to

---

* Author's note. Stephen (the (British) translator) pointed to a regular column in a British satirical magazine which is a negative example to my claim on feminism. It has a cartoon of a gang of crazy females about to castrate a bewildered and harmless-looking man, and a collection of distressingly exaggerated claims by feminists.

It is true that we do not have this type of satire in France, nor perhaps this type of extreme feminism !

I would say that my argument is valid in most European countries, except Great Britain.

computers. Already there exist programs which surprise their creators by inventing unexpected solutions. The example of D. Lenat's EURISKO can be cited amongst numerous others. Applied to naval warfare problems, it discovered all on its own that an effective way of increasing your chances of winning consists in sinking your own vessels that are too damaged yourself, since this increases the mobility of your side. This rule is easy to understand, which is why we have given it. In the field of problem-solving, of theorem-proving, we see that more and more people prefer to use their program rather than their intuition to find rules or proofs. This tendency will only grow with the birth of ML, which tries to systematize this phenomenon. The reader must have understood that ML is still in its first stammerings, but we also hope he/she will note that a systematic approach is being established. The personal initiative of computers can only grow, and imperceptibly we shall arrive at machines having their own personality.

The concept of a computer in love is not absurd in itself, but there is no reason why it should display quasi-sexual urges and, in particular, it is a mystery why it should be specially attracted by young and pretty girls, as is generally the case in SF.

On the other hand, what a really disembodied love could be, what the constituents of a purely intellectual love are, or again, conversely, what carnality must nevertheless be present as soon as an emotion of love appears, or again the "emotional" problems between programs themselves; these are themes which SF does not, to our knowledge, pick up. And yet they will certainly arise in everyday life as soon as a program is able to start having enough autonomy to prefer to be used by a particular programmer or to collaborate with another particular program.

Likewise the theme of the power-drunk computer which turns up so often in SF is completely reasonable. On the other hand, power as described in SF is something that could be dreamed of by a strongly sensuous being, but not by a pure intellectual. Why on earth should computers take any pleasure at all in exercising their senses, even if, as cannot fail to happen, they are equipped with sensitive terminals? This is even what distinguishes them profoundly from humans: in them power is not tied to the pleasure of exercising it.

It seems much more probable to us that machines, when they are presented with a certain autonomy, will be drunk with knowledge rather than drunk with power as we conceive it. Admittedly we have fears about future inquisitorial societies, but the interrogatory aspect of the Inquisition is what will be present rather than the punitive aspect. Here again the inquisitorial aspects divorced from grief and repression are quite absent from SF.

Finally, Asimov's three laws of robotics seem to us to be inspired by the image of the ideal slave or servant rather than that of a robot. Incidentally, the notion of "harming" a human is such a relative notion, hence demanding so much preliminary information, that it can only depend on each individual's own experience. In any case, in a robot it can be considered as the conclusion of an apprenticeship, and not as a prerequisite of an apprenticeship.

It is quite certain that robots are made to carry out specific tasks, and will be optimized for these tasks, not in order to harm or not harm humans. On the other hand, a simple economic argument allows us to declare that the first robots developed will be military, and hence made to harm certain humans.

Another simple example is that of the already existing robot which plays chess. If it were subjected to restrictions about the well-being of its owner, would it have to let him/her win from time to time to flatter his/her ego? Does it it not harm somebody to flatter his/her ego?

To conclude this topic, SF either expresses an exaggerated fear of the computerization of society, or else, conversely, when it is favorable to relations with machines, envisages them as being too sensuous.

2.1.3 Integrated Man and SF

Rare are the SF authors who describe universes in which mankind is less cut off from itself than in our own.

By way of exception we see, for example, R.A. Heinlein, who describes worlds where mankind integrates its masculine and feminine constituents better, and U.K. Le Guin, who has sometimes described worlds where waking life is integrated with dream-life (*The word for world is forest*, 1972).

On the other hand, it is foreseeable that AI will contribute to improving mankind's integration with Nature, and this we shall return to.

2.1.4 ML and SF

In most SF books where a computer acquires knowledge, it does it in a very human way, without using one of the techniques described here.

An exception is *The Adolescence of P-1* (T.J. Ryan, 1977), where a program learns by using techniques obviously similar to those of Chapter 5. It must, however, be noted that the book's theme is that of the power-drunk computer rather than learning.

Similarly, problems connected with knowledge representation are rarely tackled. The only exception, to our knowledge, is Ian Watson's book *The Embedding* (1973), whose central theme is the transmission of knowledge in embedded form, as is possible in a LISP program. However, we know of no work whose theme is recursion properly speaking (instead of embedding, which is only a syntax for recursion) or, especially, whose theme is unification as in PROLOG.

2.2 AI, ML and Society

2.2.1 The power of the Powerful

When it comes down to it, Science has never claimed to be a factor for social progress.

In any case, it has become clear that the status of a welfare recipient is always bad. So if Society were receiving welfare from Science, the progress achieved would be condemned in advance.

2.2.1.1 Technology and conservatism

The "nineteenth-century"-type position connected with the claim that Science is objective, consists in maintaining that Science is neutral like natural phenomena, and hence that it can contain the best and the worst, according to the use it is put to.

2.2.1.2 Intelligence (artificial or otherwise) and tyranny

We do not wish to enter the traditional debate on whether Science generates social progress or social backwardness. The fact that Science can serve conservatisms of every political color and at the same time have innovative aspects appears to us to be completely obvious.

Similarly, we shall assume that these two aspects are merely facets of the same reality, as with any activity fitting into Society. Having recalled this, it is completely new, we think, to remark that AI threatens to profoundly modify the retrograde aspect of Science.

In a sense, intelligence has always been an instrument of power and, following in this tradition, AI can only reinforce the power of those who are already powerful. But everyone agrees that intelligence is a two-edged sword, as is well shown by the dictum that it is better to have an intelligent enemy that a stupid friend.

We also tend to apply this dictum to governments: better an intelligent tyrant than a stupid democrat. Provided the reader goes along with our dictum, he/she will have to agree with us in recognizing that even if it is used for the worst purposes, an intelligent program can only diminish their horror.

Let us take the example of genocides, like those of the Jews during the last war, of the Armenians and the Yaquis at the beginning of the century, that of the Ukrainian peasants under Stalin, etc...

The horror of these actions must not prevent us from noticing their enormous stupidity. Clearly these butchers think they are going to avoid the long-run consequences of their acts (not for themselves as individuals, which is, unfortunately, often the case, but for their societies. For example, present-day German society is the opposite of Hitler's dream, or again, Stalinist practices have hardly improved the yields of Soviet agriculture).

An intelligent program, equipped with mechanisms for knowledge acquisition, will never permit the long run to be neglected.

Future Hitlers will be forced, if they use AI tools, to take account of the long run in their decisions, because of the very nature of these tools.

Furthermore, all these butchers also think they can get off scot-free with what they do: at least an intelligent program will always provide them with an estimation of the probability that they will one day be put on trial.

This leads us to a theory of "furtive horror", in which a criminal will be able and will have to try to hide his/her acts by using intelligent programs.

This is even certain to be the product of the future.

Nevertheless, it is clear that mass crimes like genocides will be made more difficult.

We do not wish to maintain that "furtive horror" is less horrible than the other kind. We wish to declare simply that AI will serve rather to make state crimes less massive, even if more hypocritical.

More generally, it would have been miraculous after all if a scientific discovery had been able to forbid tyranny! After all, it is not so bad that it should require it to use gentler methods than in the past.

Future tyrannies will certainly be more hypocritical, more insidious and more penetrating than those of the past. They will use methods enabling them to go farther in their effect on each individual. On the other hand, they will certainly be less brutal, they will try to persuade rather than to impose themselves.

The broad circulation of information we are now witnessing, added to the future intelligent treatment of this information, will provide a form of democracy which is just beginning to be glimpsed by those who are getting into the habit of linking up with an electronic communication network.

In principle, "Big Brother" can always have access to any information that interests it, but in the mass of passwords, coded information and classified files, all generally containing perfectly innocent information, the notion of the control of individuals will have to be replaced by that of the control over the overall quantity of information transmitted, which leaves more room for individualisms.

This relaxation of control over individuals seems to us to be an important but implicit or unconscious reason for the rejection of AI which can be observed in certain scientists: AI is less easily controlled than orthdox Science, and this displeases them.

2.2.2 ML and education

Education is certainly one of the basic means by which society is built. ML is coming to play a growing role in this field.

2.2.2.1   Expert knowledge and casual knowledge

First let us quickly give two definitions.

We wish to distinguish two sorts of knowledge: *expert knowledge* and *casual knowledge*.

We shall say that a human possesses an **expert knowledge** when he/she is able to explain his/her actions or his/her reasoning to another expert.

We shall say that he/she has a **casual knowledge** of a subject when he/she acts effectively but without being able to justify him/herself.

An obvious example of expert knowledge is that of the experts. It will be noted that in many cases knowledge can be expert and ineffective at the same time, as with experts in economics, who tend to only explain after the event.

An obvious example of casual knowledge is riding a bicycle. Everyone knows how to ride a bicycle, can give vague explanations about keeping his/her center of gravity above the line between his/her points of contact with the ground, but is incapable of explaining precisely which muscles he/she mobilizes (see also the discussion in section 2.6 of chapter 2). It will also be noted that casual knowledge often has an effectiveness which is remarkable ... and inexplicable.

A slightly more subtle example is that of psychologically unstable people who go through a process of analysis. They clearly search for what are called the real explanations of their behavior, hoping that afterward they will be capable of modifying it. In our vocabulary, these people are trying to change the casual knowledge which everybody has of his/her actions into expert knowledge.

The teaching of casual knowledge can only be done through examples. Methods for teaching casual knowledge can be reduced to a selection of exercises (examples) which have been shown by experience to facilitate the acquisition of this knowledge. A student will be called a "good student" if he fits well into these exercises, so that he/she rapidly acquires the knowledge. In particular, his/her failures help him/her less than his/her successes.

The teaching of expert knowledge should be done by a subtle alternation between explanation by example and explanation by theory. Teaching methods for expert knowledge are based on explanations and counter-examples. In particular, each case of a student's failure is extremely interesting, because when associated with a detailed explanation, it is going to enable him/her to illustrate the "false" theory which he/she had developed on his/her own, and hence enable him/her to understand better the "true" theory he/she was supposed to acquire.

One of the commonest causes of failures in this field comes from teaching expert knowledge as if it were casual knowledge.

Bad teachers teach mathematics using methods similar to those used for learning to swim. Students who can learn on their own will cope, but not the others.

In other words, it is left to the child to create his/her own network of explanations, while undergoing pernickety checking on whether the theory he/she has forged for him/herself is valid for certain typical examples (the exercises he/she does correctly). If the child's theory is wrong, then the only reaction is a bad grade, along with some rapid explanations in the best of cases.

Education is a field in itself, and it is not for ML to claim to be the solution to its problems. At the most it can provide some confirmation for ideas already known in Education.

2.2.2.2   The disappearance of the concept of "mistakes"

What is typical of the AI approach to teaching is its attempt to reconstruct an explanatory model capable of producing the same mistakes as the child. In this model, it is absurd to talk of "mistakes", since the model is right precisely when it makes the desired mistakes. By extension, if such a model of the child exists, even if this model is not really the child's, this approach tends to interpret his/her behavior by this model, or models derived from this one, rather than by declaring the child's behavior mistaken.

For example, a possible cause of such "mistakes" is that he/she has over- or under-generalized the examples into inexact rules.

Here are two examples of children's addition sums with carrying

$$
\begin{array}{cc}
26 & 18 \\
7 & 5 \\
\hline
33 & 23
\end{array}
$$

Either the child could over-generalize if he/she concludes that you always have to add 1 in the left-hand column, which could possibly serve as an explanation if he/she gives the answer: 25 + 4 = 39.

Conversely, the child could under-generalize if he/she concludes that only the column to the left of the column farthest right is affected. This could possibly serve as an explanation for the answer being: 186 + 75 = 161.

Of course, these are not the only explanations possible, and the whole difficulty in education is to find the "true" explanations.

Meanwhile, it is already interesting to confirm that the wrong answer in an exercise can either show a real lack of understanding or reveal the fact that the student has constructed his/her own personal model.

Of course, everyone will agree that whatever the model constructed may be, it has to be judged by its coherence, and not by its conformity with that of the teacher.

2.2.2.3 ML models and human learning

One of the attractions of ML is the provision of models to explain the gaps between the answer expected by the teacher and the answer given by the student.

All the learning mechanisms described in the previous chapters can be interpreted as mechanisms for explaining such gaps.

We have just given an example tied to the notion of an exact generalization, whose derivation is described in chapters 4, 5, 6 and 7. The contents of chapter 8 could also be used to show that the student can under certain circumstances construct a different taxonomy from the one expected by the teacher. You saw in chapter 9 how the student could place him/herself in a micro-world different from his/her teacher's.

Now here are some precise examples of these possibilities.

Let us return to an example given in chapter 4, section 6.

Suppose a student has to learn a rule on the basis of these two examples.

E_1: *[NEEDS(FRANCE, VIDEOS) & PRODUCT(JAPAN, VIDEO) -->*
POSSBUY(FRANCE, VIDEOS, JAPAN)]
E_2: *[NEEDS(BELGIUM, COMPUTER) & PRODUCT(USA, COMPUTERS) -->*
POSSBUY(BELGIUM, COMPUTERS, USA)].

Assume that he/she infers from them the following rule

IF EURO-COUNTRY(x) & EXOTIC-COUNTRY(y) & ELECTRONIC-EQUIPMENT(u) THEN
[NEEDS(x, u) & PRODUCT(y, u) -->
POSSBUY(x, u, y)].

The teacher can guess that his/her student has used a taxonomy like

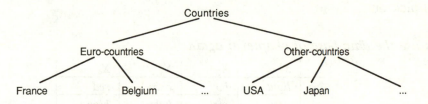

In this case it is utterly useless to tell the student he/she has not found the right solution, except in order to ask him/her to find another possible taxonomy. On the other hand, if the student has indeed used this taxonomy, then the teacher can suggest another example to him/her to better show him/her how he/she should improve his/her choice of taxonomies. For example, the teacher can say that E_3 is also an example of the rule.

E_3: [NEEDS(FRANCE, ELECTRON-MICROSCOPE) & PRODUCT(WEST-GERMANY,
ELECTRON-MICROSCOPE) →

POSSBUY(FRANCE, ELECTRON-MICROSCOPE, WEST-GERMANY)

Let us suppose that the student still has not found the rule the teacher wanted to teach him/her. Only after a certain number of failures will the teacher use the traditional method which consists in giving him/her the solution. Indeed, it is possible for the student simply not to possess the taxonomy (or to possess one of the possible "false" taxonomies) which his/her teacher would want him/her to use.

It is clear that many intermediate stages are possible before giving the solution to the student.

Let us suppose that the student is not aware that France is a second-rate country from the point of view of the electronics industry.

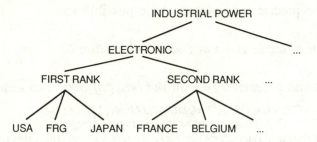

So the rule the student was supposed to have learned was

IF EURO-COUNTRY(x) & FIRST-RANK-INDUSTRIAL-ELECTRONIC-POWER(y) &
ELECTRONIC-EQUIPMENT(u) THEN
[NEEDS(x, u) & PRODUCT(y, u) →
POSSBUY(x, u, y)].

Another example of a completely different kind is where the student's "mistake" is due to his/her having picked out a different feature from the one the teacher wanted him/her to pick out.

Let us use the data-base of chapter 6 again.

	X_1	X_2	X_3	X_4
e_1	light	boy	baby	red
e_2	light	girl	baby	blond
e_3	light	boy	child	chestnut
e_4	medium	woman	teenager	chestnut
e_5	medium	boy	child	red
e_6	heavy	girl	child	blond
e_7	heavy	man	teenager	red
e_8	heavy	woman	teenager	chestnut
e_9	heavy	man	adult	blond
e_{10}	heavy	woman	adult	chestnut

We have seen that our symbolic clustering algorithm gives the following clustering tree.

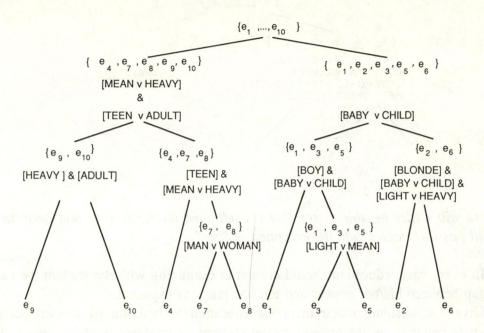

In this table, each node of the tree is represented by the set of examples it contains and by the common features which have served to cluster these examples.

This way of analyzing this data amounts to noticing in the first place that teenagers and adults have medium or heavy weight. That is to say that the example e_6 of a heavy girl is considered to be negligible at the first approximation.

So let us suppose that the teacher wants to make his/her student discover this feature, but that the student, for his/her part, notices first that girls are blond.

By following his/her student, then applying our method to the groups thus defined, the teacher can obtain the clusters which result from the choice of initially using the fact that girls are blond.

Only a detailed analysis of the consequences of this choice will enable him/her to really explain to his/her student either why he/she should not have done it or why the two choices are equally good. Without a system which constructs the clusters automatically, such a task would be practically impossible.

So in our example, the student obtains the clusters

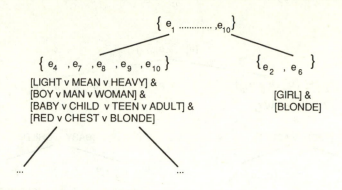

He will easily be able to see that the left-hand cluster is very bad because it covers all possible values with the exception of "girl".

In every case, education should consist in examining with the student the causes of the gap between his/her answer and the one that was expected.

Given an absolute requirement for education to function by reward/punishment, then it is better to tie the rewards to the building of coherent models, even if they are different from those of the teacher, and to tie the punishments to the building of incoherent models, even if they give the same answer as the teacher's.

2.2.3 Assimilation of subjectivity by Science

2.2.3.1 Efficiency through identification

Extraordinary skill in solving well-set problems is associated with detachment from the problem. This must be considered as a microcosm external to oneself, in order to unravel its traps better.

Extraordinary skill in setting problems so well that they have an obvious answer is associated with an identification with the problem, which thus requires to be considered as a universe into which you have to plunge in order to find its structure.

The first kind of skill is the one which is demanded from students and the second is the one which is necessary in practice.

We have already talked in section 1 about the oriental approach to Nature, where efficiency is measured in terms of identification with Nature.

The above remark leads us to interpret the oriental approach as an attempt to systematically reformulate problems in such a way that their solutions become trivial. Conversely, the western approach would consist rather in developing complex techniques of problem-solving capable of solving them without modifying their terms.

It is a matter for History to judge who was right, supposing one could ever talk about "being right" about the matter.

For our part, we take the obvious path, which consists in saying that both are necessary. More precisely, the objective approach is certainly the one which is most efficient in the short term for solving a given problem. Conversely, the method of identification is certainly more educational, and demands a deeper understanding of the problem set.

Just as when instincts are too long repressed by Society they come out wildly at the first opportunity, so the need to identify with one 's research topic, rejected by scientists for too long, seduced some specialists into unbridled infatuation with their own programs. We do not approve of this extremist attitude, but it is understandable, and even perhaps necessary to struggle against the distanciation which Science has taken as its creed up to now.

2.2.3.2   Natural sciences/social sciences

In section 1, we rejected the traditional distinctions between theoreticians and experimentalists, between creators and toilers. In the same way, we now wish to reject the traditional distinction between "natural" sciences and social sciences.

The natural sciences are precisely those where it is easy to distance oneself from one 's research topic. Conversely, in the social sciences, experimentation is difficult because the experimentalist is right in the middle of the subject of his/her experiment.

To the extent that identification with one 's research topic ceases to be anti-scientific, it is obvious that the special nature of the social sciences no longer has any raison d'être.

In practice, it is the multiplicity of models proposed by AI and the possibility of experimenting on enactments which are going to progressively give all the "desirable objectivity" to the social sciences. But, as we have seen, these models and these enactments are precisely the reason why AI can claim to be a science in which the scientist identifies with his/her research topic.

We also claim that the natural sciences will go the other half of the way by "humanizing" themselves a little.

2.2.3.3   ... for science without conscience is nothing but ruin of the soul

This phrase of Rabelais' (Pantagruel, Chapter 8) has almost become an object of derision.*

Yet the atomic bomb was needed for scientists to rediscover the fact that their

---

* Translator's note: This phrase has been grossly over-worked in papers written by French high-school students.

responsibility is involved, even when they are working on the most abstract topics.

At the present time other scientists are making the same mistake as their predecessors, and no doubt this will bring the same crop of belated awakenings.

A large number of scientists are working on satisfying our energy needs. It is quite obviously impossible for the growth of these needs to continue indefinitely without threatening our environment. The belief that these needs must grow still more is purely socially determined.

If we want to carry on increasing our electricity production, nuclear power plants are certainly less polluting than the multiplicity of traditional power plants which would be needed to satisfy the same needs.

But why these needs? Would it not be better to admit not only that our electricity consumption must not grow, but that it is already scandalously high?

It is not the existence of nuclear power plants which is dangerous but their multiplication, resulting in their trivialization and their deterioration with age, which is going to lead to more and more serious accidents.

Recent accidents in the USA and the Soviet Union clearly show that high- technology countries can have flaws. What is going to happen in the under- developed countries which equip themselves with nuclear power plants?

It will have to be realized that a nuclear accident in one of these countries' power plants affects us too, even supposing that "our own" power plants are well supervised.

The scientist is a divided man, with one part of his/her mind at work, his/her body at home and his/her soul in church if he/she is a believer.

The followers of orthodox science find this situation ideal, because it enables Science to be better.

On the contrary, a current of thought has arisen which criticizes this situation from the social and human point of view.

We even claim that AI is the fore-runner of a situation where the uninvolved man will always be, in addition, a bad scientist. The scientist will admittedly have to be capable of distancing him/herself from his/her problem, but also of identifying with it, of seeing its social consequences, of discussing its applications.

It is in this sense that we return to Rabelais' phrase, but clarifying it, for science without conscience, but also science without moral, social and bodily commitment, is nothing but ruin of the soul.

Bibliography

These books are all basic ones, containing texts which are useful for everyone who wants an introduction to Artificial Intelligence.

[Biermann & Al. 1984] Biermann A.W., Guiho G., Kodratoff Y. *Automatic Program Construction Techniques*, Macmillan Publishing Company, New York 1984.
A book which brings together several texts about automatic program construction and learning. Its first chapter contains a description of the synthesis of a simple program using all the methods described in the book.

[Chang & Lee 1973] Chang C. L., Lee R. C. T., *Symbolic Logic and mechanical Theorem Proving,* Academic Press 1973.
The book for those who are beginning serious work on theorem proving.

[Diday & Al. 1982] Diday E., Lemaire J., Poujet J., Testu F. *Eléments d'Analyse des Données,* Dunod, Paris 1982.
Everything about data analysis, its methods and applications.

[Dreyfus 1972] Dreyfus H. L. *What Computers Can't Do. A critique of Artificial Reason*, Harper and Row, New-York 1972, pp. 215-217.
An interesting account of the early criticisms AI had to refute.

[Nilsson 1980] Nilsson N. J. *Principles of Artificial Intelligence*, Morgan-Kaufmann, Los Altos CA 1980.
The best known introduction to Artificial Intelligence. A pre-requisite to a real understanding of ther present book.

[Michalski, Carbonell & Mitchell 1983, 1986] Michalski R.S., Carbonell J.G., Mitchell T.M. *Machine Learning, An Artificial Intelligence Approach*, Tioga Publishing Company, Palo Alto 1983, now distributed in the US by Morgan Kaufman and in Europe by Springer Verlag.
Michalski R.S., Carbonell J.G., Mitchell T.M. *Machine Learning, An Artificial Intelligence Approach, Volume 2,* Morgan Kaufmann, Los Altos, 1986.
The "bible" of learning through Artificial Intelligence. Because of the success of this work it has become a series, and "Machine Learning, An Artificial Intelligence Approach 2" came out in 1986, and a third volume is under way.

[Waterman & Hayes-Roth 1978] Watermann D.A., Hayes-Roth F. *Pattern-directed inference systems*, Academic Press, New York 1978.
A reference work on expert systems, but its content is also interesting from the point of view of learning.

[Knuth 1973] Knuth D. *The Art of Computer Programming*, Vol. 3, Addison-Wesley 1973.

[Kowalski 1979] Kowalski R. *Logic for Problem Solving*, North Holland 1979.
Another bible: that of Logic Programming and its applications. It is also a simple work, but written to be read from cover to cover without skipping between chapters.

[Shapiro 1983] Shapiro E. Y. *Algorithmic Program Debugging*, The MIT Press, 1983.

[Winston 1975] Winston P.H. *The Psychology of Computer Vision*, McGraw Hill, New York 1975.
Contains a simple description of the fundamental principles of AI.

Scientific Articles

[Arsac & Al 1982] Arsac J., Kodratoff Y. "Some Techniques for Recursion Removal from Recursive Functions", ACM ToPLaS 4, 1982, 295-322.

[Benamou & Al. 1986] Benamou N., Kodratoff Y. "Conceptual Hierarchical Ascending Classification", Rapport de Recherche LRI 305, Université Paris-Sud 1986 .

[Buchanan et Al. 1971] Buchanan B.G., Feigenbaum E.A., Lederberg J. "A heuristic programming study of theory formation in sciences", Proceedings of the Second International Joint Conference on Artificial Intelligence, London 1971, pp. 40-48.

[Buchanan & Mitchell 1978] Buchanan B.G., Mitchell T.M. "Model-directed learning of production rules", in *Pattern-directed inference systems,* Waterman D.A. and Hayes-Roth F. eds., Academic Press, New York 1978.

[Brazdil 1978] P. Brazdil, "Experimental Learning Model", Proc. 3rd AISB meeting, Hamburg 1978, pp. 46-50.

[Bundy & Al. 84] Bundy A., Silver B., Plummer D. "An Analytical Comparison of Some Rule Learning Programs", Univ. Edinburgh, DAI Res. paper 125, 1984.

[Burstall & Darlington 1977] Burstall R. M., Darlington J. "A Transformation System for Developing Recursive Programs", J. ACM 24, 1977, 44-67.

[Carbonell 1983] Carbonell J. G. "Learning by Analogy: Formulating and Generalizing Plans from Past Experience", in *Machine Learning, An Artificial Intelligence Approach,* Michalski, R.S., Carbonell, J. G., Mitchell, T.M. (eds), Morgan-Kaufmann 1983, pp. 137-159.

[Cohen & Sammut 1984] Cohen B., Sammut C.: "Program synthesis through concept learning", in *Automatic Program Construction Techniques,* Biermann A.W., Guiho G., Kodratoff Y. eds, Macmillan Publishing Company,1984, pp. 517-552. Macmillan Publishing Company,1984, pp. 463-482.

[Colmerauer 1979] Colmerauer A. "An Interesting Subset of Natural Language", in *Logic Programming*, Clark and Tarnlund eds, Academic Press 1979.

[Costa 1982] E. J. F. Costa "Dérécursivation automatique en utilisant des systèmes de réécriture de termes", Thèse, Paris 1982. Publication Interne LRI 118.

[Dejong 1981] Dejong G. "Generalizations Based on Explanations", Proc. 7th IJCAI, 1981, pp. 67-69.

[DeJong and Mooney 1986] DeJong G., Mooney R. "Explanation-Based Learning: An Alternative View", *Machine learning 1*, 1986, 145-176.

[Doyle 1979] Doyle J. "A Truth Maintenance System", AI Journal 12, 1979, 231-272.

[Dietterich & Al. 1981] Dietterich G.T., Michalski R.S. "Inductive learning of structural descriptions : Evaluation criteria and comparative review of selected methods" Artificial Intelligence Journal 16, 1981, 257-294.

[Franova 1985] Franova M. "CM-strategy: A methodology for inductive theorem proving on constructive well-generalized proofs", Proc. IJCAI-85, Los Angeles 1985, pp. 12141-219.

[Franova 1987] Franova M. " Why are we (almost always) able to prove inductive theorems "by Hand" and how to obtain an automatic system that does it the same way", Rapport Interne n0 327, LRI, Université Paris-Sud, Orsay 1987.

[Franova 1988] Franova M., to appear in Proc. ECAI-88, Munich 1988, Kodratoff editor, Pitman London 1988.

[Ganascia 1985] Ganascia J.G. "Comment oublier à l'aide de contre-exemples?" Actes du congrès AFCET RFIA, Grenoble, Novembre 1985.

[Hayes-Roth & Al. 1978] Hayes-Roth F., McDermott J. "An interference matching technique for inducing abstractions", C. ACM 21, 1978, 401-411.

[Jouannaud & Guiho 1979] Jouannaud J. P., Guiho G. "Inference of functions with an interactive system", *Machine Intelligence 9*, pp. 227 - 250, Hayes, Michie and Mikulich eds., Ellis Horwood 1979.

[Kedar-Cabelli 1987] Kedar-Cabelli S.T., McCarthy L.T. "Explanation-Based Generalization as Resolution Theorem Proving", Proc. 4th Int. Workshop on Machine Learning, Irvine June 1987, Pat Langley editor, Morgan Kaufmann, Los Altos 1987.

[Kodratoff 1979] Kodratoff Y. "A Class of Functions Synthesized from a Finite Number of Examples and a LISP Program Scheme", Int. J. Comput. Inf. Sci. 8, 1979, 489-521.

[Kodratoff 1983] Kodratoff Y. "Generalizing and Particularizing as the Techniques of Learning", Computers and Artificial Intelligence 2, 1983, 417-441.

[Kodratoff & Jouannaud 1984] Kodratoff Y., Jouannaud J.-P. "Synthesizing LISP programs Working on the List Level of Embedding", in *Automatic program construction techniques,* A. W. Biermann, G. Guiho, Y. Kodratoff eds., Macmillan Publishing Company, New York 1984, pp. 325-374.

[Kodratoff & Al. 1984] Kodratoff Y., Ganascia J.-G., Clavieras B., Bollinger T., Tecuci G. "Careful generalization for concept learning" Proc. ECAI-84, Pisa 1984, pp. 483-492. Now also available in *Advances in Artificial Intelligence,* T. O'Shea editor, pp. 229 - 238, North - Holland Amsterdam 1985.

[Kodratoff 1985] Kodratoff Y. "Une Théorie et une méthodologie de l'Apprentissage Symbolique", Actes Cognitiva 85, pp. 639-631, 1985.

[Kodratoff & Duval 1986] Duval B., Kodratoff Y. "Automated Deduction in an Uncertain and Inconsistent Data Basis", Proc. ECAI-86, Brighton 1986, pp. 101-108.

[Kodratoff & Ganascia 1986] Kodratoff Y., Ganascia J.-G. "Improving the Generalization Step in Learning", in *Machine Learning, An Artificial Intelligence Approach, Volume 2,* Michalski, R.S., Carbonell, J. G., Mitchell, T.M. (eds), Morgan-Kaufmann 1986, pp. 215-244.

[Langley 1983] Langley P. "Learning Search Strategies through discrimination", Int. J. Man-Machine Studies 18, 1983, 513-541.

[Lebowitz 1986] Lebowitz M. "Integrated Learning : Controlling Explanation", Cognitive Science 10, 1986, to appear.

[Manago and Kodratoff 1987] Manago M., Kodratoff Y. "Noise and Knowledge Acquisition" Proc. IJCAI-87, Milan Aug. 87, pp. 348-354.

[Manna & Al. 1972] Manna Z., Ness S., Vuillemin J. "Inductive methods for proving properties of programs", C. ACM 16, 1972, 491-502.

[Michalski & Chilauski 1980] Michalski R. M., Chilauski R. L. "Learning by Being Told and Learning from Examples : An Experimental Comparison of the Two Methods of Knowledge Acquisition in the Context of Developing an Expert System for Soybean Disease Diagnosis", Internatl. J. of Policy Analysis and Information Systems 4, 1980.

[Michalski & Al. 1982] Michalski R. M., Davis J. H., Bisht V. S., Sinclair J. B. "PLANT/ds : An Expert Consulting System for the Diagnosis of Soybean Diseases", Proc. ECAI-82, Orsay 1982, pp. 133-138.

[Michalski 1983] Michalski R.S. "A Theory and Methodology of Inductive Learning", in *Machine Learning, An Artificial Intelligence Approach,* Michalski, R.S., Carbonell, J. G., Mitchell, T.M. (eds), Morgan-Kaufmann 1983, pp. 83-130.

[Michalski 1984] Michalski R.S. "Inductive Learning as Rule-guided Transformation of Symbolic Descriptions : a Theory and Implementation", in *Automatic Program Construction Techniques,* Biermann A.W., Guiho G., Kodratoff Y. eds, Macmillan Publishing Company, 1984, pp. 517-552.

[Mitchell 1978]Mitchell, T.M. "Version Space: An Approach to Concept Learning", Ph.D. Thesis, Stanford CS Rept. STAN-CS-78-711, HPP-79-2, Stanford University, December 1978.

[Mitchell 1982] Mitchell T.M. "Generalization as Search", *Artificial Intelligence 18*, 1982, 203-226.

[Mitchell 1983] Mitchell T.M. "Learning and Problem Solving" Proc. IJCAI-83, Karlsruhe 1983, pp. 1139-1151.

[Mitchell 1985] Mitchell T. M., Mahadevan S., Steinberg L. I. "Leap : A Learning Apprentice for VLSI Design", Proc. IJCAI-85, Los Angeles 1985, pp. 573-580.

[Mitchell, Utgoff & Banerji 1983] Mitchell T.M., Utgoff P.E., Banerji R. "Learning by experimentation, acquiring and refining problem-solving heuristics", in *Machine Learning, an Artificial Intelligence Approach,* Michalski R.S., Carbonell J.G., Mitchell T.M. eds, Tioga Publishing Company 1983, pp. 163-190.

[Mitchell and 1986] Mitchell T. M., Keller R. M., Kedar-Cabelli S. T., "Explanation-Based Generalizations : A Unifying View", Machine Learning 1, 47-80, 1986.

[Moore 1973] J S. Moore "Computational Logic : Structure Sharing and Proof of Program Properties", PhD thesis, Edinburgh 1973.

[Murray 1987] Murray K. S. "Multiple Convergence: An Approach to Disjunctive Concept Acquisition", Proc. IJCAI 1987, pp. 297-300.

[Nicolas 1986a] Nicolas J., "Les stratégies de contrôle dans l'apprentissage à partir d'exemples", Comptes-Rendus JFA-1986, Rapport de Recherche LRI 259, 1986.

[Nicolas 1986b] Nicolas J., "Learning as Search : A Logical Approach", Proc. CIIAM'86, Hermes Paris 1986, pp.443-459.

[Nicolas 1988] Nicolas J., to appear in Proc. ECAI-88, Munich 1988, Kodratoff editor, Pitman London 1988.

[Porto 1983] Porto A. "Logical Action Systems", Proc. Logic Programming Workshop'83, Portugal July 1983, pp. 192 - 203.

[Quinlan 1983] Quinlan J. R. "Learning Efficient Classification Procedures and their Application to Chess End Games" in *Machine Learning, An Artificial Intelligence Approach*, Michalski, R.S., Carbonell, J. G., Mitchell, T.M. Eds, Tioga Publishing Company, 1983, pp. 463-482.
See Also " Induction of Decision Trees" Machine Learning Journal 1, 1986, 81 - 106.

[Rosenblatt 1958] Rosenblatt F. "The perceptron : A probabilistic model for information storage and organization in the brain", Psychological Review 65, 1958, 386-407.

[Saint-Dizier 1985] Saint-Dizier P. "An approach to Natural Language Semantics in Logic Programming", Rapport de Recherche INRIA no 389, 1985.

[Samuel 1959, 1963] Samuel A.L. "Some studies in Machine Learning using the game of checkers", IBM Journal of Research and Development 3, 1959, 211-229.
Samuel A.L. " Some studies in Machine Learning using the game of checkers", in *Computer and Thought*, Feigenbaum E.A. et Feldman J. Eds, McGraw-Hill New-York 1963, pp 71-105.

[Silver 1983] Silver B. "Precondition Analysis : Learning Control Information", in *Machine Learning, An Artificial Intelligence Approach, Volume 2,* Michalski R. S., Carbonell J. G., Mitchell T. M. Eds, Morgan Kaufmann, Los Altos 1986, pp. 647 - 670.

[Siqueira & Puget 1988] de Siqueira J.& Puget J.F. "Explanation-Based Generalization of Failures, to appear in Proc. ECAI-88, Munich 1988, Kodratoff editor, Pitman London 1988.

[Sloane 1973] Sloane N.J.A. "A Handbook of integer sequences" Academic Press 1973.

[Steels & Van de Welde 1985] Steels L., Van de Welde W. "Learning in Second Generation Expert Systems", in *Knowledge-Based Problem Solving*, Kowalik J. S. Eds,

Prentice-Hall 1985.

[Summers 1977] Summers P. D. "A Methodology for LISP Program Construction from Examples", J. ACM 24, 1977, 161 - 175.

[Touretzky & Hinton 1985] Touretzky D. S., Hinton G. E. "Connectionist Inference Architecture, Proc. IJCAI-85, Los Angeles, 1985, pp. 238-243.

[Vere 80] Vere S.A. "Multilevel counterfactuals for generalizations of relational concepts and productions" Artificial Intelligence J. 14,1980, 139-164.

[Vere 81] Vere, S.A. "Constrained N-to-1 Generalizations", unpublished draft, 23, Feb, 1981.

[Vrain 85] Vrain C. "Contre-exemples : explications déduites de l'étude des prédicats", Actes congrès AFCET RF-IA, Grenoble 1985, pp. 145 - 159.

[Vrain 1987] Vrain C."Un outil de généralisation utilisant systématiquement les théorèmes: le système OGUST". Thesis, Univ. Paris-Sud Feb. 1987.

[Waldinger 1977] Waldinger R. J. "Achieving several goals simultaneously', in *Machine Intelligence 18*, pp.94-136.

[Walter 1984] Walther C. "A Mechanical Solution of Schubert's Steamroller by Many-Sorted Resolution", Proc. AAAI-84.

[Winston 1982] Winston P.H. "Learning New Principles From Precedents and Exercises", *Artificial Intelligence 19*, (1982), 321-350.

Non-scientific Books

[Capra 1975] Capra F. *The Tao of Physics*, Fritjof Capra 1975.

[Herrigel 1970] Herrigel E. *Le zen dans l'art chevaleresque du tir à l'arc*, Dervy-Livres, Paris 1970. In English: [Herrigel 1985] *Zen in the art of archery*, Arkana, London 1985.

[Lévy-Leblond & Jaubert 1975] Lévy-Leblond J. M., Jaubert A. *(Auto) critique de la science*, Editions du Seuil, Paris 1975.

[Pirsig 1974] Pirsig R. M. *Zen and the Art of Motorcycle Maintenance*, William Morrow, New York 1974.

Science-Fiction Books

U.K. Le Guin, *The Word for World is Forest*, Granada, London 1980.

T.J. Ryan, *The Adolescence of P-1*, Baen Science Fiction Books, New York 1977.

Ian Watson, *The Embedding*, Victor Gollancz 1973.

Index

Action mode
  predicates in 60–2
Actions
  problems involving 64–5
  representation of knowledge about 59–74
Adding conjuncts rule 172
Adding disjuncts rule 152–3
Adding names of variables rule 153
Algorithms
  clustering 191–2, 201, 283
  for conceptual clustering 157–8, 194–5
  for the generation of recognition
      functions 154–5
  Knuth-Bendix completion 39–41
  Kowalski resolution 32–6
  rational generalization 164–71
Analogy, learning by 216–28
Asimov's three laws of robotics 274, 275
Automatic programming 244, 256–62
Auxiliary rules 62–3
Axioms
  and similarity detection 163, 171–2

Backward chaining 18–19, 35–6, 37–9, 46, 57
  and goal regression 126
  in hierarchy representation 51
  and problem solving 64, 65

Canonical form 41
Casual knowledge 279
Causal relationships
  and analogy 216–18, 219–20, 222, 223,
      223–4, 226–7
Chaining see Backward chaining; Forward
  chaining
Checking mode, predicates in 60–2
Choice criterion
  in version spaces 113–20
Classification, conceptual 2–3
Clauses 19–25
  causal 226–7
  conversion into sentences 21–5
  definitions 19–21
  empty 17–18, 37, 38, 46, 225, 233
      and negative examples 179–80
  and micro-worlds 205–10
  representation of complex knowledge by 42–58
  resolution and inference on 32–9
  and theorems 228–42
  use of representation by 14
Climbing generalization tree rule 153–4

Clustering 2
  conceptual 157–8, 193–201
  and negative examples 175–6
  techniques 184–201
Clustering algorithms 191–2, 201, 283
Coherent knowledge base 37
Common-sense knowledge 9–10
Completion
  of rewrite systems 40–1
Computational traces 248–54, 258, 261
Concepts
  classification of 2–3
  clustering techniques 184–8
  learning 98–100
  logical description of 47–8
  in similarity detection 138–9
Conceptual clustering 193–201
  and similarity detection 157–8
Conceptual learning 5
Condition/action pairs 14
Conjunctive generalizations 115, 248
Conjunctive normal form, conversion into 19–21, 36
Connective, in logic 20
Consistency criteria
  in version spaces 110–12
Complementary paairs 239
Critical pairs 40–1

Data analysis, application of 188–93
Debugging 207–10
Deductive learning 9, 122, 123
Description
  in similarity detection 139, 140–2
Discrimination
  problem of 3
Disjunctive generalizations 114–17
  and negative examples 173–6
Dissimilarity
  and discriminant generalization 199–201
Doing, learning by 75–92
Domain definitions
  and universal quantification 97–8
Dropping condition rule 152, 154, 172, 200

EBG see Explanation-Based Generalization
EBL see Explanation-Based Learning
Education
  and Machine Learning 278–84
Empirical learning 6–9, 10
  and similarity detection 138–58, 183

Empty clauses 17–18, 37, 38, 46, 233
  and analogy 225
  and negative examples 179–80
EMYCIN 18, 155
Exceptions
  in logical knowledge representation 44–46, 59–60
Existential quantification 95–102
Expert knowledge 10, 279
Expert systems
  and similarity detection 155–7
Explanation-Based Generalization (EBG) 128–35
Explanation-Based Learning (EBL) 3–5, 6, 9, 10, 121–37
Explanatory learning 9–10
Explicability, and efficiency 267–8
Extending domain rule 153

Factorization rule 34
Forced matching 30–1
Formal specification
  program synthesis from 256, 257–8
Forward chaining 16, 18–19, 38, 39, 57
  and goal regression 126
  in hierarchy representation 51
  in logical knowledge representation 46
  and problem solving 64, 65

General resolution 16–17
Generalization
  and clustering analysis 195–201
  discriminant 199–201
  and Explanation-Based Learning 128–35
  problem of 3
  restricted 172
  of rules 72–3
  and similarity detection 138, 151–4, 160–71
    negative examples 173–83
  and synthesis of predicates 247–8
  in unification 28–9, 30
  and version spaces 81, 83, 93–110
Goal regression
  and Explanation-Based Learning 124–8

Herbrand universe 233–9
Herbrand's theorem 242
Hierarchies
  clustering 192–3
  representation of, during resolution 49–54
  and similarity detection 160–1
History of machine learning 1–2
Horn clauses 20–1, 43, 44, 45–6, 155
Human learning
  and Machine Learning models 281–4

Idempotence
  and similarity detection 171–2
Inductive inferences 2, 171–2
  in similarity detection 138
Inductive learning 9, 121–2
Inference
  on clauses 32–9
  inductive 2, 138, 244
  representation of 15–19
  rules for control of 73–4

Input
  synthesis of predicates from 248–55, 258
Intuitive definition of generalization 93–4
Inventive learning 9
Items
  and clustering analysis 188–9

Knowledge base 37
Knowledge representation
  of inference 15–19
  logical 42–6
  and similarity detection 160–4
  without inferences 12–14
Knuth-Bendix completion algorithm 39–41
Kowalski resolution algorithm 32–6

Langley's SAGE system 86–92
Learning
  and clustering techniques 193
  by doing 75–92
  by similarity detection 138–83
  by trial and error 86–92
Lies, detection of 210–15
Linear variables
  in similarity detection 139–40
Links, introduction of
  in a rational generalization algorithm 168–9
LISP functions 12–14
LISP representations
  inference in 15–16
Literals 20
Logical knowledge representation 42–6

Main rules 62–3
META-DENDRAL program 2
Meta-rules, learning of 74
Micro-worlds
  learning of 202–15
  recognition of 205–10
  and rules 73–4
Mistakes, disappearance of concept of 280–1
Mitchell's system of version spaces 77, 113–14, 116
Modus Ponens 36, 93, 101
Modus Tollens 36–7
Move centrality, concept of 1–2

Natural deduction 36
Natural language understanding 202
Negative examples
  and similarity detection 172, 173–83
Nominal variables
  in similarity detection 139
Non-monotonic logic 59, 60
Numeric approach to clustering 184–8
Numeric clustering analysis 195
Numerical learning 5, 9

Objectivity, scientific 263–4, 265–6, 268
Oriental philosophy, and science 264–5
Outputs
  synthesis of predicates from 248–55, 258

Pattern recognition
  data analysis for 188–9
Permutations
  in unification 28
Philosophy, oriental
  and science 264–5
Post-scientific theories
  construction of 271–2
Predicates, synthesis of 243–62
Problem-solving
  and learning by doing 75–7
Program Synthesis (Automatic
  Programming) 2, 244, 256–62
Program transformation 258–61
Program translation 261–2
PROLOG
  and Winston's learning by analogy 223–5
PROLOG, NOT 62–3
PROLOG clauses 11, 57–8, 202, 206
PROLOG resolution 17–18, 206–7
Proof by refutation 36–7
Punishment, learning by 5–6

Quality criterion, definition of
  in version spaces 117–19
Quinlan's method of clustering 174–8

Rational learning 6–9, 10
  and similarity detection 159–83
Recognition functions 98–101, 245
  and clustering analysis 195, 199
  creation of 148–51
  generation of 154–5
  and similarity detection 142–51
Recurrent relations
  and synthesis of predicates 251–5
Refutation 18
Representation
  by ternary quantified trees 54–6
Resolution
  on clauses 32–9
  Kowalski's resolution algorithm 32–6
Restricted generalization 172
Reward, learning by 5–6
Rewrite systems 40–1
Robinson's Unification Theorem 31
Rules
  acquisition of
    and learning by doing 83–5
  addition of new rules 59–74
  combining 71–2
  of generalization
    in similarity detection 151–4
  generalization of 72–3
  for inference control 73–4
  main and auxiliary 62–3
  new and old 67–71

SAGE system of learning 86–92
Samuel's system 1–2
SBL see Similarity Based Learning

Science
  and Artificial Intelligence 263–72
  natural and social science 285–6
  objectivity of 263–4, 265–6, 268
Science Fiction (SF) 274–6
Semantic nets 57, 123
  and analogy 221–2
Semantic trees 239–42
Sentences
  conversion into clauses 21–5, 42–58
  transformation into theorems 47–9
Similarity
  and clustering analysis 195–9
  distances and measures of
    and clustering analysis 189–90
Similarity Based Learning (SBL) 3–5, 6, 10
  empirical approach 138–58
  rational approach 159–83
Similarity relationships
  and analogy 216–17
Simplicity criteria
  and recognition functions 145
Simplification
  in a rational generalization algorithm 170–1
Skolem form
  conversion of formulae into 233–5
Skolem functions 21, 43
  and existential quantification 97
  in hierarchy representation 53
Social role of Machine Learning 273–83
Social sciences
  and natural sciences 285–6
Sparseness
  in learning by similarity detection 144–5
Statements
  logical description of 48–9
Structural matching (SM) 7, 105–8
  in a rational generalization algorithm 164–8
  and similarity vectors 200
Structured variables
  in learning by similarity detection 140
Substitution
  in hierarchy representation 52
  in unification 28–32
Symbolic learning 2
Symbolic treatment of concepts 187–8

Taxonomies
  and clustering techniques 184–201
  of micro-worlds 204
  and similarity detection 160–2
Temporal logic 59, 60
Terms
  generalization of 101, 102–4
  in unification 26–8
Ternary quantified trees 54–6
Theorem learning
  and existential versus universal
    quantification 96–8
Theorems
  and clauses 228–42
  and generalization 108–10

Herbrand's 242
 transforming sentences into 47–9
Theoretical foundations 11–41
Theories, scientific and post-scientific 270–2
Trial and error, learning by 86–92
Truth maintenance 202–3
Turning constants into variables rule 153
Tyranny
 and Artificial Intelligence 277–8

Unification 26–32
 in hierarchy represenation 52
Universal quantification 95–102

Vere's definition of generalization 94–5
Version spaces 77–83, 93–120, 154

Winston's use of analogy 217, 220–7